A Thousand Years of Stained Glass

Bourges Cathedral, Jacques Coeur Chapel,
Annuciation (details); right, St James, *and,*
opposite, St. Catherine, *1448–50.*

Catherine Brisac

A
Thousand Years
of
Stained Glass

Translated from
the French
by Geoffrey Culverwell

Photographs by Yukichi Watabe

CHARTWELL
BOOKS

Text by Catherine Brisac
The chapter Collections of Stained Glass in Museums is by Chantal
Bouchon

Photographs by Yukichi Watabe
Drawings by Roberto Maresca

Translated by Geoffrey Culverwell

This edition published 2001

Published by Chartwell Books
A Division of Book Sales, Inc.
114 Northfield Avenue
Edison, NJ 08837

Library of Congress Cataloging in Publication Data

Brisac, Catherine.
A thousand years of stained glass.

Translation of: *Le Viitrail.*
1. Glass painting and staining-History. I. Title.
NK5306.B7513   1986   748.59   85-4506
ISBN 0-7858-0169-3
Printed and bound in Spain by Artes Gráficas Toledo, S.A.
D.L. TO: 249 - 2001

Contents

1
The Origins

As a material, glass has been known to man since the third millenium B.C. At that time, however, it was not blown but pressed, mainly by means of moulds. The ancient Egyptians noticed its extraordinary properties, and from then on glass was regarded as being preferable to pottery in many circumstances. It was particularly widely used for perfume vials and funerary glasses, large numbers of which can be seen in museums and archaeological collections. Glass-making was also carried out elsewhere in the Mediterranean area well into historical times. In Byzantium, for example, the majority of glass objects were still pressed, but some vases were already being made using a mixed technique, meaning that some sections were blown, while the neck and handle were always pressed. The two techniques were used in conjunction until the imposition of blown glass at the beginning of the early Middle Ages. It is important to start this chapter by drawing the reader's attention to these few facts because windows made from pieces of glass have existed since antiquity, although little is known of their origins. The Romans were familiar with flat glass panes as early as the first century A.D., when they occurred as small sections inserted into decorative mounts. Pliny the Younger describes several such pieces in his letters. The Muslim world continued to use this method of enclosing bays, and several elements from these claustra or transennae have been discovered in excavations of Umayyad palaces in the Middle East. This system was probably used fairly frequently. It would be reasonable to suppose that it was also used in the West during the early Middle Ages in conjunction with lead rods, the introduction of which as the accepted means of containing the different pieces of glass can still not be accurately dated.

It is likely that lead, which allowed for the settings to be reduced to the size of a thin and very pliable lattice, gradually supplanted the earlier plaster, stucco, or even wooden armature. These first

"stained-glass windows" were probably purely decorative, like those in the Basilique des Maccabées at Lyon described by Bishop Sidoine Apollinaire in the fifth century. They may have been similar to the pale grisaille windows with geometrical or vegetal patterns which the Cistercian monks used to adorn their churches during the twelfth century. Although there are many contemporary writings that describe early stained-glass windows, they provide no precise additional information and it is therefore impossible to restore these first translucent examples.

It is important to point out that the originality of medieval stained glass in the West lay in the fact that it was painted. It either told a story of the exemplary lives of Christ, his Mother, and the saints or illustrated passages from the scriptures. These glass pictures were presented for the contemplation of mankind, but, first and foremost, they were offered up to God and to his Son, for whom they were created. Since St. Augustine, light has been regarded as their indispensable complement, a vital element in their glorification, since God is also Light. This belief continued to develop throughout the Middle Ages, and at the end of the thirteenth century, a period when the art of stained glass reached extraordinary heights, Bishop Durand de Mende wrote: "Stained-glass windows are divine writings that spread the clarity of the true sun, who is God, through the church, that is to say, through the heart of the faithful, bringing them true enlightenment." In fact, a stained-glass window is itself a wall of light that changes throughout the day in accordance with the strength of the sun, and the people of the Middle Ages were entranced by the strange, even magical way in which stained-glass windows shimmer like precious stones. But rather than covering a small area, stained glass, being a monumental art form, would be able to extend over large surfaces. If one increases the number of coloured windows in a single structure, then a church will become a house of colours, a place filled with light for the greater glory of God, a heavenly Jerusalem. Manuscripts show that since the early Middle Ages man

strove to find ways in which to allow the stained-glass window to achieve its full potential, but building techniques were as yet unable to create churches flooded with light. The earliest stained-glass panels were probably small in size, like the windows of the churches and abbeys that they filled, but no example from the first century A.D. has ever been found in situ. All the earliest evidence has been obtained from archaeological digs, some of which were carried out many years ago. It is this fact that makes their dating so uncertain, since the techniques of archaeology were not as strict then as they are today. In addition, the evidence generally takes the form of broken pieces, the restoration of which also poses delicate problems.

Among these finds are the fragments of a crown found by the archaeologist Cecchelli during excavations at the Church of San Vitale, Ravenna, in 1930 and now in the city's archaeological museum. Unearthed together with other pieces of glass, the three fragments, painted in black vitreous paint, show Christ standing between an alpha and an omega. It has been assumed that they are contemporary with the building of San Vitale, which would mean that they date from around A.D. 540.

We have to wait until the eighth or ninth century before finding any other evidence to work on, and this takes the form of fragments discovered in France in Notre-Dame-de-la-Basse-Oeuvre at Beauvais and in a cemetery near Saint-Quentin (Aisne). These are of little interest, however, when compared with the fragments of a large head (more than 30 centimeters [c. 12 inches] high) discovered during excavations at the Rhenish Abbey of Lorsch, near Heidelberg, in 1934–35. Despite certain lacunae, it was possible to piece together these remains to form the head of a saint, portrayed in a rigidly frontal pose and surrounded by a halo made from a different type of glass to that used for the face, which is extensively pitted and discoloured. The treatment is very archaic, and the painting is restricted to straight, stylized lines, with a certain looseness creeping into the design of the curls in the hair and the lobes of the ears. A

parallel has to be drawn between this head and another, now in the Musée de l'Oeuvre Notre-Dame in Strasbourg. According to tradition, the latter comes from Wissembourg Abbey in Alsace, which was rebuilt in the mid eleventh century; hence the date ascribed to it. Like the Lorsch head, this has a rigidly frontal pose, with the hair forming a sort of yoke around it. The way in which the paint has

been applied (assuming that the head has not been retouched) appears more sophisticated, however, in that two successive layers of wash have been applied, as was the custom later on, during the Romanesque period. In view of their size (the Wissembourg head is only slightly smaller than the Lorsch one), it would be reasonable to suppose that these two works were displayed in isolation, like icons, in the

Fragments of a head discovered during excavations in 1932 at Lorsch Abbey, ninth century. Hessisches Landesmuseum, Darmstadt.

Opposite: Head of Christ, *from the Abbey Church of St. Peter, Wissembourg, Alsace, 1060 (?). Musée de l'Oeuvre Notre-Dame, Strasbourg.*

middle of a window in which they would have been the only painted element.

A complete contrast was provided by the head from Magdeburg, now lost, and the one unearthed during excavations at Schwarzach Church in Baden between 1964 and 1968. We are here dealing with much smaller works, which probably formed part of a larger scene and were not the only painted element like the two earlier ones. They show that narrative stained-glass windows were probably already a reality.

In fact, none of the examples mentioned

thus far give any idea of the extraordinary way in which the art of stained glass began to develop at the beginning of the twelfth century. These pieces are in this respect deceptive, most especially since it is from the beginning of the twelfth century that there derives a truly exceptional series, that of the prophets in Augsburg Cathedral. We are now no longer dealing with fragments, but with almost complete stained-glass windows still in position, even though they are not in their original setting and one of them, portraying Moses, is a sixteenth-century copy. By

virtue of their height (more than 2 meters [78 inches]), these figures, which originally numbered twenty-two in all, bear witness to the extraordinary level of technical expertise achieved by the craftsmen who created them. Their execution already combines the technical effects of Romanesque stained glass in the quality of the painting and in the precision of the scraping and shading of the glass, which accentuates the elaborate nature of the windows, while at the same time safeguarding the monumentality of the figures. Probably originally surrounded

by a very wide border, these figures still retain the hieratic quality of the Lorsch and Wissembourg heads in their strictly frontal presentation, but their colouring, the way in which certain pieces have been cut and inserted, together with the way in which the latter adapt to the shape of the robes, underline the fact that we are here faced by a highly important group of windows, and one which continues to amaze us by its expressive force and monumentality. Many thirteenth-century works are far less accomplished. It is certain that this series, when it was completed and filled the soaring windows of the cathedral, stirred people's imagination just as much as the processions of apostles and prophets that were to appear in church windows more than a hundred years later. In view of their extraordinary quality it is hard not to postulate the existence of earlier examples of stained glass, other than those discovered by archaeologists. However, with the exception of the Augsburg prophets, which are probably the culmination of a whole series of earlier experiences, nothing else has survived.

Augsburg Cathedral, high windows in the nave, south side, The prophets Jonah, Moses (sixteenth-century copy), Daniel, and Hosea, c. 1100.

2
The Romanesque Period

Of all the twelfth-century arts, stained glass is still one of the most difficult to appreciate in its original form. Very few examples of the period have survived and it is often hard for the public to get a close look at those which have without actually using binoculars. Even fewer are still to be found in situ, with the exception of such memorable examples as the three windows in the chevet of Poitiers Cathedral, which date from around 1160. Many of them have also had their original layout altered and been rearranged over the centuries, as is the case, for example, with the windows commissioned by Abbé Suger for the apse of the royal Abbey Church of Saint-Denis, which he had just had rebuilt (1140–44). In their anxiety to give some sort of coherence to works which no longer possessed any, restorers, particularly those working during the nineteenth century, often reassembled them with more imagination than accuracy. Unfortunately, the layman remains unaware of such alterations. In addition, there are the problems linked to aging, such as the way in which the glass has darkened, making the windows hard to interpret. And yet, twelfth-century stained glass exerts a powerful fascination, partly by virtue of its very conception. It was composed, at the time, of a mosaic of glass pieces, often painted and assembled to be viewed from afar, a technique which resulted in the creation of an impressionistic effect that changed constantly from minute to minute and from hour to hour, depending on the light. The Romanesque Middle Ages were very conscious of this idea of glittering, light-catching colour, which they likened to the power of God, who is "Light," and also the power of his Son and of the Holy Ghost. This idea, which can be traced back to St. Augustine, endowed light with a whole series of symbolic values that stained glass was able to exploit. "The stained-glass windows that are in churches and through which...

Cathedral of Saint-Denis, chevet, axial chapel, Childhood of Christ; Annunciation, *showing the donor, Abbé Suger, at the feet of the Virgin, 1140–44.*

the clarity of the sun is transmitted, signify the Holy Scriptures, which banish evil from us and enlighten our being," wrote Pierre de Roissy, a dignitary of the Chartres chapter in around 1200, at the time of the installation of the first windows in the nave of Chartres Cathedral, which was then in the process of being built. There are several other contemporary writings which give us an insight into the value placed by medieval theologians on light and on the glass panels in which this light was reflected. This symbolic significance is almost a closed book to us today, but we must have some understanding of it in order to appreciate the role played by twelfth-century stained glass. Paying homage to God did not involve just praying, but also presenting him with a stained-glass window for his house, the church. We have to view stained glass within the religious and moral context of the period if we are to understand it properly. If we fail in that, we shall see, for the most part, only an interplay of colours, distorted by the passing of the years.

THE CHARACTERISTICS OF ROMANESQUE STAINED GLASS

Unlike Gothic windows, those of the twelfth century possess their own light-giving value. They are like shafts of light with their own formal independence and their own evolutionary process, often mirroring the appearance and techniques of such nonmonumental art forms as enamelling and miniaturism. This paradox partly explains the nature of Romanesque windows. In the first place, they are often very "precious," filled with detail and with many effects reminiscent of precious metalwork. In the French districts of Champagne, Dauphiné, and the Île-de-France, for example, there are a large number of windows containing scenes that stand out against a background of small foliate scrolls which would do credit to any goldsmith. These patterns, which reveal a high degree of manual dexterity, are technically very close to the processes employed in the manufacture of niello or enamel work. The art of stained

glass was therefore still strongly influenced by the latter traditions. This phenomenon is also confirmed by an analysis of Romanesque windows. The narrative sections are generally contained within several decorative bands consisting of beading and friezes of small palmettes rhythmically interspersed with coloured lozenges. Between the medallions there are plant motifs arranged in a line or *en broche*. The borders, normally broad, are also composed of vegetal elements or bunches of leaves, sometimes enriched with decorative bands, either facing each other or back to back, which are arranged perpendicularly or vertically in relation to the axis of the window and are linked by ribbons which can be either plain or decorated. These compositions merely emphasize the plastic qualities of Romanesque decoration that appear in all artistic techniques of the period. Stained glass, however, being an art form synonymous with colour, achieves even more remarkable effects. The variety of these compositions is every bit as exceptional due to the large number of basic models. The same types were produced by different workshops; only the workmanship and use of colour varied.

And yet, unlike other delicate techniques, stained glass is also a monumental art, meaning that it can only realize its full potential when linked with architecture. During the twelfth century, however, the function of a wall was purely to hold up the ceiling structure, whether vaulted or otherwise, and the roof. This imperative prevented the creation of large windows. Romanesque windows were small in size and driven through thick walls. Since very little light penetrated the interior of the building, it was vital that the window openings should be as clear as possible and admit the maximum amount of light. This explains the often dazzling, unified colouration of Romanesque stained glass, quite unlike the gloomy windows of early thirteenth-century France. Even when, from 1140–50 onwards, the structural nature of Gothic architecture altered the way in which interiors were illuminated, as in the choir of the Abbey Church of Saint-Denis, windows still retained their

earlier shape and their pale colours. The master craftsmen only gradually succeeded in breaching the conventions of the twelfth century, but there was never any sudden break. The new ideas were introduced little by little. The original colouration of Romanesque glass, which has now often been distorted by corrosion, was pale, as in the west front of Chartres Cathedral, where the exemplary restoration work carried out between 1975 and 1977 has allowed the three windows to resume their original light-giving role, with the famous blue playing an essential part in balancing the other colours.

The originality of Western stained-glass windows lies in the fact that they are a form of painting illustrating biblical texts or episodes from the lives of the saints. The procedures involved owe much to the techniques of mural painting, with the latter being adapted to suit the new medium. The paint itself was composed of copper or iron oxide, "frit" (finely crushed glass that allows for more rapid melting), and a binding agent such as wine or urine. The glass artist was able to vary the intensity of the mixture by altering the rate of dilution. The preparation was generally applied in three layers, a technique that imitated the procedures used in painting murals, an art whose importance now began to decline as a direct result of the introduction of stained glass. A Rhenish Benedictine monk, Theophilus, who was active during the first third of the twelfth century, wrote a treatise entitled *De diversis artibus*, a veritable "technical manual" and the first of its kind to be produced in the West, in which he listed the methods of producing a stained-glass window, right down to the composition of the glass paste. As far as the application of the paint was concerned, Theophilus recommended the use of three successive layers of unequal thickness, which he called "values." Only those sections in full light were left unpainted; the others received a layer of paint of varying intensity. The lowest layer was a light wash applied over large areas while the intermediate layer acted as a means of reinforcing the shadow; the final one, which was generally strong in tone, marked the essential lines, most notably the contours. This skillful technique was followed by a large number of twelfth-century workshops and accurately mirrors the main concerns of contemporary stained-glass artists: how to vary the effects of painting by simple means, the superimposition

of flat tints taking the place of relief. However, in order to achieve different effects craftsmen began to carry out a laborious process on the freshly applied paint (before firing) that involved removing the paint by means of a paintbrush handle or a stylus to create small decorative designs or to write inscriptions.

The light-giving role of stained-glass windows during the Romanesque period, their behaviour within their architectural frame, the bay, and the development of their biblical and hagiographic iconography all combine to explain the nature of their composition. The illustration of evangelical texts or the exemplary lives of the saints by means of pieces of painted glass, often small in size and held together by means of lead rods, is governed by certain optical restraints. Furthermore, the very technique used, that is to say the act of grouping together a large number of pieces of unequal thickness within a lead lattice, imposed certain physical restrictions because of the considerable combined weight of the two materials. It therefore became necessary to divide the window into sections, the majority of which were less than one meter (39 inches) square. In order to fix these panels into the bays it also became necessary to invent a system of frames or armatures, sometimes of wood, but more commonly of wrought iron, a material which was more resistant to atmospheric changes. The most widely used system involved the division of windows by means of an orthogonal armature, as is the case with the Jesse window in the Abbey Church of Saint-Denis (1140–45). Another formula, destined to make the narrative compartments even easier to interpret, was to insert the latter in saddle bars fashioned in the shape of the compositions, as in the marvellous Crucifixion from the Romanesque cathedral at Châlons-sur-Marne (post 1145), now on display in the cathedral treasury. This solution, which was used up until the mid thirteenth century in France, gave rise to astonishingly complex jigsaw-like effects.

During the twelfth century, in fact, stained-glass windows generally possessed a fairly straightforward layout, whatever their position. In the lower story, where they were to be viewed from close to, they were composed of a series of superimposed medallions, one or two at each level, and in exceptional cases three, surrounded by wide borders. Between these elements there were decorative motifs which developed in a line or were enclosed in *broches*, with mosaic backgrounds not appearing until the end of the century. This formula, known by the experts as "legendary," was used in the lower bays and also ambulatories and radiating chapels. From the end of the century windows began to grow in size

and their arrangement changed: the narrative sections at each level increased, as in the St. Peter window in Lyon Cathedral (c. 1190), or were gathered together in groups of several medallions that acted as a means of expressing the desired narrative or theological message. This style of composition was sometimes adopted for tall windows, as in the chevet of Poitiers Cathedral (c. 1160), but the preferred composition was normally that of standing or enthroned figures, generally beneath an arcade: apostles, prophets, or other saints grouped around the figures of Christ and the Virgin, in an apostolic procession or, as at Canterbury and the Church of Saint-Remi in Reims, in a genealogy of Christ. Very few examples of these twelfth-century schemes are now in existence, however. Apart from the two cited, which in any case have survived incomplete, the majority are remnants that have been reduced to one or two figures and whose overall composition it is impossible to recreate with any accuracy.

A single window could bring together and illustrate an iconography of extraordinary exegetic density or explain the writings of some contemporary theologian, as is the case in Poitiers Cathedral with the Crucifixion window, which conveys the thoughts of Gilbert de la Porée. Unlike the thirteenth century, when the subject was spread out over a number of different windows in a single story, during the twelfth century the composition could be concentrated in just one window and could interpret one or more specific concepts that were not revealed at first sight by the image or images. Years of research are sometimes needed to fully decipher the message contained within Romanesque windows like the one in Saint-Denis or the typological ones in Canterbury Cathedral. To return once again to the five windows from the old Abbey Church of Arnstein on the Lahn (c. 1160–70), now preserved in the Landesmuseum in Münster, Westphalia: their composition reveals extraordinary iconographical maturity, dwelling on, among other things, the subtle parallels to be drawn between the Old and New Testaments. The Jesse Tree, the most spectacular iconographical creation of the Middle Ages in the West, was given pride of place in the chevet of Saint-Denis in around 1140–45, being placed in one of the two bays of the axial chapel opening onto the ambulatory. The representation of the Genealogy of Christ in accordance with the writings of the prophet Isaiah is an older practice, but the Saint-Denis version was to act as the model for other windows in France and England for more than a century, until the Holy Roman Empire added the major events of Christ's life, as can be seen in Freiburg im Breisgau Cathedral (c. 1200). The material chosen

often concentrates on the lives of Christ, the Virgin, and such major saints as Stephen, which as a rule are illustrated in a narrative way. The development of hagiography was also to the advantage of stained-glass windows, with the donors commissioning representations of the lives of either their own patron saint or the one to whom the building was dedicated, as in the St. Julian window behind the west front of Le Mans Cathedral (c. 1155–60). Events in the realm of religious politics also explain certain subjects: the restoration of the primacy of St. Peter by Pope Alexander III (1159–81) gave rise to the rebirth of his cult and to the emergence of his imagery in stained glass, as at Poitiers Cathedral (c. 1160) and Lyon Cathedral (c. 1190). Nevertheless, the disappearance of large numbers of windows means that only a partial record can be established, either on the basis of extant works or of old texts and descriptions.

In addition to these narrative or figurative windows, with pure, pale colours, there was another type, the white grisaille window, simply conceived, but with finely executed decorative ornament that often made use of such elements as palmettes and strapwork. Very few original examples of these windows, which must have been in common usage from the beginning of the twelfth century, have survived, however, apart from a few panels in churches belonging to the order of St. Bernard of Clairvaux, such as the one at Obazine in Limousin and at La Bénissons-Dieu in Forez. Spurning all forms of richness for their places of worship, the Cistercian order forbade its monks to decorate their churches with painted or coloured windows, and it was from this interdiction, which was renewed on several occasions during the course of the twelfth century and even during the thirteenth as well, that there arose the art of colourless, nonfigurative stained glass, which relied on an age-old, archaistic decorative repertoire. In fact, significant parallels may be drawn between the floral motifs that make up the earliest Cistercian grisaille windows, at Obazine, for example, and those to be found in Islamic and Visigothic transennae of the seventh and eighth centuries. This cannot be the result of any direct contact, but rather of the resurfacing of an ancient decorative vocabulary common to the whole Mediterranean world, which at certain moments in history experiences a resurgence.

CENTERS OF PRODUCTION AND WORKSHOPS

Advancing beyond these general trends,

Chartres Cathedral, interior of the west front, left bay, Passion of Christ, *lower section, c. 1150.*

Church of the Trinity, Vendôme, Chapel of the Virgin, Virgin and Child, second quarter of the twelfth century.

Opposite: Poitiers Cathedral, chevet, axial bay, Crucifixion and Ascension of Christ, 1165–70.

and despite the disappointingly limited number of surviving works, there is a synthesis published some years ago by Louis Grodecki which has led to greater awareness of the creative vitality of the art of stained glass during the twelfth century. His work, the product of extensive and laborious research, shows that stained glass possesses its own artistic geography and follows an evolutionary pattern that varies according to the different workshops. For a long time it was believed that stained glass developed only in the northwestern areas of Europe, most notably England and the regions lying between the Loire and the Rhine. It now has to be admitted that this is anything but true. Even though the surviving remains are less important than those to be found in western France or the Île-de-France, there is nevertheless contemporary evidence to be found in both the Auvergne and Lyonnais. Spain and Italy ought also to be included in this inventory: one American museum possesses a small narrative window from a church in Catalonia, while the treasury of Aosta Cathedral contains two medallions from a church in the town which can be dated to 1190–1200. Political circumstances also created similarities and disparities between different schools. In the west of France, for example, in regions such as Poitou and Maine, where the Plantagenets held sway, workshops took up Romanesque forms, thereby echoing those to be found in wall paintings of the period. It is even possible to maintain that often, as in the Ascension in Le Mans Cathedral (c. 1140), stained glass surpassed the works created on other materials, such as parchment or plaster, by virtue of its own special properties.

In spite of the wholesale destruction that took place during the sixteenth-century wars of religion and during the Revolution, France is still the country with the richest heritage of stained glass. There are, however, provinces such as Burgundy in which nothing has survived, even though written accounts tell us that buildings of the region, such as the Abbey Church of Saint-Bénigne at Dijon, did indeed possess stained-glass windows. All physical traces of them have vanished and our knowledge is restricted to what can be gleaned from old descriptions, which do not, unfortunately, allow us to reconstruct the style and iconography of the original works. In Normandy only a few fragments have survived, unearthed during nineteenth-century excavations at Mont-Saint-Michel, even though there are references in old books to several

Norman churches containing stained glass. We possess no indications as to the general nature of Norman stained glass nor any important series; works such as the Virgin and Child at Vendôme exist in isolation and today form no part of any overall picture. Given these circumstances, many of our studies and conclusions are, and will continue to be, provisional. The region that now possesses the greatest number of stained-glass windows is western France, with three main centers, Le Mans, Poitiers, and Angers, which were active for several decades. In Le Mans Cathedral no fewer than seven schools of craftsmen are recorded between the years 1130–40 and 1190–1200, a phenomenon that is unique in twelfth-century French stained glass, and not all of them followed the same iconographic or stylistic traditions. The famous Ascension (c. 1130–40), a major work of Romanesque art, displays an astounding graphic and chromatic authority which places it in the same league as such masterpieces of wall painting as the vault of Saint-Savin-sur-Gartempe or such masterpieces of miniaturism as the illuminations of the Sacramentaire de Limoges, now preserved in the Bibliothèque Nationale in Paris. But the Ascension outstrips these works in the expressive qualities and formal tension that lie beneath its surface. The composition, which is incomplete in its present state (the figures of Christ and the angels have disappeared from the upper register), has an alternating blue and red background reminiscent of a mural. Against this background there appear the figures of the Virgin and the Apostles, grouped in twos or threes, each one balanced on a small mound in dance-like poses, their feet at different angles, their faces upturned, and the palms of their hands outstretched.

There was a whole succession of workshops in Le Mans that lasted right up until the end of the century, some of which, like the one responsible for the panel portraying St. Peter's deliverance from prison (c. 1150), adhered to the graphic and pictorial traditions of the Ascension; while another echoed the techniques employed by Anglo-Norman illuminators working at Mont-Saint-Michel, a third found inspiration in the wall painting of the Loire valley, and a fourth, active after 1150, betrayed the insidious influence of the new, Byzantine-style of art that was beginning to infiltrate Romanesque forms. A fifth master, who painted the life of St. Stephen (Saint Étienne) between 1156 and 1160, exploited and surpassed the style of the three windows in the west front of Chartres Cathedral. Le Mans is the only French city in which it is possible to trace the existence of such an important amount of activity, but it was undoubtedly not alone in playing host to workshops and master glaziers from neighbouring regions, who transformed local traditions.

Neither Poitiers nor Angers reveals the same diversity. At Poitiers, the three windows of the cathedral's chevet form an exceptional group, with the Crucifixion in the axial bay displaying an iconographical interpretation that is unique in twelfth-century stained glass. On the north side the windows portray the life of St. Lawrence, and on the south side, the lives of St. Peter and St. Paul. This group was created by the same workshop and dates, in all probability, from 1165–70. The center window reunites the three essential elements of the Redemption. An enormous Crucifixion occupies the central part: Christ, his eyes wide open, is nailed to a purple cross that evokes both his suffering and his royalty, while beneath one arm of the Cross stand the Virgin and St. Stéphaton and, beneath the other, Longinus and St. John, the traditional witnesses to the Crucifixion. The sun and moon have been consigned to the border, where they lengthen the arms of the Cross. The image is accompanied by a very small Resurrection, represented by the episode of the women visiting the tomb, which is placed below the Crucifixion (not shown here). Above the Crucifixion, and almost overlapping it, there is the contrasting image of Christ in Glory, as symbolized by the Ascension. The Saviour, triumphant, with one hand in a gesture of benediction and the other holding a book, stands inside a mandorla with a red background dotted with blue rectangles and flanked but not supported by two angels. Beneath this Ascension stand its historical witnesses, ten Apostles and the Virgin, whose poses recall the Ascension in Le Mans Cathedral, which is several decades earlier in date. There are, in fact, numerous similarities in the draughtsmanship and the pictorial execution of the two works that prove they were both products of the same artistic milieu. The Poitiers window, however, displays such a high degree of formal and chromatic coherence that it must belong to a later stage in the development of Romanesque painting in western France.

The series of Romanesque windows in Angers Cathedral possess neither chronological nor stylistic homogeneity. The oldest sections, such as the Annunciation (c. 1155), have now become hard to decipher and it is the later windows, portraying St. Catherine, the Dormition of the Virgin, and the Martyrdom of St. Vincent (c. 1180) and still possessing a very strong luminous quality, which now attract attention. Although their ornamentation and their draughtsmanship are derived from the works already observed at Le Mans and Poitiers, their compositions, which involve several historiated sections grouped around the main medal-lion, and the very organization of the scenes, in which the figures are no longer tightly serried, show a stylistic evolution that already reflects the conventions of Late Romanesque Art.

This western French "school" possesses a stylistic coherence that results from the inspiration that it shared with both the mural painting of the region and the style of illumination practiced in Limousin and Poitou. Although the workshops evolved along parallel lines and although styles differed locally and influences were not always the same, this group is nevertheless the one which best reflects the stylization of Romanesque art in stained-glass windows: the elongation of their figures, the feeling of tension in their movement, and the decorative treatment of the folds and drapery. In fact, there are a number of stained-glass panels and windows in churches in Touraine and Anjou, evidence of the flourishing nature of the art in these regions during the twelfth century, which can be grouped around these three main centers. They include the Virgin and Child at Vendôme, which may be contemporary with the Ascension at Le Mans, created during the 1140s, and which possesses an exceptional formal quality. The iconographical design of this Virgin and Child in Majesty is traditional: Mary, portrayed in a rigidly formal pose and wearing a crown surrounded by a halo, is seated, holding the Child in front of her and with her right hand raised in a gesture of benediction. And yet there is such a strong formal symbiosis between the drawn-out shape of the mandorla surrounding the Virgin and the hieratical outline of her figure that the significance of this cult image undergoes a metamorphosis and, despite its monumentality, achieves the status of an icon. Contrasting with this truly Romanesque movement is the group of windows from the Île-de-France, which already display early Gothic qualities. The most notable of these are the Abbé Suger windows at Saint-Denis (c. 1140–44), the three windows in the west front of Chartres Chatedral (1150–55) and, from the end of the century, the medallions depicting the life of St. Matthew (c. 1180), which were redeployed in the rose window in the southern arm of the transept of Notre-Dame Cathedral in Paris, and the christological panes in Saint-Germer-de-Fly (Oise), an old Benedictine abbey on the borders of the Vexin region. This group evolved essentially from the experiences at Saint-Denis, where, as Abbé Suger himself wrote, he summoned masters from "divers nations." It is still difficult, however, to compose a register of these painters, as the works of Louis Grodecki have shown. Some of the Saint-Denis windows are known solely from old drawings or archaeological documents.

Le Mans Cathedral, nave, south aisle,
Ascension of Christ, *c. 1140(?).*

There are few of the original elements still in situ and these have been incorporated in windows restored during the nineteenth century by craftsmen who understood neither their original composition nor the thought that lay behind them. Other panels have been dispersed through American and European museums and collections. In addition, the chevet and the ambulatory of the Abbey Church of Saint-Denis mark the introduction of new building techniques involving the use of intersecting ribs, which created a whole structure and a whole series of architectural effects that are clearly Gothic in style. Paradoxically, however, the windows' composition was still Romanesque and remained relatively untouched by these innovations. Despite the enlargement of chapel windows, large murals retained their importance, while the window still maintained its characteristically Romanesque colouring. Apart from the Jesse Tree, which achieves a new spatial quality through the use of large blue areas in its background, the other medallions—whoever made them—adhere for the most part to the earlier conventions derived from other areas of figurative art, such as, for example, Mosan enamelling (champlevé enamels from the valley of the Meuse) and miniaturism in the case of the "Signum Tau," the sole surviving section of a typological window dedicated to Christ's Passion.

Almost everyone is familiar with the three west windows of Chartres Cathedral, which must be the most famous in the world. Situated in an axial bay, they comprise an enormous Childhood of Christ, flanked to the south by a Jesse Tree and, to the north, by a Passion, all of which have been restored to their original glory by the exemplary restoration work carried out between 1975 and 1977. Their original position, that is to say prior to the fire that devastated Chartres Cathedral in 1194, was in a gallery above the monumental doorway built between 1135 and 1155, from whence they illuminated a long, dark Romanesque nave, a fact that the modern visitor is often unaware of. Rescued from the fire and preserved in their original setting, they were incorporated in a marvellous Gothic edifice, but their role as a means of transmitting light became profoundly altered. Their brilliance is magnified by the famous "blue which excites us like the revelation of another world" (Émile Mâle). The remarkable thing about this vast theological lesson on the glory of Christ and the Virgin, the patroness of the building, is the alliance of a monumentality previously unknown in stained glass to a decorative style that still retains the old "precious" quality. The Childhood is the earliest surviving example of a composition made up of three illustrated compartments at each level, and it contains a very comprehensive treatment of this period of Christ's life and also of two later events: his Baptism and the Entry into Jerusalem. Some episodes are dealt with in a sequence of several compartments: there are six, for example, in the case of the Adoration of the Magi. The Passion cycle occupies the whole window and is spread over a double row of superimposed medallions, starting with the Transfiguration and ending with Christ's posthumous appearance to the disciples at Emmaus. The Jesse Tree reverts to the formula used at Saint-Denis, but with the injection of a feeling of monumentality, as well as a greater degree of clarity in its layout. The technical procedures are also changed. The outline is stronger, to the detriment of the wash beneath, a feature which reflects the speed of execution that characterizes Gothic technique.

The Romanesque cathedral at Chartres was embellished with other stained-glass windows, the only surviving sections of which are a border panel that has been reused in a transept window and, most importantly, the *Vierge de la Belle Verrière*. This figure, created around 1180, probably for the axial bay of the Romanesque building, was salvaged from the 1194 fire and incorporated in the new Gothic structure around 1215, at which point a new series of figures and scenes were added that broadened its original meaning, endowing it with a liturgical and typological significance in keeping with scriptural interpretations of the first quarter of the thirteenth century. The master craftsmen of Chartres also created stained-glass windows for buildings other than the cathedral. There is one panel, for example, now in poor condition, which came originally from the old Abbey Church of Saint-Pierre and which predates the *Vierge de la Belle Verrière* by a few years; this shows how the old Romanesque forms were still persisting, particularly in the ornamentation, which retains the earlier feeling of delicacy. Its subject is the Ascension, in which the representation of Christ "disappearing from view" follows an iconographical type created in England around 1000.

During the final decades of the twelfth century Paris entered a period of flourishing artistic activity that was to reach its culmination during the reign of St. Louis. Very little, however, has survived from this early period, apart from seven medallions depicting the life of St. Matthew which have been reused in the south rose of Notre-Dame and whose provenance is uncertain. These sections must originally have come from a low window, as is shown by their small scale and the delicate precision of their workmanship, both of which are qualities that recur in Champagne and in the Holy Roman Empire. A similar style of draughtsmanship occurs in the poorly preserved panels from the old Abbey Church at Saint-Germer-de-Fly (Oise), to the northwest of Paris. Like the St. Matthew series, these must have been made in the 1180s, which would prove a common inspiration for the two groups that has yet to be explained. But there is also a final medallion (now in the Musée de Cluny), probably a remnant of a rose window because of its shape and subject matter, which relates to the Last Judgement, and this section, whose style already contains elements characteristic of thirteenth-century aesthetics, has a markedly Parisian feel to it.

The art of stained glass in Champagne displays trends that vary according to the region's different centers of production (Châlons-sur-Marne, Reims, and Troyes) and according to the dates of the panels or full-scale windows still preserved in these towns. The oldest, those from the Romanesque cathedral at Châlons and now on display in the cathedral's treasury, are thought to be contemporary with the building's consecration (1147) and probably adorned the choir, which was rebuilt during the thirteenth century. The most important element is a Crucifixion, accompanied by scenes from the Old Testament, which is all that is left of a window dedicated to the Passion. As was the case with the Ascension in Le Mans, which paid tribute to the western French style of painting, this Crucifixion epitomizes Mosan art. Both in its composition and its iconography it resembles the Stavelot altar, a masterpiece of Mosan enamelling now in the Musées royaux d'Art et d'Histoire in Brussels. The striking similarities between the two works are proof of their common inspiration, but the pictorial treatment of the window displays a technical mastery and a chromatic harmony that have rarely been equalled. The paint is applied in three layers in accordance with the principles laid down by the monk Theophilus: a wash to temper the translucence of the glass, an intermediate layer to strengthen the shaded areas, and then a strongly defined outline. The other elements in Châlons Cathedral lack this formal authority, even the fine medallion depicting the story of St. Stephen's relics, which is only slightly later in date (c. 1155) and whose division into four scenes exemplifies the illustrative development of stained glass at the beginning of the thirteenth century.

This dependence on Mosan art lasted right up until the end of the twelfth century, whether in the typological window in the ancient Abbey Church of Orbais near Épernay (c. 1190) or in the remains at Troyes. The latter probably come from the old Collegiate Church of Saint-Étienne, which was attached to the palace of the Counts of Champagne that

Le Mans Cathedral, nave, south aisle, The Angel Frees St. Peter from Prison, *c. 1150.*

has since been destroyed. The formal and chromatic qualities of these remains, now scattered through a number of museums and collections in France and elsewhere, usher in the relaxed, archaistic art of the thirteenth century by means of original stylistic formulas that closely reflect those seen in manuscripts from the Abbey Church of Clairvaux in southern Champagne. Of the different series of windows in the famous Church of Saint-Remi at Reims (traditionally believed to have been built above the tomb of the bishop responsible for baptizing the Frankish King Clovis), which were installed after the 1160s, when the abbey church was partially rebuilt, or possibly even earlier, some follow trends that still reflect Mosan art, while others take the form of early Gothic windows, with a graphic quality and a sense of monumentality that closely resembles contemporary examples in Canterbury Cathedral. There is a last group, which comprises topographically disparate remains, but ones whose iconography and style, although different, incorporate Byzantine-style elements originating in either Venice or Sicily, one of the most brilliant and innovative artistic centers of mid-twelfth-century Europe.

These works, which are to be found in Auvergne and the southeast of France, are evidence that the art of stained glass was not the exclusive domain of the north. Unfortunately, however, very little has survived of this work: some unmatched panels, made during the course of the last three decades of the century, in the Gothic cathedral at Clermont-Ferrand, and a window dedicated to St. Peter in Lyon Cathedral (c. 1190). Conversely, this stylistic group also contains one of the best-preserved examples of Romanesque stained glass: the window in the small country church of Champ-près-Froges (Isère), to the northwest of Grenoble. It most probably comes from a ruined priory, which can be dated to the 1160s, and has colours of astonishing freshness and purity. It is a distillation of the particular qualities to be found in stained glass of the region, which can still be seen in several windows in the lower story of the chevet of Lyon Cathedral (1215–25), with the Byzantine traditions persisting and resisting the penetration of Gothic innovations.

It is almost impossible to retrace the activities of Germanic stained-glass workshops. With the exception of the Arnstein group, now on display at the Münster Landesmuseum, Westphalia and the series preserved in Strasbourg Cathedral, which can be dated to between 1180 and 1200, the only other survivals are unmatched panels of uncertain date and origin. Yet it was in a monastery in the Rhineland or in Lower Saxony that Theophilus wrote his famous treatise, a section of which is devoted to the manufacture of stained glass (incidentally, the only known signature of a stained-glass artist is that of Gerlachus, who included his own likeness at the base of one of the Arnstein windows). Many examples of Germanic stained glass have been destroyed over the centuries, however, some even during the Second World War.

The Arnstein group was probably destined to adorn the choir of the Premonstratensian abbey, founded in 1139. The windows were originally five in number and followed a typological pattern illustrating highly sophisticated comparisons between the Old and New Testaments. The axial window, two of whose three original panels have survived, contained a Jesse Tree, which was surrounded by Christological scenes that have since disappeared. Of the Old Testament scenes, which were consigned to the farthest-flung windows of the axis, only five panels now remain and these show a minute and delicate style of execution, with great attention paid to detail. The technique of painting is very precise and there are also certain pieces painted on the outside, as was often the case during the Romanesque era. It is likely that Gerlachus's workshop originated in Koblenz, since his non-monumental style is linked to the painting traditions of the mid-Rhine area, especially those of the illuminated manuscript, an art form which flourished there. These links enable us to date the Arnstein windows to around 1160 and also to tie them in with such isolated panels as the small Crucifixion in the Church of Sainte-Ségolène in Metz (c. 1160). In Westphalia, the St. Patroclus group at Soest (post-1165), now corroded and in a fragmented state, reflects influences from the same artistic milieu, that of the scriptorium at Helmarshausen. The Rhineland, in fact, played an essential part in the development of stained glass during the twelfth century: the formulas perfected by the workshops of the region lasted into the first half of the thirteenth century, as can be seen in the chevet of St. Kunibert in Cologne (1215–25).

The most remarkable testament to this activity along the banks of the Rhine, however, is provided by the windows in Strasbourg Cathedral. These panels, the most important of which number twenty in all, are hard to locate in the building, let alone study, but there are others in the Musée de l'Oeuvre Notre-Dame. Originally created to adorn the nave of the Ottonian cathedral and for the Romanesque choir built during the closing decades of the twelfth century, these windows, which can be dated to the same period, were of much greater importance: Strasbourg was, in effect, an "imperial city" during the period of the Hohenstaufen, who came originally from nearby Haguenau, where they owned a castle. There is one series, the remains of a Jesse Tree that once adorned the axial bay of the Romanesque apse, which depicts a praying Virgin and an angel and dates from 1180–1200. The composition and iconography of these panels, now placed in windows in the north arm of the transept, incorporate numerous elements derived from Byzantine art: the Virgin is portrayed as *Theotokos* and the angel wears the court dress commonly used in Constantinople. An awareness of this Byzantine contribution is essential to our appreciation of the originality of Strasbourg Cathedral's stained glass, which can be explained by the political links that existed between southern Italy, Sicily, and Alsace. It is of prime importance, for example, in understanding the original nature of the portrayal of the two St. Johns, the Baptist and the Evangelist, who had been widely associated with each other since early

Christian times. Both their pose and their treatment recall the mosaic tradition of Sicily, while their flowing drapery recalls the famous manuscript created in the Abbey of Mont-Saint-Odile during the time of Abbé Herrade of Landsberg. Like the glass panels, this manuscript, which was burnt during the 1870 fire in Strasbourg Library, showed very clear links with the Byzantine-style art of Sicily. The most important series, however, is the one depicting the emperors of the Holy Roman Empire, now in the windows of the north aisle of the Gothic nave, to which must also be added the figure thought traditionally to be that of Charlemagne, but which is in reality a symbolic image of imperial power and is now on display in the Musée de l'Oeuvre Notre-Dame. This element, whose original position is open to discussion, can be dated to the tail-end of the twelfth century or the very beginning of the thirteenth. The emperor is shown wearing a crown and with a halo round his head, bearing an orb and scepter, the insignia of his power, and there are two attendants at his back, as in representations of this type in very early manuscripts. The Byzantine character of the work, which is very marked in the figure's pose and shape, is further emphasized by the meticulous nature of its execution, which dwells extensively on the decorative detail of the costume. It is likely that this "picture" was the central element of a large group that covered the whole nave, with the emperors occupying the north side and the prophets occupying the south. The position allocated to this imperial iconography in Strasbourg's Romanesque cathedral was exceptional: the emperors were probably situated on the north side, in the upper story, while their companion figures, to the south, were prophets, apostles, and martyr saints such as those of the Theban Legion, slain at Agaune in Valais at the end of the third century A.D. Some figures have survived from this vast scheme and have been reused in bays in the north aisle, but originally they were placed beneath an arcade, with one window for each arch. The imperial theme also appears in three medallions belonging to a Judgement of Solomon (1180–1200), a biblical example of a just and temperate prince, and can be explained by the link between the archbishops of Strasbourg and Frederick Barbarossa, who was fighting against the Papacy.

The peripheral influence of this Strasbourg school remains hard to assess: contemporary remains from the surrounding areas, on both sides of the Rhine, do not follow the same stylistic principles, whether they be the panels from Alpirsbach (c. 1170), now in the Württembergisches Landesmuseum, Stuttgart, or the Virgin and Child from the old Abbey Church of Wissembourg (c.

1200), which is Byzantine in style. This phenomenon is not unique in the Holy Roman Empire: there are several stylistically isolated panels (ones which cannot easily be linked with any known work shop), such as the ones that formerly belonged to Goethe and which are now on display in the Goethe Nationalmuseum, Weimar, or the small Mary Magdalene from Weitenfeld Church in Carinthia (c. 1170), now in the Diocesan Museum in Klagenfurt (Austria). These examples all provide proof of the way in which the art of stained glass flourished throughout the Holy Roman Empire, even in its farthest-flung corners.

The old Romanesque forms lingered on in the Holy Roman Empire, hindering the new spatial and pictorial concepts of Gothic art. And yet this late Romanesque style, which was equally dominant in the other areas of art, did not atrophy: on the contrary, it took on new strength, as in the Church of St. Kunibert in Cologne, the chevet of which was decorated with stained glass between 1215 and 1230. It was the same in Strasbourg Cathedral, where reconstruction of the building was carried out through the transept and where two rose windows were installed to illuminate the south arm (1220–30). Despite being restored on numerous occasions, one of these windows, which portrays scenes from the New Testament, remains firmly wedded to Romanesque tradition; the other, by contrast, reveals certain elements characteristic of Gothic art, such as a technically less complicated composition. In England, a country which enjoyed a brilliant artistic flowering during the twelfth century, very little stained glass survives from the period before the great building program in Canterbury Cathedral. From the first half of the century almost nothing remains, although numerous illuminated manuscripts of the period have survived. It is at York Minster, in the north of England, that the earliest examples of stained glass are to be found, albeit often in a parlous condition. The best-known example is a king from a Jesse Tree, datable, like all the other fragments, which include elements from a Life of St. Benedict, to the third quarter of the century. The king is shown seated and holding the branches of a tree, in a pose closely resembling the earlier French forms that we have already seen at Saint-Denis and Chartres from the middle of the century. Despite its present poor state, the style of this very elegant figure can be compared to that found in contemporary manuscripts from the north of England. Another trend can be seen in the

Temptation in the Wilderness; Satan Carries Christ Up to the Pinnacle of the Temple, c. 1170, from Troyes Cathedral(?). Victoria and Albert Museum, London.

Head of the Patriarch Shem,
c. 1180–90, fragment of a window, from
Canterbury Cathedral. Victoria and Albert
Museum, London.

Canterbury Cathedral, choir, north side,
Parable of the Sower, c. 1200(?).

Canterbury Cathedral, Corona Chapel, sixth typological window; detail, The Bunch of Grapes from the Promised Land, *before 1200.*

panel portraying St. Nicholas, all that remains of a window dedicated to one of the Middle Ages' most popular saints. Its less contrived pictorial technique is very different from that of the preceding panel, a fact that underlines the presence in York of several workshops, the activities of which are hard to trace.

Canterbury Cathedral, by contrast, like Chartres, possesses a marvellous collection of windows, the majority of remarkably high quality. They have, however, been mistreated over the centuries. A large number have been moved and different panels have been reassembled, making it hard to work out their original relationships. The twelfth- and thirteenth-century elements were created for the east side of the cathedral, England's most important ecclesiastical foundation, which was rebuilt following a fire four years after the murder of Thomas à Becket in 1170. The new building was erected in honour of the dead primate, at whose tomb numerous miracles had been performed. The rebuilding of the eastern section, which was the first part to be restored, was entrusted to a French architect, Guillaume de Sens (William of Sens). In 1180 the monks took possession of the new choir, but there were still extensive works to be carried out, and these were not completed until 1220, when the relics of St. Thomas à Becket (canonized in 1173) were solemnly transferred to the Trinity Chapel situated directly behind the choir. The majority of the windows were put into position between 1180 and 1220 in accordance with an ambitious program carried out by a large number of workshops and master glaziers. A vast typological series dedicated to the Life of Christ was placed in the twelve lower windows of the choir and the east transept. It represents the most complex example of its types to have survived from the twelfth

century. Each Christological scene was accompanied by at least two scenes from the Old Testament with explanatory inscriptions. Only four windows have been partially preserved and these are now situated in the northern bays of the choir; they include a Genealogy of Christ, which begins with a representation of Adam digging and probably culminated in a portrayal of Christ and the Virgin. A certain number of these figures are still to be seen today, but none of them is in its original position. There was also a third series illustrating the lives of such venerable archbishops of Canterbury as St. Dunstan and St. Alphege, who lived around 1000. Both the Trinity Chapel and the little chapel called the Corona, which is situated directly behind it, were adorned with stained-glass windows in 1184 and 1220; apart from another cycle depicting the Life of Christ, the windows were decorated with scenes telling the story of the numerous miracles achieved through the intervention of Thomas à Becket and scrupulously recorded by the monks. Seven partly original windows still survive from the original group of twelve. Despite all the losses, no other building possesses such a coherent series of windows as Canterbury Cathedral, which during the closing decades of the twelfth century acted as a magnet for lay pilgrims and, more especially, the regular clergy of Europe. On a stylistic level, this group marks a high spot in the art of stained glass. Although there are clearly great differences between the elements created by the first master glaziers who worked there as early as 1180, and those active during the 1220s, all of them, while continuing to use old Romanesque formulas in the windows' execution, also introduced forms that were to be adopted in thirteenth-century art, as well as injecting a spatial quality that was already Gothic in feeling.

Opposite: Canterbury Cathedral, Bishop (believed to be Thomas à Becket), before 1200.

Canterbury Cathedral, Trinity Chapel, north side, Miracles Performed at the Tomb of Thomas à Becket; the Healing of Eilward of Westoning, c. 1200(?).

Canterbury Cathedral, choir, nave, north side, Noah's Ark, c. 1200(?).

3
The Thirteenth Century: the Great Cathedral Series

The thirteenth century is quite rightly regarded as the heyday of stained glass. As early as the end of the twelfth century, French Gothic architecture entered its "classical" period, starting with the rebuilding of Chartres Cathedral in 1194. Architects were now able to reduce the surface area of walls and replace them with numerous bays, enlivening the end walls of transepts and the interiors of façades with large rose windows. In the nave of Chartres Cathedral the bays are composed of two lancets surmounted by a rose, a prelude to the more sophisticated and airy compositions in which the distance between the lancets became reduced to a thin mullion, as happened as early as 1220 in Amiens Cathedral. This transformation was greatly to the benefit of stained glass, which now filled the spaces no longer occupied by the walls, allowing either for the introduction of large groups that fulfilled the requirements of contemporary Christian thinking or for the insertion of windows illustrating devotional scenes appropriate to some particular church or religious community. It is at Chartres, however, more than in any other building of the period, that one gains the best idea of the essential part now played by stained glass. This cathedral contains some one hundred and sixty stained-glass windows and three roses, created, in the case of the earliest ones (in the nave), around 1200, and, in the case of the later ones, between 1235 and 1240. Windows became much darker than during the previous period because of their increase in size, and their relationship with architecture also changed. They were to remain the same, at least in the *Domaine royal* and the adjoining regions, up until 1250–60.

During the first half of the thirteenth

century, France under the Capet dynasty was a kingdom in full expansion; in a way it was the flagship of Christian Europe. During the reign of Philip II (Philip Augustus) it had grown considerably, and Paris had become an artistic capital in which numerous craftsmen flourished, their professions becoming secularized in the second half of the twelfth century. In the case of stained glass, it is difficult to prove Parisian supremacy until after the program of building works carried out at Saint-Germain-des-Prés and the Sainte-Chapelle in Paris, which, from 1240–45 onwards, were to be the dominant influences on French stained glass. The situation elsewhere in Europe was much more complex and changed from period to period.

Although stained glass, an essential element of religious architecture, became increasingly monumental during the thirteenth century, it continued to be an art whose style and treatment could vary from region to region and workshop to workshop or even be affected by the personality of an individual, innovative artist. The number of windows to be worked on was, in fact, so high that several master stained-glass artists were often summoned to work together on a single project. Three were used for the ambulatory and radiating chapels of Bourges Cathedral, for example, where the bays were filled with stained glass between 1210 and 1215, while three were also employed on the windows in the upper story of the Sainte-Chapelle in Paris, which were completed between 1242 and 1246. Artists sometimes came from far away in search of work and, once they had fulfilled their task, returned home again. At the turn of the twelfth century, members of workshops in the regions around Laon and Soissons, for example, showed considerable enterprise in leaving their home territory in search of work. Not everyone, however, went as far afield as the master glass-artist responsible for the St. Eustache window in Chartres Cathedral (c. 1210). Pierre d'Arras was active in Lausanne in around 1230, when he worked on the famous rose window that dominates the southern arm of the cathedral's transept. And when work was finished on the

windows in the triforium and the upper story of the nave in Strasbourg Cathedral, in about 1265, the artists moved eastwards into the farthest corners of the Holy Roman Empire, where their hand can be seen in Brandenburg Cathedral in Prussia and the one at Wiener Neustadt, not far from Vienna. Although many stained-glass artists never ventured beyond the boundaries of the provinces in which they worked, the mobility of many of their fellows is an essential element in understanding the links existing between different workshops that were sometimes geographically very far apart. As during the previous century, stained-glass artists continued to be anonymous. Very few of their names are known to us, although there was a certain Clement, a glazier from Chartres (*Clemens vitrearius carnotensis*), who signed a window in the ambulatory of Rouen Cathedral around 1235, and there are other names contained in archive documents, such as Étienne, a glazier from Bourges, who lived in a canon's house in that town in around 1220.

Such information is very incomplete and it does not enable us to trace the activities of a single workshop or to know the number of artists and assistants who comprised it. All we know is that the craftsmen generally lived in lodgings near the building on which they were working, grouped around a master glazier who was the head of the workshop. From the end of the thirteenth century there are written references which give us a clearer idea of how the work was organized. In the royal Abbey Church of Saint-Denis, for example, a glazier was employed to maintain the stained glass and was paid eight livres a year, a considerable sum of money in those days; the materials that he needed, the glass and the lead, were provided by the monks. Many other important buildings, such as cathedrals, employed a man with similar responsibilities.

The methods of commissioning stained glass, on the other hand, are much better known. The donors often had themselves portrayed in the window that they had presented, not forgetting to "sign" it by means of an inscription bearing their name and rank. In addition, they had their gift recorded in the archives. The obituary list of Lyon Cathedral provides us with the names of a dozen such donors, who include church dignitaries, monks, and members of the gentry. Generally speaking, trade associations and guilds such as the furriers or tanners chose to be portrayed going about their daily activities, whereas nobles and prelates preferred to be shown kneeling in prayer, holding a small model of their window. These gifts sometimes commemorated a special event, like the one presented by the vine growers of Le Mans, who were obliged to present a window to the cathedral for having arrived late at the consecration ceremony of the new choir on April 20, 1254. Since the cost of erecting any building, particularly a cathedral, lay far beyond the financial capabilities of any religious foundation, whether an abbey or a cathedral, those in charge of the project turned for help to anyone in a position to assist them. Most of the stained glass in Chartres Cathedral was obtained in this way between 1200 and 1240. Some was paid for by the guilds, like the Charlemagne window presented by the furriers, and some was donated by canons or illustrious *seigneurs*, like the rose window in the north arm of the transept presented by the Dreux-Bretagne family. In the majority of cases these donors would have vanished from our collective memory, were it not for the fact that they recorded their generosity by "signing" these windows with a portrait and their name.

THE FOUNDATIONS OF GOTHIC STAINED GLASS

In the thirteenth century any religious building, especially a cathedral, was both a monument erected by skilled architects with the help of workmen, of whom undoubtedly much was asked, and a representation of the heavenly Jerusalem, the ideal city according to the Apocalypse. This concept, which was developed in many writings of the period, such as those of Bishop Sicardus of Cremona and Durand de Mende, partly explains the nature of the development of stained glass during the period. Windows became light-filled compartments at every level of Gothic architecture: in the low windows of the ambulatory and of the chapels radiating from the chevet, in the upper story and, after 1230–35, in the triforium as well, when that too began to be pierced. A sort of rivalry sprang up between the architect, who increased the number of openings in the wall in order to make his buildings lighter, and the stained-glass artist, who took advantage of these openings, while at the same time realizing that his work had to blend in with the architecture and not clash with it. This realization explains the increasingly strong palette used by glaz-

iers, the darkest example of which can be seen in the choir of Le Mans Cathedral (1255–70). But this chromatic progression reached a critical point when the bays attained their maximum size and Gothic architects found themselves obliged to follow more restrictive principles, since the optics of mass, volume, and perspective tended to heighten naves and make them seem larger. A sort of impatience led them to exploit the marvellous possibilities offered by the Gothic system and to research new models for the interior and exterior of buildings. From 1260 onwards we witness a complete change from the trends prevailing during the first half of the century: the first tentative experiment can be seen in Tours Cathedral (after 1260), while a more fully developed example of this phenomenon is provided by the Collegiate Church of Saint-Urbain at Troyes, which has already been mentioned. Brightly coloured stained-glass windows were now replaced by mixed windows: these juxtaposed coloured panels (the iconographical sections) with pale ones (decorated with foliar motifs), which were to become more and more important and ultimately relegate the scenes and figures to the status of vignettes, as in the chevet of the Abbey of Saint-Martin-aux-Bois in the Vexin region (c. 1260). This evolutionary process, which involved a large part of both France and England, did not follow the same course in the Holy Roman Empire, where stained glass conformed to the architectural styles favoured by the mendicant orders and resulted in the introduction of a distinctive style characterized by the enlargement of the architectural canopy over the scenes, creating a sort of magical tabernacle.

These modifications could never have been achieved without the accompaniment of important technical innovations in the way that stained glass was made. Although at the beginning of the thirteenth century artists still followed the traditional principles of Romanesque stained glass, such as the delicate cutting-out process, and enlivened their works by means of abrasion, as, for example, in the Passion window in Bourges Cathedral (c. 1210), they soon realized that it was vital to speed up the process because of the increase in size of windows. They would have to abandon the old processes, resort to ever larger and simpler, more geometric cutting-out, and begin to paint in a more summary way. In fact, they would have to abandon the old doctrine of "three values" preached by Theophilus in the previous century and use just two painting processes, a wash—and even that ended up being omitted from the Bishop Bernard d'Abbeville window in Amiens Cathedral (1269)—and an outline. Glass artists forfeited the subtleties of Romanesque stained glass in favour of expressive effects

and pictorial simplification, particularly since many windows were now placed high up in buildings, far from ground level, where the human eye could not discern the same amount of detail as in the lower windows, such as the ones in the ambulatory or in radiating chapels.

A formal reaction was to occur in France, particularly in the workshops of the Île-de-France and Normandy, and also in England. Stained-glass artists returned to a much more refined and expressive style of painting, as in the window portraying the Life of the Virgin that adorns the east bay of the south aisle in the small Church of Saint-Sulpice-de-Favières, to the southwest of Paris, the choir of which is a masterpiece of Rayonnant architecture (the so-called "Court Style") from the time of Louis IX. In fact, during the first half of the century stained glass became the most important artistic technique, dominating the other pictorial arts, most notably miniaturism, where, in such famous works as the French *Bibles moralisées*, one can see compositions very similar to those found in stained glass of the period, with superimposed medallions standing out against mosaic backgrounds. During the second half of the century, by contrast, Miniaturism regained prominence and stained glass began to imitate it by adopting the same formal mannerism, by evolving towards a smaller and more detailed style and by refining its pictorial technique, a process that had spread to most European workshops by the end of the thirteenth century and the beginning of the fourteenth. These alterations did not affect just the way in which the paint was applied; some of them occurred earlier on in the process and related to the actual way in which the glass was made, which became less empirical. At the end of the thirteenth century greater control began to be exercised over the raw materials from which the glass paste was made, notably the river sand, thereby permitting the creation of glass with a more uniform colouring; this was particularly true of pale glass, which now became white. The methods of blowing glass were also perfected, resulting in the creation of larger and thinner panes, which in France at the time were generally made by the *cives* or crown process. The conditions under which stained glass was made changed. The scale of the individual pieces increased and the leads became lighter, while a new stain, silver salt, was introduced, the application of which was to free glass windows from the constraints of the lead lattice. It represented a technical revolution, and its introduction coincided with a desire in France and England to make stained-glass windows lighter. Known

Chapel of Baye Castle, Marne, Jesse Tree; *detail,* Head of Christ, *c. 1220.*

Jesse Tree; *detail, King, c. 1220, provenance unknown. Victoria and Albert Museum, London.*

since antiquity, silver salt had been used for the manufacture of vases in Egypt since the sixth century. It was an element that allowed a piece of clear glass to be coloured without resorting to cutting and it also enabled the shading to be varied in accordance with the laws of complementary colour. What is more, the silver stain was applied to the outside of the glass, with the glazier then painting on the internal surface in the usual way, which allowed him to vary the amount of light passing through the glass. The formula for silver stain is thought to have reached the West at around the end of the thirteenth century through the *Lapidary*, a written compilation of the processes used in Moorish Spain and translated into Castilian on the orders of Alfonso X, "the Wise." A copy is believed to have been presented to the French court in about 1300, perhaps a little earlier, and the preparation of silver stain was soon being carried out in a number of workshops, probably in Paris, Normandy, and England. The new stain was ideally suited to the formal and chromatic refinement that these workshops were striving to achieve, since just a few touches of silver stain were enough to bring a piece of glass to life. Its introduction met a very real stylistic need and within less than twenty-five years glaziers throughout Europe had adopted it wholeheartedly, thereby revolutionizing the development of stained glass.

At the beginning of the thirteenth century the increase in the size of bays also began to have an effect on the actual composition of historiated windows. Instead of a single medallion per register, a layout that persisted in the Holy Roman Empire and in certain other centers, such as Lyon, several narrative elements were now brought together in a single group, often in very inventive shapes such as quadrants and elongated diamonds, which were themselves divided into four or six, with each of these shapes corresponding to a scene. In Chartres Cathedral there are a large number of star-shaped compositions, while in the window of the ambulatory in Bourges Cathedral the principle was used for the purpose of theological illustration. The center depicts the most significant episode, with the side sections being treated as illustrated glosses whose function is to explain and emphasize the lesson contained within the axial medallion. This formal evolution began as early as the end of the twelfth century, most notably in Canterbury Cathedral, and was taken up by a great many French workshops at the beginning of the thirteenth century. Between these compartments, often held together by wrought-iron bars that mirror their outline, there developed small-scale decorative motifs. During the first half of the century these mosaics, often in two colours, consisted of

Jesse Tree; *detail*, Daniel, *c. 1210, originally from Troyes Cathedral (?). Victoria and Albert Museum, London.*

Overleaf: Chartres Cathedral, nave, south side, Death and Assumption of the Virgin; Death of the Virgin, *1205–15.*

37

Chartres Cathedral, nave, north side, Parable of the Good Samaritan; *detail,* Expulsion of Adam and Eve from the Garden of Eden, *1205–15.*

delicate floral ornament, later to be replaced by heraldic motifs such as the fleur-de-lis and the *château de castille*, as in the Sainte-Chapelle in Paris. Soon they became purely decorative and did not correspond, as has all too often been maintained, to any royal or princely liberality, except in certain cases, such as the lancets of Saint-Urbain at Troyes. At the beginning of the century, certain workshops, notably in Canterbury and northern France, replaced these mosaics with small foliated scrolls coiling round the sconcheons of the window, between the historiated compartments. Although this decorative device, which was difficult to achieve, was soon abandoned, it re-emerged in a rather dull and lifeless form in Burgundy during the 1230–40 period.

Scenes were often linked together by large ornamental devices known to French glaziers as *fermaillets*, whose decorative repertoire was similar to that of the mosaics. As for the borders, these soon narrowed down and, although during the first part of the century their typology stayed close to that of the Romanesque period, their decorative elements, by contrast, grew simpler and thinner and their execution became rapid, even sketchy. Starting with the Sainte-Chapelle, they became overrun with heraldic devices,

which made them seem increasingly banal since there was very little innovation, except at Saint-Urbain in Troyes, where a number of windows from around 1270 possess some very fine and inventive borders based on the arms of Count Thibaud V of Champagne and Pope Urban IV.

The narrative and pictorial image tended to occupy the entire window and reduce the space reserved for border decoration. This practice was slowly introduced, but the upper windows of the Sainte-Chapelle in Paris mark the culmination of a trend that prevailed before 1250. The narrow division of the lancet, fifteen times as tall as it was broad, here played host to a large number of superimposed scenes, albeit small in size, and compelled glaziers to return again and again to the same layouts. One image blended into another, almost identical one, and the biblical narratives, of which there were many in the Sainte-Chapelle, became incomprehensible.

The story of Esther and Ahasuerus, for example, is told in one hundred and twenty-nine scenes and thus loses its narrative precision. Hagiography also became similarly watered down. One episode was stretched out over several scenes, and even in the windows of the inner ambulatory of Le Mans Cathedral,

Chartres Chatedral, ambulatory, north side,
Story of Charlemagne; *detail,* Vision of
Constantine, *c. 1225.*

completed between 1250 and 1260, the same subjects are repeated. After 1260, however, there was a complete about-turn. Just at the moment when windows containing a mixture of pale grisaille panels and historiated ones were developing, there was a return to the portrayal of two or three scenes per window. The actual image then regained the impact that it had lost in the Sainte-Chapelle in Paris and the choir of Tours Cathedral, whose windows were created between 1255 and 1265.

Another iconographical formula, one dating back many years, enjoyed a great revival during the thirteenth century: the portrayal, in the axial bay, of important personalities, prophets, apostles, martyrs, and legendary bishops grouped around Christ and the Virgin. Slowly but surely, however, this basic formula grew increasingly complicated. The figures were now superimposed in twos and threes and were accompanied in the lower registers by donors, as in the choir of Le Mans Cathedral.

But what meaning did these light-filled panels hold for the faithful? First of all, the way in which the images were understood varied from cleric to noble and from monk to peasant or burgess. Laymen were granted only limited access to cathedrals. They were normally restricted to the nave, being allowed into the choir only during processions. We must therefore dispense with the idea expounded by certain historians during the nineteenth century, and repeated by the French poet and dramatist Paul Claudel in the twentieth, that stained-glass windows were the "catechism of the poor." Placed too high up, these glittering, glowing images cannot have conveyed any spiritual message that would have been understood by all, although there were some, situated in the axial bay of the chevet, for example, which were more accessible. The same was true in the case of the interior of the west front and the far walls of transepts, which were often occupied by immense rose windows. The development of these windows, which had been a slow process during the twelfth century, gained extraordinary momentum during the thirteenth century, when increasingly daring architectonic formulas were sought to accommodate glorifying series like the one in the interior of the west front of Notre-Dame in Paris (c. 1220), dedicated to the Virgin; cosmic ones, as in the northern arm of the transept of Laon Cathedral (c. 1200) and, later on, the one in Lausanne Cathedral completed prior to 1235 by a master known as Pierre d'Arras; eschatological ones, as in the interior of

the western façade of Chartres Cathedral (c. 1215), where a Last Judgement evokes the Second Coming of Christ. Sometimes, as in the southern arm of the transept at Chartres, these compositions are completed by five immense bays that form, together with the rose above dedicated to the Glorification of Christ surrounded by the Old Men of the Apocalypse, a marvellous series that focuses on the role of the Virgin as personification of the Church by having her accompanied by the four Evangelists borne aloft on the shoulders of prophets. Such a scheme could also revolve around just a few windows, as in the chevet of Laon Cathedral, or a whole series, as in the ambulatory of Bourges Cathedral. Put into place between 1210 and 1214, these windows convey a powerful theological and moralistic lesson through their choice of theme and subject matter, while the ones in the chapels are devoted to the saints most commonly venerated in this foundation. In the upper story of the Sainte-Chapelle, the Life of Christ, his royal Genealogy, as well as those of his closest companions, St. John the Evangelist and St. John the Baptist, are framed by several biblical cycles, whose protagonists, such as Tobias, Judith, and Job, in different ways exalt piety, a moral

virtue that profoundly influenced thirteenth-century exegesis. The windows of the Sainte-Chapelle illustrate the story of Man's redemption through Christ's suffering on the Cross. The relics of this event, which was of such decisive importance for the future of mankind in the eyes of thirteenth-century theologians, are also preserved in the chapel. But the series of windows has a royal significance in that it emphasizes the continuity between biblical royalty and that of the Capet dynasty, as embodied by Louis IX, founder of the chapel. The Sainte-Chapelle is exceptional, but in buildings as important as cathedrals the men responsible for the commission, generally the bishop and his chapter, would seek to glorify the saint or saints that had been patrons of the building since its foundation, and would choose the lives of the apostles upon whom their building's Christian antiquity rested, such as St. John the Evangelist in the case of Lyon. The windows of chapels generally illustrated the life or lives of the saints to whom they were consecrated. These could change from one diocese to another, while certain saints, such as St. Eustace, a Roman general martyred for his faith, enjoyed a high degree of popularity that they have since lost, but the choice of

Chartres Cathedral, ambulatory, north side, Life of St. James the Greater; *detail,* Donors *(furriers), c. 1220.*

Opposite: Chartres Cathedral, north arm, group of windows presented by the royal house of France. In the central lancet, St. Anne Carrying the Virgin, Flanked by Kings and Great Priests of the Old Testament *(from left to right,* Melchizedek, David, Solomon, *and* Aaron); *in the rose,* Glorification of the Virgin, *c. 1235.*

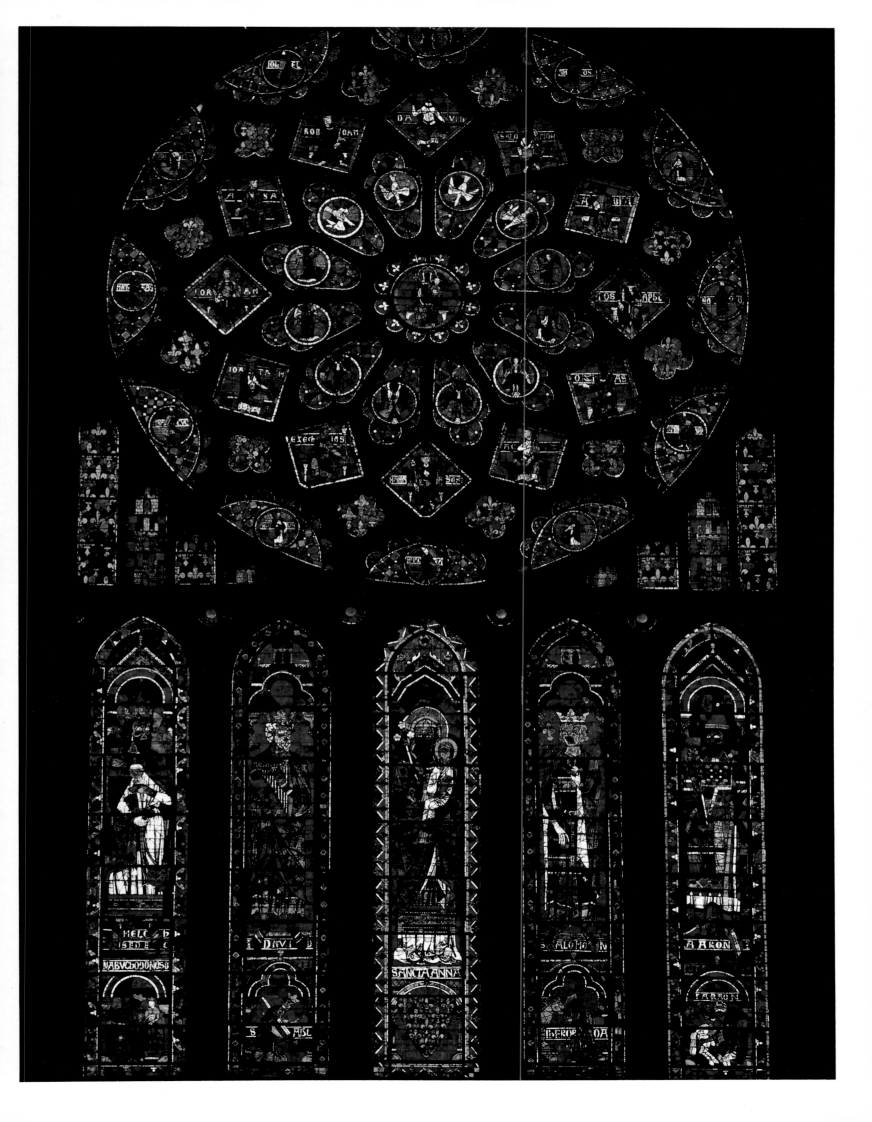

Chartres Cathedral, chevet, north radiating chapel, Life of St. Pantalion; *detail,* Donors *(stonecutters and sculptors), c. 1220–25.*

episodes depicted was not necessarily the same and neither, sometimes, was the layout. In the same way, the windows of axial chapels in cathedrals, as a rule dedicated to the Virgin, would contain Marian subjects, such as her life, her relationship with her Son, her powers of intercession, exemplified by legends such as the one relating to deacon Théophile, and her miracles, like that of the Jewish child of Bourges. It can therefore be seen that there was often a correlation between a building's dedication and the subject or subjects depicted in its bays. On the other hand, it is sometimes hard to imagine that it was the donors who chose the subject of their gift. The butchers of Bourges, for example, donated a window dealing with the dogma of the Redemption and the link between the Old and New Testaments. The significance of this theological lesson, one of the most profound to emerge at the beginning of the thirteenth century, must have escaped them, at least in part, and the subject may have been selected by the man commissioning it, who was undoubtedly Archbishop Guillaume of Bourges. Forty years later, by contrast, it was certainly the donors who themselves chose the images to be portrayed in the windows of the

inner ambulatory of Le Mans Cathedral: the repetitions reveal a lack of discipline and an absence of coordination and basic direction. An overall program has been abandoned in favour of individual devotionalism, a spiritual attitude that presages the direction taken by fourteenth-century thinking.

Another type of window enjoyed great success during the thirteenth century: the clear grisaille window. This was not an innovation, since the Cistercians had made great use of such windows during the twelfth century and other buildings probably had their bays filled with these decorative windows. During the first half of the thirteenth century, however, they were frequently used, either for reasons of economy or to complete a window quickly, and numerous examples have survived in European cathedrals and monastic buildings, not only abbeys, but also monasteries and chapter houses. On the other hand, except in the Holy Roman Empire, the Cistercians did not always adhere to the rules laid down by their order, preferring sometimes to install coloured windows. And yet the tradition of unpainted grisaille in the Cistercian manner lasted throughout the thirteenth

century in buildings as disparate as the Abbey Church of Saint-Jean-aux-Bois, near Beauvais, the Cathedral of Châlons-sur-Marne, and Beauvais Cathedral. The majority of them, however, were enlivened with floral decoration whose motifs followed no set pattern up until 1260. For the most part, they stand out against a fine trellis-work background, called by French glaziers "*cage à mouches*," and are grouped into geometric figures held together by coloured, thread-like lines. From the 1260s onwards these foliar designs were freed from their lead setting and traversed it like branches spreading freely over a trellis. The "woven" background disappeared and the vegetal repertoire of the design became naturalistic, with the English and French using ivy, strawberry, or columbine leaves. In the Holy Roman Empire, however, grisaille windows did not evolve along the same lines. The decorative motifs were on a larger scale and were represented straight on rather than in profile, as was normally the custom in France, with the favourite leaves being those of oak and holly. In around 1300 these windows altered considerably and began to make more and more use of colour, introducing lively animal elements such as lions and parrots.

STYLISTIC DEVELOPMENTS IN EUROPEAN STAINED GLASS DURING THE THIRTEENTH CENTURY

A stained-glass window is also a "painting on glass," meaning that each one possesses its own stylistic personality, which varies according to its artistic context and according to the workshop that creates it. Production during the thirteenth century was so extensive that one can detect a large number of different trends and nuances within a single building. The Gothic aesthetic was not adopted everywhere at the same time. In fact, it sometimes took several decades to attain formal and expressive maturity, which was then immediately transformed by new variations in line and colour. These modifications, accompanied on occasion by experimental elements that sometimes worked and sometimes failed, give thirteenth-century stained glass a very contemporary feel, as well as an exceptionally dynamic quality; in the Holy Roman Empire, for example, Romanesque art lasted well into the second half of the thirteenth century,

inventing new stylistic formulas and evolving towards an almost abstract graphical quality, as well as increasing the angularity of its compositions.

At the beginning of the thirteenth century the position of stained glass in Europe was paradoxical. There were whole regions still unfamiliar with the new ideas of Gothic art, where the new style of architecture had still not been imposed, most notably Italy and Spain. The west of France continued to remain faithful to the traditions of Romanesque painting, as was also the case with the southeast, where Byzantine-style influences, strong since the beginning of the twelfth century, prevented the adoption of less conservative formulas. In the north of France, however, in Champagne, the Île-de-France, and the southeast of England, as well as in some neighbouring centers, the majority of workshops adopted stylistic criteria that differed totally from those of the preceding century and which revived "antique" formulas, thereby following in the artistic footsteps of the great goldsmith Nicolas de Verdun. It is now some thirty years since scholars such as O. Homburger in Germany and L. Grodecki in France pointed out the "independence" of

Chartres Cathedral, nave, north aisle, Legend of St. Lubin; *detail,*
Donors *(left, a vine-grower; right a tavern-keeper), c. 1205.*

the 1200 style, which must, however, be regarded as an epiphenomenon lasting only a few decades, since it disappeared after 1220–25. It was a brief moment of stylistic change that affected not only stained glass, but also sculpture, Miniaturism, and the goldsmith's art. The style, which was no longer Romanesque, but still not yet Gothic, was characterized by a return to antique forms drawn in supple, fluid lines in which folds were arranged in undulating drapes in the Classical manner (*Muldenfaltenstil*). In addition, it was influenced to varying degrees, depending on the workshop, by the Byzantine formulas emanating from Venice and from Sicily, which had formed part of the Holy Roman Empire since 1180, having previously been a Norman kingdom. The formal qualities of the Byzantine works of Venice and Sicily, which were known in northern Europe through manuscripts or small objects brought back by travellers or Crusaders, were adapted and allowed artists to free themselves from the constraints of Romanesque art. Faces became more human and expressions more natural and closer to reality. At the same time, ornamentation passed beyond the bounds of abstract convention in favour of broad foliar motifs in which the foliated scroll assumed an important role. Among the earliest works to bear witness to this trend in European stained glass, mention should be made of the remains from Troyes (c. 1170), originally from either the city's Romanesque cathedral or the collegiate church situated within the palace of the Counts of Champagne, which are now scattered through various museums and collections in France and elsewhere, and also several marvellous figures from a

Genealogy of Christ (prior to 1180?) in Canterbury Cathedral. These masterpieces proclaim the existence of many other similar examples, since the graphic and pictorial qualities of this intermediary phase achieve an astonishing impact in stained glass, comparable and even superior to those found in illuminated manuscripts and sculptures.

There is one region which is particularly favoured, that of Laon-Soissons, in the northwest of France, because of the number of examples that have survived, the earliest of which date from around 1200. In Laon Cathedral, the rebuilding of which began in the 1160s, the rose in the northern arm of the transept still retains a few medallions, the majority portraying the Liberal Arts, which represent this new stylistic trend in stained glass around 1195. The silhouettes show a new formal fullness, while the fluid, undulating drapery betrays the harmonious shape of the bodies. It is, however, the windows of the chevet and the rose surmounting them which best express the Classicism of the 1200 style. The three lancets illustrate the Passion of Christ in the center, his Childhood accompanied by symbolic figures to the south and, to the north, the legend of deacon Théophile, the outline of a Marian series, and the martyrdom of St. Stephen, all grouped together. The conjunction of these two subjects has led Florens Deuchler to suggest that these windows were made for the original ambulatory, demolished at the beginning of the thirteenth century in order to make way for the present chevet. In addition, the pictorial technique of the three windows betrays the presence of several artists. Certain scenes of the Passion are still very clut-

tered, while others, by contrast, are very airy and herald the spatiality of Gothic art. Their colouring is characteristic of the beginning of the thirteenth century and also of this style, with lots of pale colours, especially white, used in large swathes, as in the clothes, for example. The center window, which is closest in style to the rose crowning the group, has as its subject the Glorification of the Virgin, who occupies the center and is surrounded by the twelve apostles and the twenty-four old men of the Apocalypse, from whence came the cathedral's designation as a Marian foundation. Nowhere else does the design achieve such cohesion; the harmony of the figures is "Classical," almost antique. In the window portraying the Childhood, on the other hand, the iconography, as in the Ingeborg Psaltery in the Musée Condé at Chantilly, a masterpiece of contemporary illumination created between 1193 and 1213 for the queen repudiated by Philip II, revives Byzantine-style formulas.

The characteristics of the Laon style recur in Soissons Cathedral, but the windows of this building have been the subject of such extensive depredation and destruction that the best panels are no longer in situ, having been sold to the United States by antique dealers. However, the main window in the choir, probably a Jesse Tree, was donated by Philip II, probably somewhere between 1210 and 1215. The likeness of a royal ancestor of Christ, now in an American collection, allows us to appreciate the extraordinary formal and pictorial quality of the figure, the draughtsmanship of which is as rigidly Classical as that of the contemporary figures in the east rose

Chartres Cathedral, choir, north side, Legend of St. Julian the Hospitaller; *detail,* Donors *(left, a cartwright and a cooper; right, carpenters), 1215–25.*

window at Laon mentioned earlier. The two panels of the Life of St. Nicholas, recently discovered in the same collection, underline the fact that the legendary windows possessed the same formal coherence. They display, albeit on a smaller scale, a graphic inventiveness and mastery of painting similar to that encountered in the Jesse Tree. The same quality can also be seen in the panels of the Life of St. Nicasius, bishop of Reims at the beginning of the fifth century, most of which are now preserved in the Isabella Stewart Gardner Museum in Boston. No other panel better expresses just what the "1200 style" means in a legendary window: the harmonious groupings of figures of slender proportions, in calm poses, wearing antique styles of dress, with elongated faces and noses that are a continuation of the forehead. This sense of the antique can be further seen in other legendary windows, the finest panels of which are also in American museums or collections, such as those portraying St. Crispin and St. Crispinian.

The dynamic quality of this group of windows affected other buildings in the region, such as the Abbey Church of Saint-Yved at Braine, some 15 kilometers (9 miles) from Soissons, but the surviving medallions are now preserved in a window of Soissons Cathedral and in an American museum. Of greater significance for the 1200 style are the two windows in the Chapel of the Virgin at the Collegiate Church of Saint-Quentin, one of which is dedicated to the Childhood of Christ and is accompanied by Old Testament episodes that presage similar events in the New Testament, while the other is dedicated to the Glorification of the Virgin.

The two works, of similar composition, take the form of half medallions grouped around compartments placed on the point, with the spaces in between filled with foliate scrolls instead of the usual mosaic. Compared to the windows at Laons and Soissons, the scale is much smaller, but there is greater graphic detail and precision. There is a connection to be made between this group and a window in the ambulatory of Chartres Cathedral, the one depicting St. Eustace, which was probably executed around 1215 by an unknown master who had arrived from the Saint-Quentin region. This too uses foliate scrolls as a background motif, which is rare in Chartres, and the figures recall the same Classical quality as those in the Laons-Soissons group. This case is by no means isolated and it is probable that craftsmen from this region of France travelled to other places in search of work during the opening decades of the thirteenth century, and not only in areas bordering on Champagne, but further afield as well.

Several buildings in Champagne possess windows that bear witness to the flourishing nature of this trend. The castle at Baye, for example, a small village to the south of Épernay, has preserved its chapel in almost pristine condition, whereas the other buildings have been rebuilt on several occasions. This annex, dating from the beginning of the thirteenth century, is one of the oldest buildings of its type in France and the only one to have retained its original glass. The windows, five in number, all follow the same style, which echoes the artistic criteria of the Laon-Soissons group, notably in the colouration, which is still pale. Farther south,

Overleaf: Chartres Cathedral, chevet, upper story; in the axial bay, Annunciation, Visitation, *and* Virgin and Child, *1210–25; left, north side,* Aaron *and* Angel Bearing a Censer, *with the donors (Gaufridus and his family) beneath, 1210–25; right, south side,* Donors *(bakers),* Moses and the Burning Bush, Isaiah with a Flowering Staff, *and* Angel Bearing a Censer, *1210–25; far right,* Donors *(money changers) and* Scenes from the Life of St. Peter, *1210–25.*

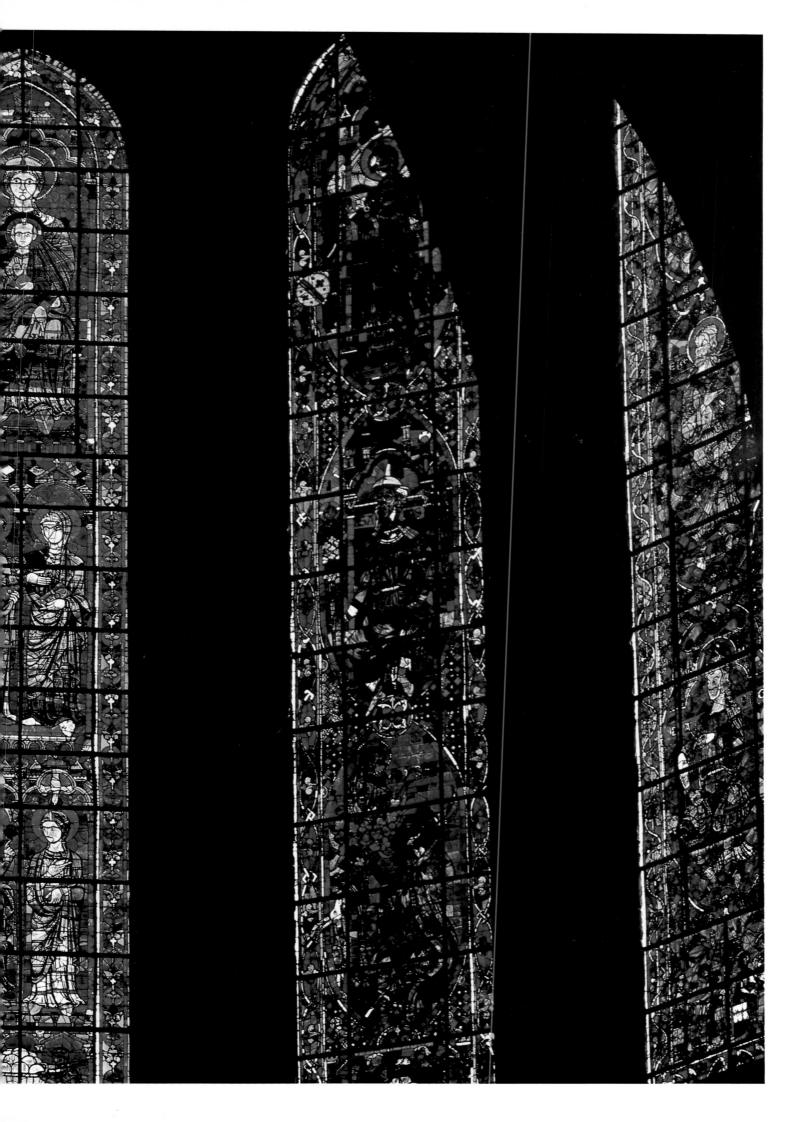

the ancient Abbey Church of Orbais possesses a small Crucifixion whose more metallic style recurs in several of the windows in the ambulatory and radiating chapels of the Gothic cathedral at Troyes, which was rebuilt from 1205 onwards. The persistence of the style at Troyes during the 1210–20 period emphasizes how firmly it had become rooted in Champagne, although it remained less monumental than at Laon or Soissons and nearer in style to the goldsmith's art. Of the other cities, Paris must have occupied a truly unique position. Although it appears that it had been an important artistic center since the end of the twelfth century, only one example of stained glass from the early decades of the thirteenth century has survived, namely the west rose window of Notre-Dame, which is unfortunately in a very poor state. Only a dozen or so of the medallions are original; the remainder date from the beginning of the sixteenth century or from the 1800s. Nevertheless, the old medallions display a monumental authority comparable to that seen in the north rose at Laon, although they also possess a distinctive graphic elegance and a vigorous outline that herald the advent of a truly Gothic style.

In Rouen Cathedral, a highly individualistic artist created at least two windows, one depicting the Seven Sleepers of Ephesus and the other, St. John the Baptist, which must originally have adorned the bays removed at the beginning of the fourteenth century to allow for the addition of the side chapels. The John the Baptist window was reused in the third and fourth north chapels of the nave, when it was combined with others to form a set of composite windows called *Belles Verrières* in the fifteenth century, but only a dozen or so panels of the Seven Sleepers window have survived, the finest of which is now in the Worcester Museum of Art in Massachusetts. The formal graphical and pictorial qualities of these two works link them to this northern French movement; the elegance of the gestures and the balance of the poses are beautifully controlled, surpassing even the best panels at Laon or Soissons.

At Bourges Cathedral, this noble, "antique" style of northwest France can be seen in two ambulatory windows situated on both sides of the axial chapel, one depicting the Passion and the other the Apocalypse, which can be dated to between 1210 and 1214 because of a contemporary document informing us that the ambulatory and the radiating chapels of Bourges Cathedral were used for worship. Nothing is known of the earlier history of this Bourges master, or

Bourges Cathedral, ambulatory, north side,
Discovery of the Relics of St. Stephen, *upper
section, 1210–15.*

of his origins and training, but stylistic
analysis shows that the two windows are
the work of the same artist, who was using
pictorial forms current in northwest
France. The presence of a window in
Freiburg im Breisgau Cathedral which,
even if it was created in Basle in around
1215, reveals the same stylistic trends, can
only be explained by the arrival of artists
from other regions, as is also the case with
another window, some ten years later in
date, in Lyon Cathedral. The truth of the
matter is that although we can today
presume that the origins of this 1200 style
probably lie in northwestern France, we
are still unable to understand the ways in
which it was spread.

THE GENESIS OF THE GOTHIC STYLE

While the 1200 style was evolving, elsewhere in France the old traditions persisted. This was particularly true of western France, where Romanesque painting,
most notably in stained glass, had reached
its zenith as far back as the 1160s. There
was some resistance to the penetration of
new, northern ideas, that is, Gothic art,
and several centers, such as Poitiers,
Angers, and Le Mans, refused to abandon
their traditional stylistic criteria, at best
merely modifying them. The windows
installed in Poitiers Cathedral at the
beginning of the thirteenth century mirror
the characteristics of those in the chevet,
which had been put into place forty years
earlier. Unfortunately, however, they
have now become barely legible, in addition to which large numbers of them
were destroyed during the city's bom-
bardment by the Protestants in 1562. The
series must have been among the most
interesting northern French examples
from the beginning of the thirteenth
century. The north windows were probably devoted to the Old Testament and the
south ones to the New Testament and,
contrary to northern French custom, they
were designed to be read from top to
bottom. Although the figures remain
stylistically close to the old Romanesque
types, there is nevertheless a certain elongation and a lighter feel to the design of the
drapery, while the shapes are smoother
and no longer possess that feeling of
restlessness found during the twelfth century.

The situation at Angers was the same as
at Poitiers, and it was not until after 1230
that the new ideas of Gothic art gained
acceptance among Angers workshops.
Until this time they had remained faithful
to the styles promulgated by Romanesque
painting. The same applies at Le Mans

Bourges Cathedral, ambulatory, third south radiating chapel. Above, detail from Life of St. John the Evangelist *showing bakers (the donors) at work.*

Right, detail from Story of the Patriarch Joseph *showing a wheelwright (a donor), 1210–15. Opposite: Bourges Cathedral, ambulatory, south side; detail from* Parable of the Good Samaritan *showing the encounter between the Samaritan and the traveller stripped naked by thieves.*

Overleaf: left, Bourges Cathedral, chevet, third south radiating chapel, Life of St. John the Baptist, *1210–15; right, Bourges Cathedral, ambulatory, south side,* Last Judgement, *lower section, 1210–15.*

Cathedral, where several series dating from the end of the twelfth century reveal a strict adherence to the old forms. And yet, paradoxically, these works, despite their opposition to Gothic ideas, contributed towards the development of the thirteenth-century Chartres style.

Chartres Cathedral is a whole world unto itself which overawes all who enter it. It is a supernatural place, unique on earth. Work on its rebuilding began immediately after the 1194 fire and the final windows were installed in around 1235, which means that the whole colossal undertaking took a mere forty years to complete. As far as the stained glass was concerned, this meant that two successive generations of workers were involved in glazing the one hundred and seventy-five windows and three rose windows. Chartres was an exceptional testing ground for the various teams of glaziers, even though some of them were less inventive than others. What is more, the enterprise acted as a training ground for artists who, after the work was completed, moved on to other places, such as Le Mans Cathedral.

The first bays to be fitted with stained glass were those in the nave, but the first task was to repair the three windows in the western façade, which had been damaged in the 1194 fire. This was entrusted to an artist still strongly influenced by the Byzantine-style art of the 1200s, and it is possible to detect, if not the same hand, the same tendencies in the scene depicting the Death of the Virgin that adorns a window in the south aisle. A second workshop perpetuated Romanesque traditions, while at the same time introducing new expressive forms by "Gothicizing" the style of drawing; the same team was also responsible for the famous St. Lubin and Noah windows. A third workshop lies behind three other windows: the ones depicting the Death of the Virgin, Mary Magdalene, and the symbolic Passion. Its style is one of great harmony, with well-balanced compositions and a more conventional, almost predictable style. The work of this group is very important in defining the Chartres style of 1220, which developed out of compositions whose sense of balance derives from their formal and pictorial expression. Apart from these workshops, there were individual craftsmen using completely different formulas, a phenomenon which underlines the powerful attraction exerted by this vast architectural enterprise. Some of these individuals, such as the master of the St. Eustace window, were responsible for only one work, while others appear to have had links with projects elsewhere, such as the master of the Parables, who was connected with the workshop responsible for the Parable of the Prodigal Son. There were therefore a large number of glaziers present in Chartres from 1200–10

onwards, a state of affairs which lasted throughout the period of building, but the physical state of certain series has prevented scholars from carrying out as deep an analysis as they would like; this is particularly true in the case of the high windows in the nave, which portray standing figures of saints and martyrs, many of whom have become too darkened by the effects of corrosion to be decipherable.

Passing from the nave to the transept, one moves from one generation of artists to another. One workshop, called by some scholars "Classical," was responsible for about ten windows. Certain individual touches can be detected in all these works, but the graphic and pictorial style of the workshop is characterized by balanced compositions. Each scene is endowed with great "readability" and has restrained, well-modulated colouration. This workshop, whose greatest achievement was the marvellous Charlemagne window, characterized by the extraordinary fullness of its compositions, continued in the same tradition as the team responsible for the Death of the Virgin in the nave and may be regarded as one of the "pivots" of Chartres stained glass.

The second trend displayed in the windows of the choir and chevet of Chartres Cathedral was one that influenced stained glass throughout the second quarter of the thirteenth century. The final elements in the *Belle Verrière*, illustrating episodes from the Life of Christ, already revealed a formal tension never found in the works executed by the Charlemagne "master," but the artist responsible for the St. Chéron window and his workshop were to transcend this energetic style. This master was working at a time of increasing formalism, as can also be seen in sculptures created during the 1220s in Paris and Amiens. In contrast with the feeling of freeness that characterized the style prevailing around the turn of the century, this new form of expression made shapes sparer and more schematic, with volume being accentuated by the interplay of broken, even pointed folds. The St. Chéron window, donated by the sculptors and stone-cutters who had themselves depicted going about their daily work, marks the inauguration of this stylistic phase at Chartres, but its greatest works, whose expressive force proclaims a truly Gothic style, are the famous window depicting St. Denis handing over the oriflamme of the Abbey of Saint-Denis to Marshal Jean-Clément de Metz, created between 1228 and 1231, and the group donated by the Dreux-Bretagne family, which consists of five lancets occupied by the Virgin, personification of the Church, flanked by the Four Evangelists borne aloft on the shoulders of prophets and surmounted by a rose window glorifying Christ.

Still other artists worked on the windows of the choir of the chevet. In the windows of the apse one can see the conjunction of several stylistic trends. Beside the archaic style of the axial window dedicated to the Virgin, patroness of the cathedral, the style of the archangel in the neighbouring bay to the north seems very powerful. This figure, like the one of Moses facing it, appears to come from another group that was never completed. In the final works produced at Chartres, the styles began to lose their coherence and also their expressive qualities.

Another monument, Bourges Cathedral, possesses series of windows that played just as important a part in the development of Gothic painting at Chartres. We have already mentioned this building in connection with the 1200 style of art, since a master working in this tradition created two windows in the ambulatory, while the remaining windows in this section were entrusted to two other artists. The first master glass painter, the so-called "master of the Good Samaritan," completed, together with his workshop, eight of the twenty-two windows still in position. His work is distinguished by its graphic intensity, its taste for the exaggerated and, on the iconographical level, a readiness to introduce new ideas. He probably came from the west of France, which for a long time remained hostile to the new principles of Gothic painting. The second master, dubbed the "master of the Relics of St. Stephen" after his greatest work, increased the number of original compositions and displayed an extraordinarily lively spirit of invention, while still remaining faithful to the old Romanesque formulas. Unlike the previous master, he was a local man, whereas the third came from the northwest of France. Subsequently, he was to complete most of the windows in the inner ambulatory and most of the high windows, trying to adapt his style to the new spatialism of Gothic art.

Of the other buildings to receive stained glass during the opening decades of the thirteenth century, Sens Cathedral retains four windows in its side ambulatory. The date of these four works, which is open to dispute, is probably between 1210 and 1215. The first series depict parables, those of the Prodigal Son and the Good Samaritan, and are probably the work of a master who had trained locally or in the Île-de-France, possibly even in Paris. His

Auxerre Cathedral, ambulatory, south side, Stories of Noah, Abraham, and Lot; detail, The Angels Announce the Destruction of Sodom to Abraham, c. 1235.

Overleaf: Sainte-Chapelle, Paris, upper chapel, general view of the windows in the chevet, 1243–48.

Sainte-Chapelle, Paris, upper chapel, north side. Left, the Deuteronomy
Window; *details,* Moses Builds the Cities of the Jews *(above) and*
Moses Appoints Joshua His Successor *(below).*
Right, the Exodus Window; *detail,* Moses Is Saved from the Waters.

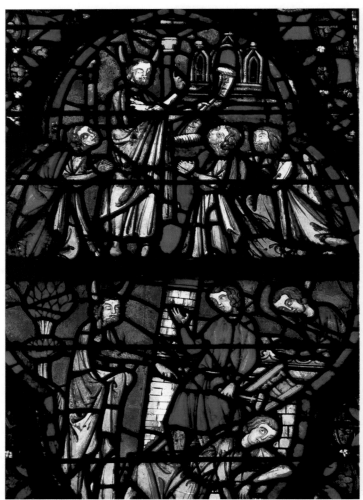

style displays a great feeling of formal energy and his compositions reveal a surprisingly uncluttered quality that has a strong Gothic feeling to it, while his figures still retain certain echoes of the period around 1200, particularly in the arrangement of the drapery. The second series comprises a window dedicated to St. Eustace and another dedicated to St. Thomas à Becket, the English archbishop murdered in 1170 by King Henry II and canonized three years later. Since the nineteenth century these windows have been compared to those at Canterbury, with which they have much in common, but close examination shows that their style is an intermediary style between those of Canterbury and northern France. Once again, it is difficult to ascertain the origins of this master and additional research needs to be done on the subject.

The last group from this period is to be found in the lower story of the chevet of Lyon Cathedral. The work was carried out between 1215 and 1225, when the seven bays were filled with windows whose subjects matched the political and religious preoccupations of the Church in Lyon at the beginning of the thirteenth century. A powerful religious and feudal institution, it was trying to strike a balance between the Holy Roman Empire, in whose fief it still remained, and the increasingly powerful France of the Capetian dynasty, a situation reflected in these windows, the originality of which was grasped by Émile Mâle at the beginning of this century. This great historian drew attention to the Byzantine-style character of several of their number, which is in direct contrast to the contemporary windows at Chartres. In fact, four of them obey these conventions, which had become firmly rooted in the region since the beginning of the twelfth century, while the others are based on schemas imported from the north of France or even Burgundy. This blend of different stylistic formulas is typical of the period and of the regions bordering the Capetian kingdom, with the Gothic style gaining the upper hand and gradually supplanting the old Romanesque and Byzantine-influenced traditions. This process is underlined by the fact that the windows carrying on the old traditions were the first to be installed.

During the second quarter of the thirteenth century stained glass evolved almost everywhere towards a harder style of drawing and a more summary style of execution, thereby following in the steps of the simplified technique practiced by such masters as the one responsible for the St. Chéron window at Chartres. The latter artist was not unique, however, since the same reactions occurred elsewhere during the same period, both in sculpture and in painting, as at Amiens, for example. It seems as though as early as 1225–30 Paris became affected by this renewal of form, known as the Rayonnant style, which introduced new solutions to every aspect of art, particularly architecture. It was not until this period that the Gothic style reached its maturity in the realm of figuration and spatiality thanks to stained glass, which began to occupy more and more space in buildings. And yet, between

Cathedral of Notre-Dame, Paris, north arm, Glorification of the
Virgin, *c. 1255.*

Overleaf: Cathedral of Notre-Dame, Paris, south arm, Glorification of
Christ, *c. 1260.*

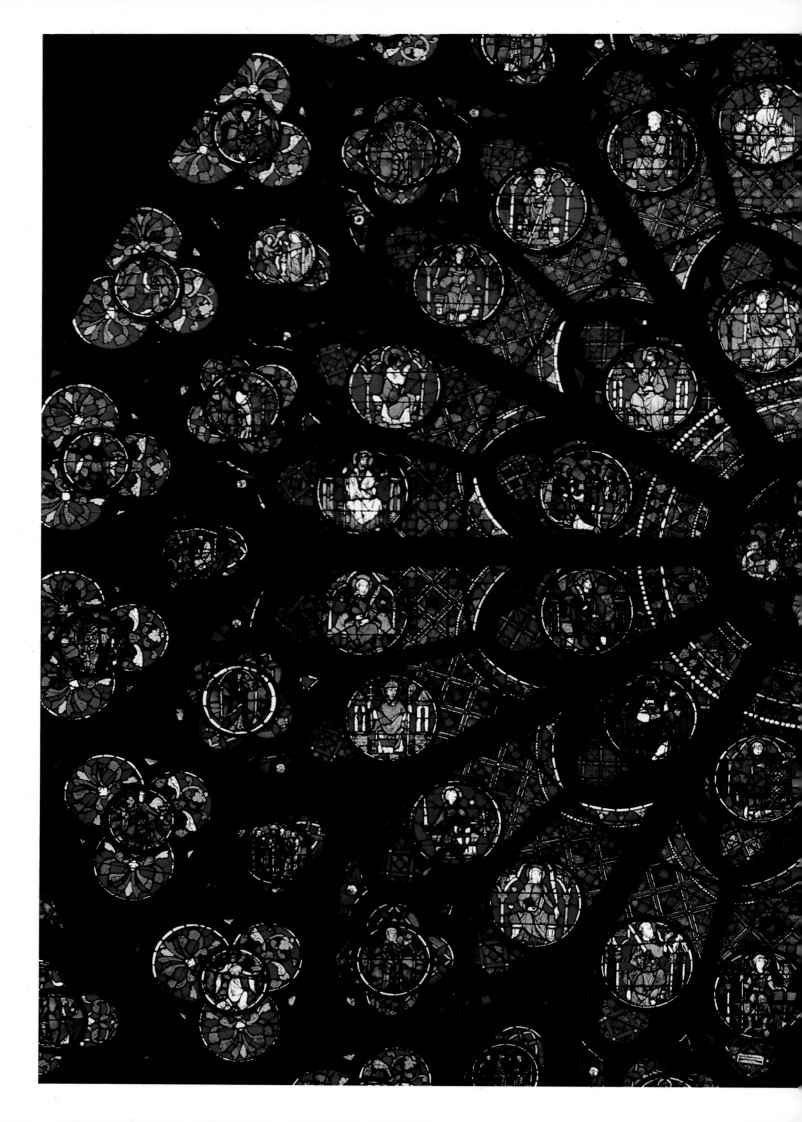

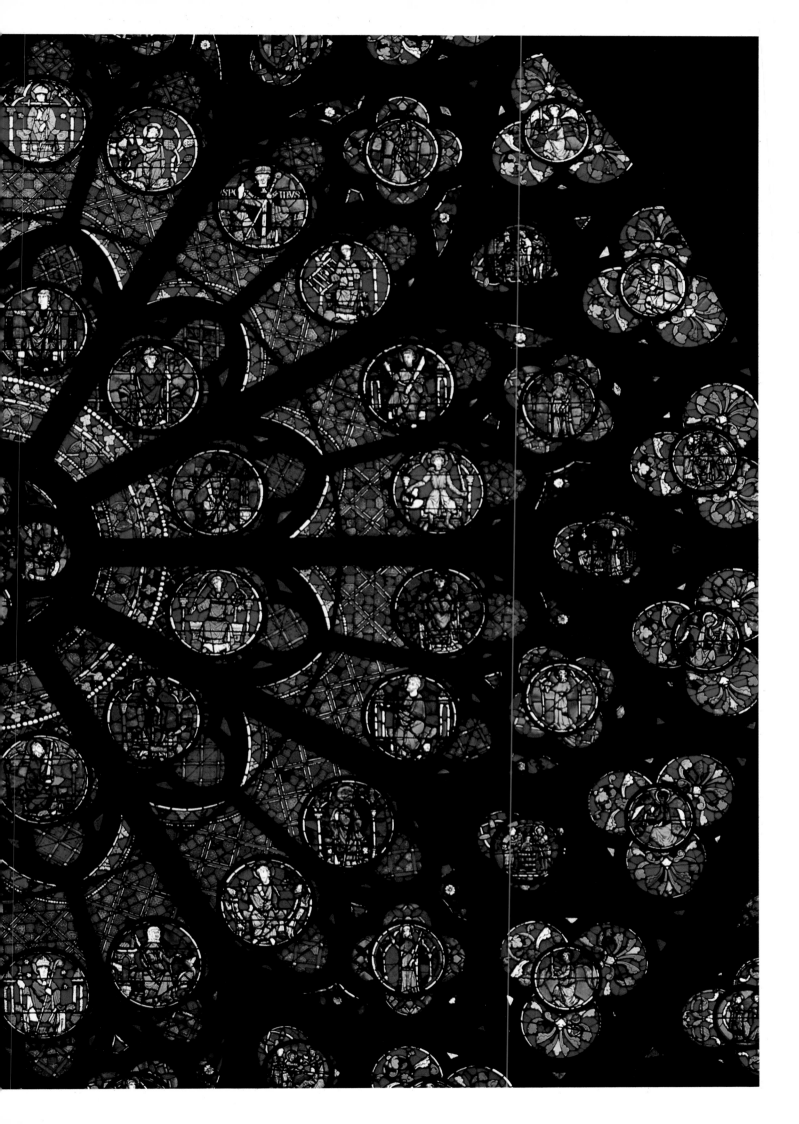

the west rose window of Notre-Dame in Paris, completed around 1220, and the works undertaken at Saint-Germain-des-Prés and the Sainte-Chapelle, which, in the case of the refectory of the famous abbey, was begun around 1235, nothing of any importance has survived. It is some small churches of the Paris region which provide evidence of the changes occurring in stained glass: works such as the panels, now in the Musée de Cluny in Paris, from the ruined Abbey of Gercy, near Corbeil, to the southeast of Paris. Some are the remains of a Jesse Tree and others come from a Life of St. Martin, but they already display rigidly stylized faces, which in a way counter the fluidity of the clothes. A strengthening of outline can also be seen in two other works, the rose in the Church of Donnemarie-en-Montois, near Provins, in Seine-et-Marne, and the group of windows in the chevet of Saint-Germain-lès-Corbeil. Like the Gercy panels, these works can be dated to between 1220 and 1225 and they all, in varying degrees, show that the old tradition of the *Muldenfaltenstil* was fading away in the face of a more nervous, less harmonious style of drawing. The new technique affected faces much more than clothes and drapery, and the experiments conducted by different workshops and painters undoubtedly helped Parisian craftsmen to develop the style that characterizes their output during the years between 1235 and 1245, a period that coincided with the middle period of the reign of St. Louis.

The first major building program undertaken in Paris from which elements of stained glass have survived are the refectory and the Chapel of the Virgin, at Saint-Germain-des-Prés, constructed by the famous architect Pierre de Montreuil. The former was begun in 1234–35, the latter around 1243–44, the same time as the Sainte-Chapelle, but both were demolished at the very beginning of the nineteenth century and most of their glass destroyed, with the exception of a few panels. Four of these panels are still to be seen in situ, having been reused in one of the church's radiating chapels, but the majority are today scattered through various overseas museums and collections: the Victoria and Albert Museum, London, the Germanisches Nationalmuseum, Nürnberg, the Metropolitan Museum of Art, New York, and the Walters Art Gallery, Baltimore.

Their original arrangement is still the subject of controversy: the art historians who have studied these remains, L. Grodecki and P. Verdier, are divided over the origins of the panels, which fall into three iconographical series. The majority, however, seem to have come from the Chapel of the Virgin which, according to old texts, was adorned with full-colour windows in the apse and pale grisaille ones in the lateral bays, in accordance with a new practice that was increasingly widely adopted during the second half of the thirteenth century. One group of panels, dealing with the Life of the Virgin, certainly come from the chapel. Technically, this series is surprisingly clumsy and poorly finished, but its style, very different from that of the windows in the Sainte-Chapelle, possesses an expressiveness similar to that present in certain windows in the upper ambulatory of Le Mans Cathedral, which were completed a few years later. Other panels, whose original themes it has not been possible to identify with any certainty, portray royal cavalcades and pious donations and should be viewed within the context of the illustrious past of this Parisian abbey, founded during the sixth century. Their provenance, however, is still in doubt and there is no way of knowing whether they came from a chapel or a refectory. But the most interesting work, which leads into the art of the Sainte-Chapelle, relates to the Life of St. Vincent, in whose name the abbey had been founded. Of the fewer than twenty panels that have survived from the original forty, all are now outside France. The finest panels of this series, especially the one in New York depicting St. Vincent and Bishop Valerius in chains, clearly reveal the changes that had occurred since 1220. The contours have become geometrical and the clothes hang straight, with stiff folds, while the faces, by contrast, are calm and expressive. A perfect balance has been struck between line and volume, a feat that was later repeated with even greater mastery in the Sainte-Chapelle.

Built to house the relics of Christ's Passion, bought some years earlier from Emperor Baudouin II of Byzantium, this two-story palatine chapel was conceived as a reliquary. In fact, it is the building which best expresses the degree of perfection achieved by stained-glass artists during the reign of St. Louis. Despite the fact that they have been restored on many occasions over the centuries, the fifteen high windows of the upper chapel still create a strong impression by the power of their colour, their formal variety and, paradoxically, their conceptual unity. A single overseer, doubtless assisted by theologians, created this group, which was installed in record time between 1242 and 1248. We must rid ourselves of the once common notion that the glaziers came from Chartres. Certain of the compositions follow the Chartres pattern, with the saddle bars forged to match the outline of the compartments, but in the majority of cases the formulas chosen are more modern, consisting of half medallions, as in the Esther window. The speed with which the man responsible for the commission, namely St. Louis (King Louis IX), wanted to complete the enterprise resulted in repetitions and accidents in the firing of the glass. Nevertheless, the Sainte-Chapelle is the building which best expresses the qualities of the Rayonnant style in stained glass. The elegance of the figures, the fragility of the slightly disjointed silhouettes, and the precision of the gestures are achieved with extraordinary verve. Three master craftsmen created this amazing group, with the principal master being responsible for ten of the fifteen windows in the upper chapel. This artist, creator of the axial window devoted to the Passion, favoured symmetrical compositions, filling the frame around the compartments, which he also embellished with artichoke-shaped trees or architectural elements; the figures are always calm, even in the battle scenes, with the supple folds of their dress conveying little feeling of bodily movement. This style is similar to that of the St. Vincent window at Saint-Germain-des-Prés, which is a few years earlier in date. The second master, the so-called "Ezekiel master," is harder to place within the evolutionary process of Parisian stained glass. He created much livelier windows than the other masters, and although his compositions are just as balanced, his figures, on the other hand, are much more elongated and emaciated; their faces are angular, with long, thin noses and almond-shaped eyes. The final artist was perhaps not just a glazier, but maybe also an illuminator, since his style is similar to that found in royal manuscripts from the middle of the century. He was a very attractive glass painter, expressive and inventive, who did not hesitate to vary the poses of his figures or to introduce new and surprising compositions. The scope of this whole enterprise, its technical qualities and the speed of its execution, a factor which people nowadays sometimes forget, emphasize the high level of expertise achieved by Parisian glaziers in around 1245. This group of windows both crystallizes and surpasses all earlier experiences in the bold way that it strove to simplify the cut of the glass, accelerate the work process, and speed up the application of the paint.

This style enjoyed immediate success and its effects have already been assessed and often exaggerated. The presence of glaziers from the Sainte-Chapelle can be detected in Paris itself, in the two rose windows in the transept of Notre-Dame: the one in the northern arm, completed before 1255 and depicting the Glorification of the Virgin, and the one in the southern arm, which has been heavily restored and completed with medallions from other sources, whose original subject was the Triumph of Christ. In addition, Parisian stained-glass artists worked in Soissons Cathedral, where they created several biblical windows, and undoubtedly also in the Collegiate

Cathedral of Notre-Dame, Paris, ambulatory, Temptation of Adam and Eve, 1225–30. Only the central roundel is old; the grisaille lobes of the rose are modern.

Church of Saint-Julien-du-Sault in Burgundy. We must, however, reject the attribution of the windows in the radiating chapels of Clermont-Ferrand Cathedral (after 1260) to these workshops, as has only recently been admitted. It is simply a question of Parisian influence at the time being so great that the formulas invented there were adopted by craftsmen elsewhere.

A parallel process of evolution, leading to a hardening of forms, also occurred in other regions, but this stylistic transformation did not develop along the same lines, nor did it have the same origins. And yet this trend extended to the majority of French workshops between 1225 and 1250, creating a truly Gothic sense of style. Some workshops readily adopted these new formulas, whereas others took several decades to embrace them. A large number of cathedrals were furnished with stained-glass windows during this period and often several different stylistic trends

will appear side by side in different windows, as at Rouen Cathedral. Frequently, it is difficult to understand the relationship between certain workshops and to show how their styles complement one another. In many cases one can do nothing more than record these differences, since so many works have been destroyed over the centuries that we lack stylistic guidelines. Sometimes a window will possess an archaic composition while the style of its configuration is, by contrast, "modern," which makes analysis a tricky process. An example of this phenomenon can be seen in Rouen Cathedral, in the ambulatory windows. In some respects, certain of them carry on the traditions emanating from Chartres, such as the symbolic Passion window, while others have evolved towards a more incisive style: the outline has become very precise and the modelling more subdued. In Coutances Cathedral, on the other hand, the numerous windows from the

second quarter and middle of the thirteenth century show a clearly conservative quality and appear to be untouched by the conventions of Gothic painting.

Picardy and the north of France seem to have more readily adopted a "tighter" style, as can be seen in the Jesse Trees at Beauvais (c. 1240) and Amiens (c. 1245), the remnants of which are soon to be replaced in the cathedral. The outline has, in fact, become sparer, but in a different way to that chosen by the Parisian workshops. It has become sharper, like that of the "Ezekiel master" in the Sainte-Chapelle. In Champagne, the choir of Troyes Cathedral possesses a group of windows with strikingly powerful colours, in which the figures are also characterized by a stiffness unrelated to Parisian art. The contemporary works in the choir of Reims Cathedral (c. 1240–45) form an original series dedicated to the glory of the Church in Reims which comprises pictures of apostles standing on small buildings representing the churches and suffragan bishoprics of the province. Several workshops were involved in this program, some of which were still using the old formulas dating back to around 1200, while others adopted the new, rigid style of the second quarter of the century. The same is also true of the figures of the choir of Châlons-sur-Marne Cathedral (c. 1240–45), which stand out against plain

backgrounds. Stained glass enjoyed a period of intense activity in Burgundy during the second quarter of the century. In Auxerre Cathedral, for example, several workshops were active between 1230 and 1250, but the windows are hard to date with any accuracy because of the extensive alterations that have been carried out over the centuries. Their quality is uneven, but most of them display an expressive figurative style, sometimes rather summary in its execution, with strongly defined outlines. Two other series in this region are worthy of mention: the one in Saint-Julien-du-Sault, partly created by a team from the Sainte-Chapelle, and the few windows in the Church of Notre-Dame at Dijon, which use the old formulas dating back to around 1225 and whose date of completion cannot have been before the middle of the century.

Up until the 1240–45 period the west of France remained immune to change and carried on in the old Chartres or Romanesque formulas of the 1220s. A good example of this is the choir of Le Mans Cathedral, the rebuilding of which was begun in 1217–18. Of the two sole surviving ambulatory windows, one is linked to the western French tradition and the other to the workshop responsible for the Charlemagne and St. James windows at Chartres. This latter form of Chartrain art

also lies behind the style of the original windows in the Chapel of the Virgin and the axial window in the inner ambulatory, donated by *seigneur* Rotrou de Montfort in the 1245–50 period. The glaziers of Le Mans subsequently turned towards more "modern" solutions for the majority of these ambulatory windows which, although situated fairly high up in the building, follow the layout favoured in legendary windows, with several medallions per level. The scale of the figures became attenuated, while the glass artists used a more geometrical cut for their glass and simplified the painting process, thereby following a trend that had already been introduced in Chartres, Paris, Champagne, Burgundy, and even Berry, where a small number of historiated medallions designed for rose windows in the nave adopted the same stylistic technique.

From 1255–60 onwards, however, the situation regarding stained glass changed radically in France. On the one hand, it enjoyed a period of relatively rapid expansion in provinces that had previously been little affected by it, such as Languedoc and Lorraine, where Gothic architecture arrived later than elsewhere. On the other hand, it became lighter and "whiter" by including pale grisaille panels round the full-colour panels that contained the iconography. The figurative style changed as

Opposite: Le Mans Cathedral, choir, upper ambulatory, Childhood of Christ, *detail depicting* Adoration of the Magi, *c. 1250.*

Below: Châlons-sur-Marne Cathedral, nave, north side, Donors *(furriers), end of the thirteenth century.*

illumination became the artistic technique that other artists sought most to imitate. Like miniatures, stained glass lost its monumental character in favour of a "mannerism" that varied according to the different workshops and became more like conventional painting. This change was to create considerable confusion for several decades, since some teams, like the one working in the cathedral at Clermont-Ferrand in around 1265, continued to use full-colour windows, while others adopted the system of mixed windows, as in the choir of Tours Cathedral. The pattern followed in the windows of that building's choir appears to have played a decisive part in the development of French stained glass. All the windows are in full colour except for two, at the entry to the choir, whose figures of canons and bishops are framed by grisaille panels in what the French call a *litre* or "hatchment" layout. The style of the figuration developed a "mannerist" tendency, with the scenes in the full-colour windows reflecting the style found in royal manuscripts created after the return of St. Louis from captivity (c. 1255–60).

One of the difficulties in studying French stained glass of the 1260–1300 period lies in the highly fragmentary nature of the works to be studied, the only exception being the west of France, where there were some extremely active work-shops. Even in Paris extremely little of what we know was created has survived. The small church of Saint-Sulpice-de-Favières, near Corbeil, to the southeast of Paris, contains a window depicting the Life of the Virgin and the Childhood of Christ that gives a good idea of the degree of formal and stylistic refinement achieved by Parisian workshops in the 1260s. The scale of the scenes has diminshed and the figures now develop freely, with slender and often disjointed silhouettes, within airy compositions. Only a few lines are used to suggest movement, with greater stress being laid on pose and gesture than on facial expression, a principle used by contemporary Parisian illuminators. It is also a technique that can be seen in several Norman series in the Abbey Church of Fécamp and in the cathedrals of Évreux and Rouen. The graphical and pictorial treatment ushers in a stylistic phase that lasted up until the fourteenth century and which created graceful, freely drawn figures endowed with a feeling of nervous yet precise movement. This mannerist trend was not, however, exploited solely in the Île-de-France and Normandy, but also in Lorraine and Champagne. The new mood in painting is very well illustrated at Saint-Urbain in Troyes, a church built by Pope Urban IV on the site of his birthplace and on which work began in 1262. On the lower story, the white grisaille windows are enlivened by a historiated quatrefoil, while on the upper story the figures of the prophets, which accompany a Crucified Christ surrounded by the Virgin and St. John, are placed beneath architectural baldachins in the midst of fields of grisaille traversed by thin lines of colour and enriched with delicate foliar motifs. Portrayed either in full or three-quarter profile, with a strongly expressive feeling of action, these figures seem to be endowed with some sort of supernatural force, while the interplay of folds and sharply broken drapery accentuated their formal authority. These Troyes windows, which were not only well ahead of their time, but almost revolutionary in their composition and their pale colouring, marked the beginning of a new era in the evolution of stained glass, not only in France, but throughout Europe. When, some thirty years later, the first work-shops began to use silver stain in the Île-de-France and in Normandy the process was finally complete. A mosaic of colours at the start of the century, stained glass a hundred years later had become a form of painting, losing its impressionistic effects for a pale, well-regulated luminosity. Never again would it undergo such a radical period of change.

The transition from Romanesque to Gothic in Europe was never an easy one and it followed different paths, sometimes

Châlons-sur-Marne Cathedral, nave, mixed window with figured full-colour panels and grisaille panels, end of the thirteenth century and nineteenth century.

in direct opposition to the course taken by French stained glass of the period. In the Holy Roman Empire, for example, the conventions of Romanesque art lingered on in a large number of workshops during the first half of the thirteenth century. From 1240 onwards it even combined with certain fully fledged Gothic elements to give rise to an original style called the *Zackenstil*. This phase was to last for several decades in the Empire, where Germanic stained glass never expressed the forms that characterized the French Rayonnant style. England, on the other hand, followed trends that ran parallel to those prevailing in France and, from the 1260s onwards, embraced mannerist, nonmonumental formulas closely resembling those found in illumination. The rapid spread of Gothic architecture was to ensure a dominant role for stained glass throughout the century, even in regions such as Italy and Spain, where it tended to take the place of wall painting. As in France, the building of the Sainte-Chapelle excited the admiration of those in a position to commission similar monuments, who now wanted to erect buildings along similar lines. Each region, however,

reacted differently, absorbing the new formal, pictorial, and chromatic modes into their own vernacular, often combining the two and producing original forms that sometimes even surpassed the French styles. At the end of the thirteenth century European stained glass was on the whole governed by mannerist formulas that varied from region to region and from workshop to workshop.

In the cathedral at Strasbourg, the Imperial capital, teams of glass artists in around 1200 were still working along Romanesque lines, as is shown by the portrayal of the figure alleged to be that of Charlemagne, an impressive image of calm and authority. Now in the Musée de l'Oeuvre Notre-Dame, it probably comes from a window in the west of the cathedral, where it formed the central element of a program depicting those who served God, from prophets to emperors. Despite losses and major alterations that are hard to unravel, the windows in Strasbourg Cathedral show how Germanic stained glass developed during the thirteenth century. Up until 1230 they retained a Romanesque style, barely touched by Gothic forms, although their execution becomes sparer and loses some of its more overtly Romanesque elements. Around 1235, building of the nave began along Gothic Rayonnant lines, but the glaziers were working at the time in the *Zackenstil* and the rose windows in the aisle represent some of the finest examples of this style. This stylistic phase was to last for several decades, and not just in the cathedral, but in other churches in the city as well. The building work in the cathedral then became one of the crucial transmission points of Parisian art to the Empire during the 1260s. French forms, except in the case of the figures of Christ's ancestors at the triforium level, which were probably created by a workshop from Reims, soon became transformed and distorted by influences that reflected the trends inherent in the development of Germanic stained glass, for example the architectural element.

During the 1260s the workshops of Strasbourg evolved a type of window that was later adopted not only in Alsace, but in regions of the upper Rhine such as Swabia. It consisted of a single figure in a lancet, sheltered beneath an architectural canopy or "baldachin" which was no longer just a simple dais, but a tabernacle with several tiers that later became enlivened with birds. These structures in glass were to transform the composition of windows and become independent forms governed by their own typology, the final climax of which was the group of windows in the St. Catherine Chapel in Strasbourg Cathedral (c. 1340). Of the eight layers in each lancet, only two are reserved for the actual figures of the saint; the remainder are taken up by the tabernacle. As for the style of the figuration, that became increasingly mannerist in feel, with the figures often looking almost lost in the midst of all this architecture, which occupied more and more space in the windows, as can be seen in the Crucifixion from the church at Mutzig, now in the Musée de l'Oeuvre Notre-Dame in Strasbourg, which can be dated to around 1310. In fact, the first truly Gothic manifestations in the Empire, as represented by this type of window, appeared rather late and lasted up until 1340–50, showing how this phase straddled two centuries.

The example of Strasbourg illustrates how for a large part of the thirteenth century Germanic stained glass did not model itself on French principles. And when it did adopt the latter, it promptly either diverged from them or drew on them to create original formulas such as the *Zackenstil*.

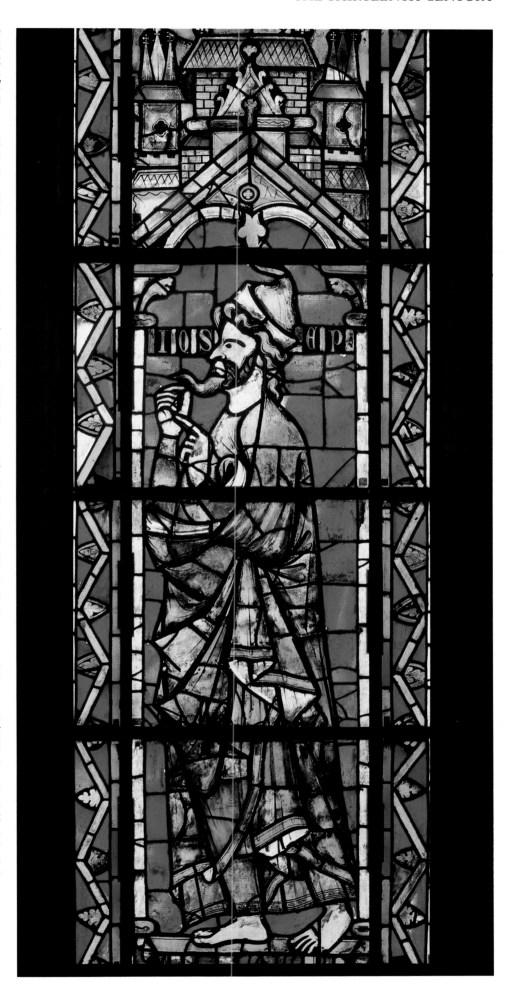

Church of Saint-Urbain, Troyes, upper story, choir, Patriarch Joseph, *c. 1270.*

Enthroned Emperor *(traditionally believed to be Charlemagne)*, *c. 1200, from Strasbourg Cathedral. Musée de l'Oeuvre Notre-Dame, Strasbourg.*

Opposite: Mary Magdalene at the Feet of Christ, *c. 1250, from the Monastery of la Haguelonette, Haguenau, Alsace. Musée de l'Oeuvre Notre-Dame, Strasbourg.*

Cologne Cathedral, Chapel of the Magi,
Bibelfenster *or typological window; detail,*
Adoration of the Magi, *c. 1250.*

Opposite: Church of St. Kunibert, Cologne,
south arm, St. Cecilia, *c. 1230.*

At the beginning of the century some workshops, such as the one responsible for the Jesse window in Freiburg im Breisgau Cathedral, had been attracted to the freer quality of the 1200 style. At Cologne, where one of the masters of this style, the goldsmith Nicolas de Verdun, worked on the shrine of the Three Magi for several years, the windows of the apse and transept of St. Kunibert, datable to 1215–30, still fall within this stylistic domain, while at the same time displaying a large number of Romanesque traits. The high windows of the two-story apse are occupied by a Jesse Tree which, in accordance with the miniaturist tradition, embraces the main events of Christ's life and the stories of St. Clement and St. Kunibert, the patron saint of the building, while the lower story contains a wonderful series of female saints, among them St. Cecilia. The composition of the latter windows, which are quite unlike their French counterparts, is characteristic of the late Romanesque art of the Empire. The saint is portrayed almost full face, within a many-lobed frame composed of numerous thin, threadlike lines. This formula, used for historiated and figurative windows alike, gave rise to numerous variants, some of which achieve truly exceptional effects in the arrangement of this internal framework, which can be divided into as many as twenty lobes and oblique lines. This practice, which persisted up until the fourteenth century in the Empire, especially in the easternmost areas that now form part of Austria, represented a form of resistance to the new ideals of Gothic art. Similarly, there were still windows with very broad borders consisting of extremely rich arrangements of foliar elements, although the style of the figuration retained an elegance that was further accentuated by pale, brilliant colours, quite unlike those of French stained glass of the period, which had already darkened. This Cologne style continued for several decades in the Rhineland, in the parish church of Heimersheim-an-der-Ahr, for example, and also in other more distant regions, as in the group of windows in the church at Bücken in Lower Saxony, which date from the middle of the century.

Several parts of the Empire still clung to Romanesque traditions, like Ratisbon, for example, where a flourishing school of painting on parchment and in fresco had developed a style totally independent of other German cities. The same considerations apply to the analysis of works from the valleys of Austria, the most important of which is the window devoted to the Life of St. Margaret in the Collegiate Church at Ardagger in Lower Austria. Completed between 1230 and 1240, this work displays astonishing technical qualities, worthy of the goldsmith's craft, as well as brilliant colours and a very small figurative scale. In the northern reaches of the Empire there are several windows that reveal a provincial style which, although betraying the presence of teams of glaziers, cannot be compared with the style of Cologne and the Rhineland. Mention should also be made of a little-known series of windows on the Swedish island of Gotland, notably in the churches of Dalhem and Endre, which possess striking pictorial qualities that orginate in the workshops of northern Germany, although these actual windows are probably the work of local artists.

It was the great German art historian Arthur Haseloff who, in his analysis of the windows in St. Elizabeth's Church at Marburg, at the beginning of the twentieth century, produced a definition of the *Zackenstil*, one of the most creative manifestations of Germanic art during this period. This surprising development can be seen not only in stained glass, but also in illuminated manuscripts and sculptures. Its origins are to be found in the pictorial art of Thuringia and Saxony, but it also contains traces of other influences, such as the Byzantine-style art of Sicily. Endowed with great graphical vigour, the *Zackenstil* developed a system of abruptly breaking folds, while at the same time, in a way that may seem paradoxical, giving the faces an almost melodious gentleness. Subsequently, however, in accordance with the trends that characterize Germanic stained glass from the second quarter and middle of the thirteenth century, it weighed down the background and the clothing of the figures with decorative patterns, while simultaneously increasing the number of decorative bands surrounding the scenes. It had considerable impact throughout the Empire—from the west, where it resulted in the marvellous rose windows in the aisles of the nave of Strasbourg Cathedral, as far as Naumburg and Erfurt, where the first windows portraying the Life of St. Francis of Assisi were installed in that city's Franciscan church. Far from being monolithic, the *Zackenstil* was interpreted in different ways by different workshops; it absorbed extraneous influences and also introduced elements from French Gothic art, as in the typological window at München-Gladbach (c. 1250). It was even exported to Italy, where the three windows in the apse of the upper church at Assisi were probably created by a German workshop around 1250.

During the second quarter of the century these formulas lingered on in certain regions, such as parts of Austria, as, for example, in the figures of prophets and the half-length figures of angels in the Abbey Church of Heiligenkreuz (1190–1200). Around 1265, however, the work in Strasbourg Cathedral was finished, an event which released onto the market painters who were inclined to adopt the new ideas of Gothic art and who had already begun to display the early mannerist tendencies of the 1260s, investigating more sophisticated techniques and reverting to paler colours. This circle of Strasbourg painters was to prove highly active and its influence spread beyond the borders of Alsace to affect the artists of the upper Rhine and Swabia and form a vast community creating windows that acted as models for other craftsmen in the Empire throughout the fourteenth century.

The development of English stained glass during the thirteenth century is hard to reconstruct and there are still many gaps to be filled. There were extensive losses at the time of the Reformation and again after 1543, when royal envoys were dispatched to verify whether the destruction had been properly carried out. Finally, many of the rare surviving examples are no longer in their original positions, while others are merely fragmentary remains, like the sections of glass from the first quarter of the thirteenth century in Lincoln Cathedral which are, nevertheless, of exceptional formal quality. At the beginning of the thirteenth century, the building work at Canterbury Cathedral, which had begun in 1180, was still under way. A number of painters still followed the antique style that prevailed at the turn of the century, whether it was the "master of the Parable of the Sower" or the "master of Petronilla," named after a nun who was cured at the tomb of Thomas à Becket. Their activities came to a temporary halt, however, between 1207 and 1213, during the exile of the archbishop and the chapter in France. It is now thought that some of the painters accompanied them to France, where they probably worked, perhaps creating cartoons at Chartres and Sens, but it is still too soon to evaluate the extent of this collaboration. On their return, some continued the same style for the windows of the Trinity Chapel illustrating miracles performed at the tomb of Thomas à Becket, while others evolved towards graphic and pictorial schemas closer to those used at Chartres during the 1220s. A similar development can be seen in the disjointed panels in Lincoln Cathedral, which probably formed part of a program comparable to that at Canterbury. This alone gives an idea of the high degree of skill achieved by English glaziers during the first third of the thirteenth century.

The pale grisaille window seems to have been in widespread use in England. As in France, the surviving examples are not exclusively Cistercian. The majority decorate windows in cathedrals and

Calvary, *Alsace, first third of the thirteenth century. Musée de l'Oeuvre Notre-Dame, Strasbourg.*

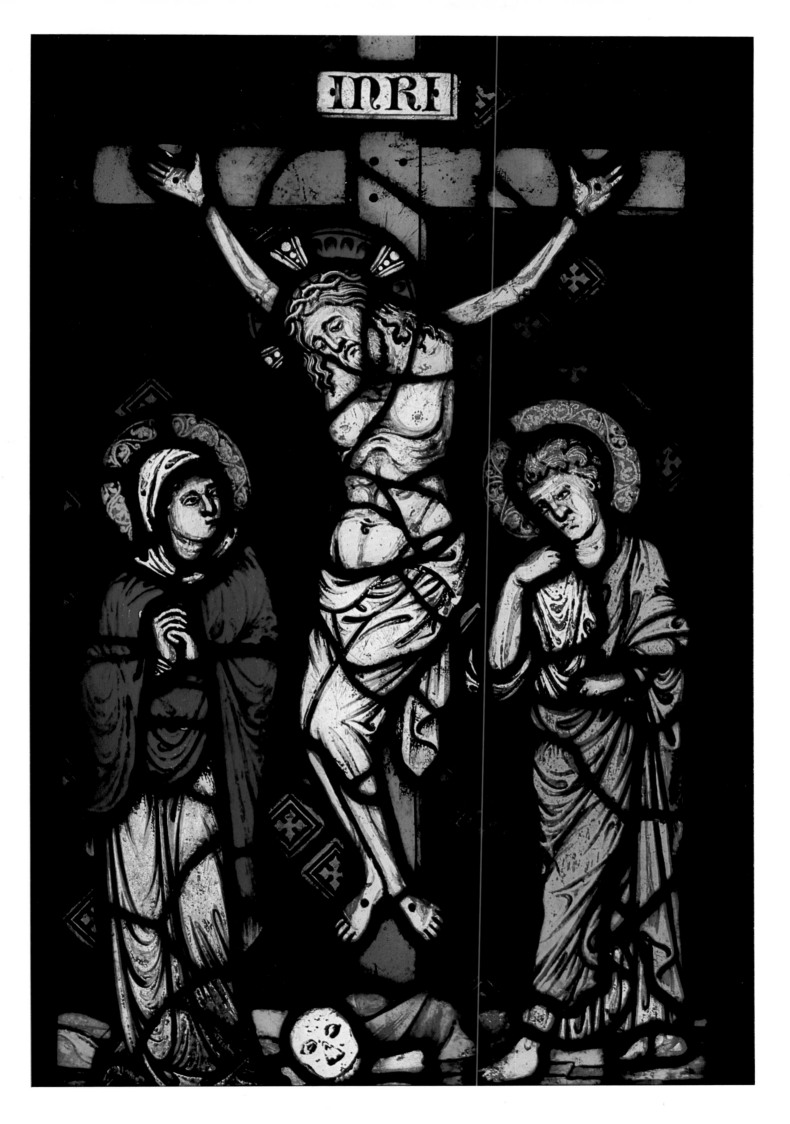

Angel, *c. 1250, medallion from Frankfurt Cathedral. Hessisches
Landesmuseum, Darmstadt.*

Baptism of Christ, *panel of the* Bibelfenster *from the Dominican
Church in Wimpfen im Tal (Swabia), 1270. Hessisches Landesmuseum,
Darmstadt.*

chapter houses. In York Minster, the famous Five Sisters window (c. 1260), so called by Charles Dickens, epitomizes this type of non-iconographical window in its breadth and its striking degree of formal compactness, a far cry from the airier French tradition. These formal divergences appear to have persisted for several decades. Foliar motifs continued to take the form of palmettes arranged in symmetrical scrolls contained within medallions emphasized by a coloured mesh, as at Salisbury Cathedral (c. 1280), whereas in France these foliar motifs were already adopting recognizably botanical forms.

The rebuilding of Westminster Abbey undertaken by Henry III, brother-in-law to St. Louis, marked the beginning of a brilliant period for English stained glass, which now strove to adopt and even surpass the formulas used in France. Unfortunately, however, the abbey's few remaining medallions of this period, now preserved in the Jerusalem Chamber at the west entrance, are not enough to allow for any real assessment of the work carried out there. From the 1270s onwards the concept of the mixed window became firmly established in England. The spread of the Court style was also to exert a considerable influence on this technique and, as in Normandy and the Île-de-France, it forfeited its monumental character in favour of a refined, mannerist quality that imitated the style found in manuscripts of the day. Using the delicate shapes of tracery windows and copying the drolleries in the margins of manuscripts, the glaziers placed their figures beneath tiered niches that were like architecture in miniature. They began to reduce the scale of their figures, which now moved in the midst of panels of almost white grisaille painted with such botanical motifs as strawberry leaves. The earliest example of this new form of stained glass are the windows in the choir of Merton College Chapel, Oxford. Completed at the tail-end of the thirteenth century or the very beginning of the fourteenth, these windows, which portray apostles, saints and, first and foremost, their donor, Henry de Mamesfeld, who had himself depicted some twenty times on his knees holding a scroll with his name inscribed on it, show the transformation undergone by English stained glass at the end of the thirteenth century. During the succeeding decades it continued along this mannerist path and ultimately achieved an often astonishing degree of graphic and chromatic subtlety.

Spain and Italy, home of the fresco, were in their turn to be attracted to stained glass, even though it always remained a marginal phenomenon. Spain was a country in which French influence played an important role during the thirteenth century, particularly in Aragon and Castile. Although Gothic architecture had begun to infiltrate Christian Spain towards the end of the twelfth century, its decorative motifs for a long time remained faithful to Islamic traditions. Only León Cathedral retains series of windows that can be dated to the second half of the thirteenth and the beginning of the fourteenth century, but the structure of the building is French in concept, with its ground plan derived from that of Reims Cathedral and its elevation from Rayonnant architecture. The insertion of stained-glass windows was, if not vital, at least logical. The first series, dating from the 1260–80 period, are windows of the legendary type, using formulas inherited from French stained glass of the 1240–50 period. Their graphical quality, however, is poor, even in the series portraying historic personages that occupies the windows in the upper story of the nave. Only one window is rescued from this monotony, the Hunt window, so called because three of the five lancets depict a royal cavalcade. They are thought to have come from a window in the royal palace of Alfonso X the Learned and to have been installed in the cathedral at the beginning of the fourteenth century. The subject is unique in European stained glass of the period and consists of a line of horsemen accompanied by archers in the midst of animals which are running beneath the legs of the horses. Their lively style would appear to derive from that of manuscripts commissioned by Alfonso X, such as the *Cantigas*, dedicated to the Virgin.

Stained glass in Italy evolved along very different lines. The earliest surviving examples are Romanesque. Dating from around 1200, they comprise two medallions in the treasury of Aosta Cathedral. Provincial and even clumsy in style, these fragments are of little importance in the development of Gothic stained glass in Italy. The oldest Gothic windows in Italy are, in fact, Germanic and belong to the *Zackenstil* period, even though their colouring betrays a certain French influence. They take the form of the three typological windows in the Upper Church at Assisi. Begun in 1228, two years after the death of St. Francis, and built to house his body, the church, which was probably completed in 1240, was consecrated by Pope Innocent IV in 1253. Historians have established that the windows had been put into position by the middle of the century, whereas the painting of the interior was begun at a later date. It is interesting to note that this relatively unknown group, which is of exceptional spiritual density and embraces several iconographical traditions, should have been installed before the frescoes in a country where stained glass was still in its infancy. Work on the windows was only resumed after the death in 1274 of St. Bonaventure, a man who had lived his whole life in accordance with the ideals of poverty. The first windows to be installed were those in the transept, which were the work of craftsmen from differing backgrounds, some of whom used German formulas and others, French. Sometimes the two conventions intermingled, producing works of great originality.

The other area where the art of stained glass developed at the end of the thirteenth century is Siena. One early example, a Virgin and Child from the oratory of the Madonna della Grotta, datable to the 1280s, is very similar in style to the Sienese madonnas of the period, which still bore strong signs of Byzantine influence in their doleful and monotonous facial expressions.

The rose in the cathedral apse is of such higher quality that it has been attributed to Duccio. Everything, or almost everything, is new about it: for example, the checkerboard division of the panels instead of stone tracery in the French style and the arrangement of the scenes like independent paintings, despite their common theme of the Glorification of the Virgin. Her death surrounded by the apostles appears in the lower section; in the center she is enthroned within a mandorla supported by four angels; at the top she is shown being crowned by her Son. At either side of the central scene, in pairs, but with each figure standing in its own panel, the protecting saints of the city, Bartholomew, Ansano, Crescenzio, and Savin, look straight out at us from within many-lobed frames, the final concession to German tradition. In the corner panels the Four Evangelists, accompanied by their symbols, are shown seated with their gospels; the way in which they are portrayed marks the first occasion on which the laws of perspective were used in stained glass. The spatial organization of the window also surpasses Franco-Germanic conventions: each figure possesses its own plastic authority and stands out against a clear, single-colour background. The date of execution of this rose, which is no longer in its original position, can be pinpointed to 1287–88 thanks to documentary evidence. Its graphic style and design are similar to that of Duccio and his workshop. It has even been suggested that Duccio created the cartoons for it, but this theory must now be treated with some caution; if, however, it was not the master himself, then its author was in all likelihood one of his pupils, and from this probable collaboration there emerged in Siena the first "modern" stained-glass window.

York Minster, north arm, Five Sisters Windows, c. 1260.

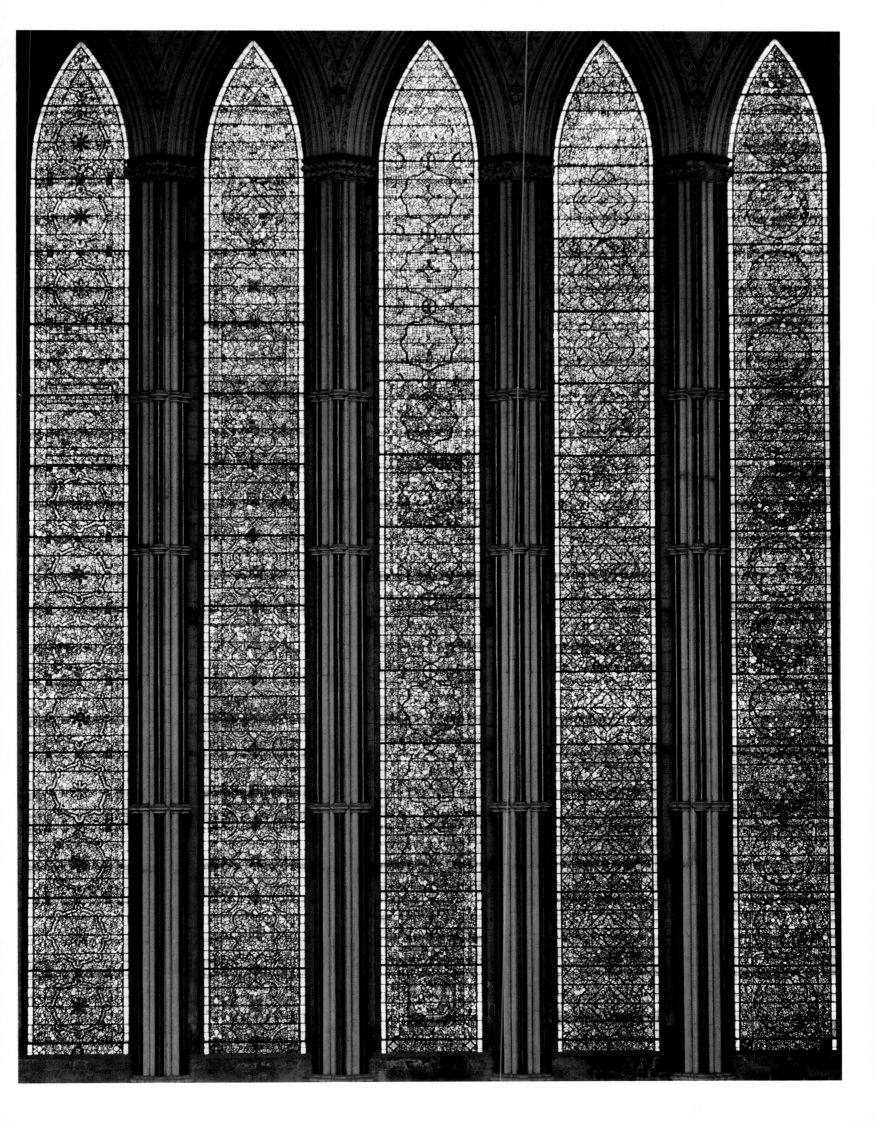

*Siena Cathedral, apse, rose window.
Central section (from below),* Death of the
Virgin, Assumption of the Virgin, *and*
Coronation of the Virgin; *central panels
(from left to right),* St. Bartholomew the
Apostle, St. Ansano, St. Crescenzio, *and*
St. Savin; *corner sections,* The Four
Evangelists and Their Symbols, *1287–88.*

Siena Cathedral, apse, rose window. Detail,
Coronation of the Virgin, *1287–88.*

4
The Fourteenth Century:
Silver Stain, a Revolutionary Technique

"Nothing resembles a thirteenth-century stained-glass window less than one of the fourteenth," Émile Mâle observed in the early years of the twentieth century. In fact, more than just a change in form and colour, there was a true revolution in stained glass, probably the most important in its entire history. But the new style of combining historiated panels with ones of pale grisaille, which rapidly turned to white, did not originate solely in the fourteenth century. The earliest surviving examples date from the 1260–70 period and can be seen in the choir of Tours Cathedral and in the upper story of the chevet at Saint-Urbain in Troyes. This style became, apart from a few exceptions, the general rule during the fourteenth century and, in France and England especially, it resulted in some beautiful windows, which gained in formal and chromatic subtlety what they lost in monumentality. The Germanic workshops, by contrast, which were enjoying a period of rapid expansion at the time, continued to favour windows with strong colours, while also adopting a mannerist figurative style.

GENERAL CHARACTERISTICS

The direction being taken by architecture, which was now tending towards a reduction in space, while at the same time increasing the number of chapels needing illumination, obliged glaziers to abandon the old thirteenth-century colour combinations in order to preserve a harmonious relationship between stained glass and architecture. Windows could no longer be that mosaic of colours which they had been in France during the first half of the thirteenth century. Bays began to be divided into even more lancets, which were surmounted by a pierced tympanum, and the wall area became reduced even further. Architectural proportions grew increasingly

Wells Cathedral, Lady Chapel, Virgin and Child Surrounded by Old Testament Figures; *in the tympanum,* Angels Bearing Candles and Instruments of the Passion, *c. 1310.*

sharp, with a tendency to develop tall, pointed niches around windows and doorways, similar in style to the architectural elements that had become so widespread in stained glass. Glaziers therefore had to make allowances for these changes, which were particularly prevalent in the northwest of Europe, most notably France and England.

In other areas as remote as the south of France, Italy, and the Holy Roman Empire, architects gained inspiration from the buildings of the mendicant orders, which had become firmly established in certain parts of Europe. The single-story church hall, with no ambulatory, in which the choir and nave form a single area, was often the chosen model. The bays, particularly those in the chevet, which was now very shallow, began almost at ground level and soared upwards for almost the entire elevation of the building, still preserving, however, rudimentary tympanums, while the lancets continued to grow. The glaziers therefore had to find original solutions, and even the arrangement of windows changed. A desire to provide every corner of the interior with the maximum amount of light, combined with the greater expense of coloured windows over plain glass, led to the invention of formal combinations that provide a startling comparison with the earliest mixed windows, such as the ones in the choir of Tours Cathedral (before 1260). At that time the "hatchment" arrangement was the rule: figures or scenes arranged between decorative grisaille panels that were still tinged with colour. What is more, windows of superimposed medallions, the so-called "legendary" type, began to fall into almost universal disfavour. The sections reserved for imagery were reduced to one scene or figure per lancet and seemed almost lost in the midst of the architectural surrounds in which the glaziers gave full rein to their imagination, creating a miniature world inhabited by birds, angels, and grotesques peering out from behind tympanums and hiding between the turrets that make up these immense niches or tabernacles. This was not a new practice—for two hundred years stained-glass win-

dows had been using canopies over figures—but what was new was the way in which these niches developed, particularly in the Holy Roman Empire. In Alsace, their outline was inspired by the shapes of contemporary Gothic architecture, but their pale, golden colouring, the unreality of their composition, and the diversity of their decoration transformed them into fairy-tale structures, which began to be portrayed in accordance with the laws of perspective around 1325.

Certain technical innovations allowed stained glass to accomplish this transformation. It is possible that these were brought about by its formal evolution, which links it to that of conventional painting. Since the closing years of the thirteenth century the quality of glass had changed. The manufacture of the glass paste had become less empirical, thanks to closer control over the types of sand used, and the melting process became more regular. The means of blowing glass was also perfected, allowing for the creation of larger and thinner panes, manufactured in France during this period by the muff/crown process. These discoveries were also of benefit to the colouring of glass: white glass, which had previously been cloudy and translucent, became more and more clear and transparent, while coloured glass gained in clarity, with pale shades, such as a pinkish purple, beginning to emerge. In order to make it easier to create elements involving detailed cutting work, such as armorial bearings, the practice of engraving on glass developed out of the process known as "flashing." Instead of being coloured all the way through, these panes of glass, such as red glass, are transparent, but covered in a thin film of coloured glass or "flash" which can easily be removed by means of abrasion. The original colour thus revealed can be either left in its original state or painted. The enlargement of the manufactured sections of glass also affected the size of the individual pieces, which now became much larger and less geometrical. Only one section was now needed for a face, its hair, and the surrounding halo, instead of the previous three.

This reduction in the number of pieces

was also largely attributable to the use of a new stain, silver. In fact, its application to stained glass was completely to transform the future of the technique, freeing it from the restraints of the lead lattice and allowing it to become painting on glass. The silver salt allowed glaziers to make a piece of white glass shade into yellow without resorting to cutting and also to alter the tone of a piece of coloured glass, which could now be given two colours without the addition of a lead bar. The stain, which was generally applied to the outer surface of the glass, penetrated during firing, after which the artist painted the inner surface in the usual way. Stained glass could now achieve new, richer effects, while the task of the glazier was also made easier. The recipe for silver stain, which had been known since the sixth century to the Egyptians, who used it to decorate vases, is thought to have reached Europe from the East at the end of the thirteenth century through a treatise, based on Moorish traditions, which was compiled at the bidding of Alfonso X the Learned, King of Castile. A copy is believed to have been brought to the French court a few years later, meaning prior to 1300, and the preparation of silver stain was soon being exploited by the workshops of certain glaziers thanks to the entourage of Philip the Bold. Its use in stained glass responded to a very real need at the time because of the way in which the technique was evolving, but the first verifiable instance of its application in France does not occur until 1313, the date that appears in an inscription on a small window in a church in rural Normandy, at Mesnil-Villeman (Manche). It seems, however, that some workshops had used it earlier, as, for example, in the cathedral at Sées, also in Normandy, around 1300, or in England, at York Minster, at some date prior to 1310. The adoption of this process fitted in with the formal preciousness and refined colours called for at the time: a few touches of silver stain were enough to enliven the outline, removing its harshness and creating an almost ethereal brilliance. This harmonious matching of style and technique, which is still hard to explain, filled a very real need and, within twenty-five years, a large number of workshops in Europe were employing it with varying degrees of skill.

Since the closing years of the reign of St. Louis, meaning prior to 1270, stained glass had been losing its primacy to the art of illumination, which became increasingly precious and refined. Paris continued to be the artistic capital of France and still attracted the country's best artistic talents, who were, from the end of the century, the illuminator Master Honoré and then, from the 1320s, Jean Pucelle. The changes taking place in illumination were also felt in the realms of stained glass,

the figuration of which began to follow the same principles: the scale of its figures began to grow smaller and its graphic technique became much finer, while gaining a feeling of great plastic precision. From now on, glaziers tried to convey the effects of conventional painting, using new types of brush: ones which made the relief smoother and fitches which lightened them. This subtle application of the paint resulted in a return to the qualities found in painting on parchment or panel, while at the same time retaining such characteristic technical procedures as abrasion. As a result of this more painterly technique, the outline contour lost the strength that it had previously possessed, becoming supple and flexible and creating a more harmonious silhouette.

In the same way as nontranslucent painting, stained glass began to absorb the new Italian concept of perspective during the 1325–30 period, the earliest example of this phenomenon being the group of windows in the choir of the Cistercian Abbey Church of Königsfelden (Canton of Aargau, Switzerland), the mausoleum of the first Habsburg emperors. Gradually this spatial innovation was to be adopted by the majority of workshops, altering the very composition of windows. After 1350, the workshops of northern Europe became anxious to translate reality, basing their style on direct observation of life and nature. During this period the principle of patronage developed, not only in the courts of Europe, but also among the wealthiest middle-class families, who began to play an increasingly important economic role. New cultural centers developed in Europe, for example at Avignon, where the Papacy was installed in 1309. As well as summoning artists to their residences, patrons also bought manuscripts and objets d'art throughout Europe. The art trade expanded rapidly, reflecting the new trends. All these collectors wanted to acquire works of a similar style, in which the still vigorous traditions of French Gothic art were mingled with such Italianate elements as perspective and a preoccupation with realism which had previously been the preserve of northern artists. Known by the name of "International Gothic," this stylistic phase, which emerged around 1360, was heralded in stained glass by groups such as the one already mentioned at Königsfelden.

Decoration took advantage of this new concern with refinement and this new taste for naturalism to renew itself. Many windows still retained heraldic borders with fleurs-de-lis, lions rampant, and Germanic eagles, but between these motifs, grotesques, derived from illuminated manuscripts, gradually crept in, together with birds, wild men, and monkeys. As in uncoloured decorative win-

dows, the floral ornament became more and more naturalistic, making use of oak leaves and vine tendrils. These are the same miniature elements that can be seen covering the damascened backgrounds against which the scenes and figures stand out, creating a screen that further accentuates the delicate and unreal character of the glass. These damascened backgrounds, which developed from the mid thirteenth century in Germanic stained glass, were later taken up by French and English workshops at a time when their contemporaries in the Holy Roman Empire were placing their figures on a red or blue ground painted in small squares or circles reminiscent of the backgrounds found in French legendary windows from the first half of the thirteenth century. Regional characteristics became blurred through being taken up by other workshops which then reinterpreted them.

These formal changes also affected iconographical traditions. Legendary windows, for example, with multiple medallions, allowed stories to be told with extraordinary narrative diffuseness, whereas in the fourteenth century only the most salient events of their subject's life were portrayed; in the case of saints, for example, it would be their meeting with Christ or their conversion to Christianity, one of their miracles, and finally their glorious death. All the subsidiary episodes are dispensed with and the "reading" of the window becomes much easier. On the other hand, the likenesses of donors began to invade windows. Some of them even elected to have themselves represented several times, like canon Raoul of Senlis in Beauvais Cathedral or the chancellor of Oxford University in the choir of Merton College Chapel. Others showed no compunction in taking up an entire lancet, like Raoul de Ferrières in Évreux Cathedral. But it was this lay and religious patronage which fostered the new lease enjoyed by stained glass, since it ensured that the workshops received more and more commissions, many of which were secular. In fact, by the end of the thirteenth century most of the great cathedrals had received their stained glass, which, being more recent in date, is still in good condition. Without these donors, the painter-glaziers and their teams of craftsmen would have been unable to find so many commissions. Some of them even worked in the full-time private service of rich and powerful lords, while others were merely summoned for specific enterprises.

Tewkesbury Abbey, apse, north side, Knights in Armour Beneath Architectural Baldachins, *c. 1320.*

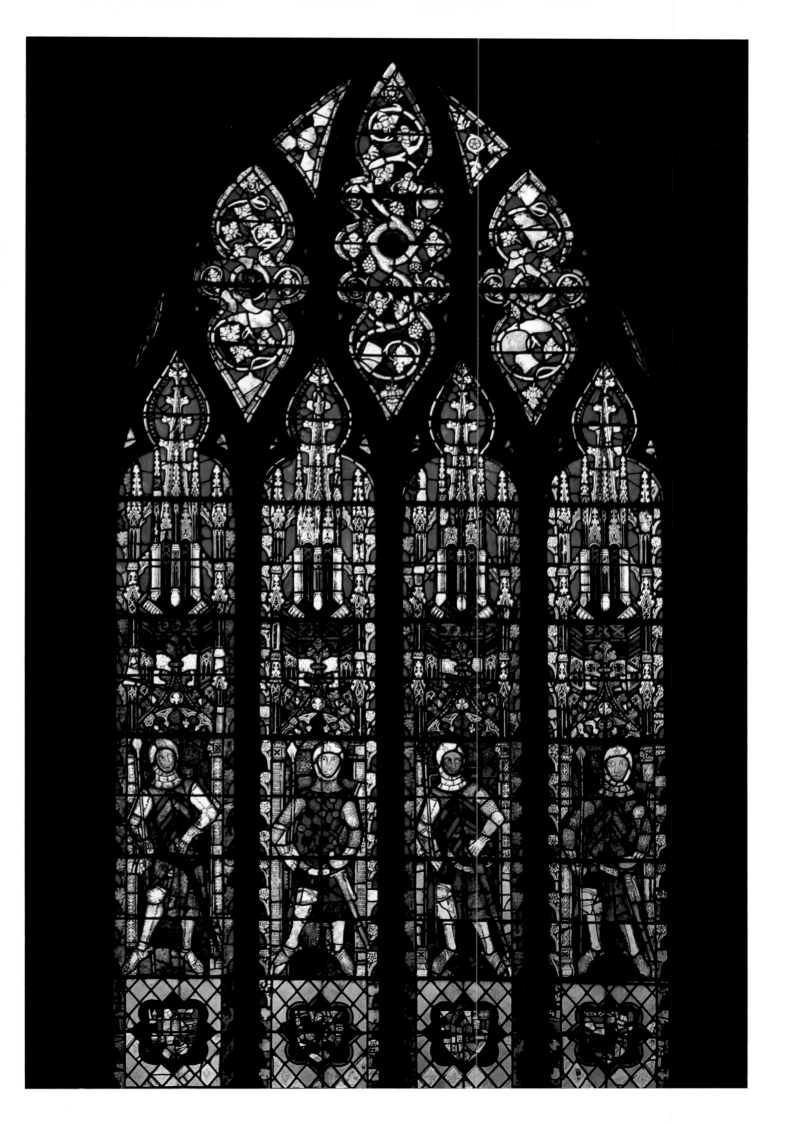

HISTORICAL DEVELOPMENT

The fourteenth century was a difficult period, notably in France, which became embroiled in a very lengthy war with England. In addition, Europe suffered several epidemics of plague, which decimated its population. These events brought with them great changes in the evolution of Europe's artistic life and France gradually lost its supremacy. Instead of there being a single artistic magnet in Europe, as during the thirteenth century, there were now a large number of princely and royal courts attracting artists, whether in England or Alsace or even in the easternmost reaches of the Holy Roman Empire. This dispersal proved

Évreux Cathedral, Angel Playing a Musical Instrument, *fourteenth century.*
Opposite: Deerhurst Priory Church, Gloucester, nave, south aisle, west window, St. Catherine, *beginning of the fourteenth century.*

very beneficial to stained glass, since it created rivalry among different artists.

IN FRANCE

The prestige of Paris persisted for several decades, but difficulties arising from the Hundred Years War soon diminished the role of the French court as an artistic powerhouse. All the stained glass produced in Paris during the fourteenth century has disappeared, with the exception of some figures of apostles, datable to the second half of the century, which come from the chapel of the famous Collège de Beauvais. But this series, which has been heavily restored, gives no idea of the important role still being played by Parisian stained glass at the time. Before the Revolution, there were still churches and palaces in Paris that possessed stained glass from this period and which can be identified from descriptive accounts. The region surrounding Paris is scarcely better endowed, the only examples being the remains in the Chapelle de Navarre, now known as the Chapelle du Rosaire, in the Collegiate Church of Mantes (Yvelines), which are not in their original position. Datable to the first quarter of the fourteenth century, these elements bear witness to the high degree of formal and chromatic refinement that had been reached at the time. The medallions relate to the Passion of Christ and are wonderfully "readable" despite their small diameter; the silver stain, used in light touches, underlines the expressive interplay of the poses, while the architectural elements are enlivened with lions and leopards, which also appear in the borders. It is, however, to Normandy, most notably Rouen and Évreux, that one must go in order to appreciate the high standards of stained glass during this period. The series of legendary archbishops in the Chapel of the Virgin at Rouen Cathedral, which dates from the beginning of the century, reveals those tendencies peculiar to the fourteenth century and the transformations that had been accomplished. The sixteen figures are sheltered beneath tall niches enriched with naturalistic decoration and stand out against damascened backgrounds. The draughtsmanship and elegant modelling of the faces contrast with the heaviness of the drapery, which reflects the actual material of the costumes. The overall effect is much lighter, not only as a consequence of the repeated use of white glass, but also through the extensive use of very pale or lightly coloured glass. Such innovations were made possible by a high degree of painting skill; the outline is reduced to a thin and

Angel Appearing to the Shepherds, English, second half of the fourteenth century. Victoria and Albert Museum, London.

sinuous line emphasized by a wash which was applied with a brush and then enlivened by details worked with a stylus. The decorative elements were equally innovative, using motifs copied from nature, in which flowers intermingle with parrots and angelic musicians. A few years later the windows in the choir of the Abbey Church of Saint-Ouen, not far from the cathedral, were decorated along similar lines, but with the forms introduced in the cathedral chapel being exploited in a much more grandiose way. In fact, the windows in the choir of this ancient abbey church, rebuilt between 1318 and 1339, represent the most outstanding series of French stained-glass windows from the first half of the fourteenth century. Endowed with exceptional stylistic unity, they are the product of a single workshop and reflect formulas which, although perhaps introduced from Paris, were interpreted by local artists.

In the wake of this skillfully mastered trend, other works appeared as further proof of the flourishing nature of Norman stained glass during the first half of the fourteenth century. But it is in Évreux Cathedral that one finds the window which exemplifies the formal and chromatic subtlety achieved by stained glass in Normandy. The window in question is the one presented by canon Raoul de Ferrières, dedicated to the Virgin, who is shown suckling the Child. An image of extraordinary authority despite its pictorial delicacy, this work, which dates from before 1330, the year of its donor's death, is the culmination of more than half a century of striving for perfect mastery over this new style. Between the mixed windows in the upper choir of Tours Cathedral and this figure of the Virgin, to whom the canon is offering a stained-glass window with great deference, there lies the work of hundreds of nameless, toiling artists. There are several windows in the upper choir of Évreux Cathedral which follow in the same stylistic vein, thereby betraying a link with the Rouen workshop, whose creations must have been close to the ones produced in Paris that have since disappeared. No fewer than some fifteen Norman churches contain evidence of this brilliant phase in the history of Norman stained glass. Its fame even spread to other regions in the west of France, notably Touraine, where its influence can be seen in the chapel of Mézières-en-Brenne (Indre), but one may generally assume that Parisian works provided the main inspiration, as in the Saint-Piat Chapel in Chartres Cathedral (before 1350) or the St. John the Evangelist window (c. 1340) in the Cathedral at Beauvais.

During the last three decades of the thirteenth century stained glass in the west of France entered a period of remarkable expansion that was to last into the first

Church of St. Florian, Koblenz, Life of Christ.
Above, from left to right and top to bottom,
Annunciation, Adoration of the Magi,
Betrayal, *and* Flagellation.

Opposite, Nativity *(formerly in Dausenau
Church, West Germany), second quarter of the
fourteenth century.*

decades of the fourteenth. The rebuilding
or modernization of several large Benedictine abbeys was the basic reason for this
phenomenon, as in the case of Saint-Pierre
in Chartres or the Church of the Trinity in
Vendôme. Although some of the windows created during this period mirror the
characteristics of Parisian art, the majority
follow an original trend whose origins are
still difficult to ascertain. The latter trend
counteracted the delicate formulas of Paris
with a bold, almost brutal graphic quality
and an emphatic use of colour. The design
was summarily drawn in large sweeps,
with extraordinary freeness, often producing a strikingly expressionistic style.

In the same way, the stained glass of
southern France, whose great period of
development followed the introduction
of Gothic architecture, still remained

highly coloured, while also adapting the
principle of the mixed window. It may be
that stained glass was used as a complement
to wall painting, a tradition that lasted
beyond the Middle Ages. At the Church of
Saint-Nazaire, in the heart of the medieval
city of Carcassonne, some of the windows
in the chevet, installed during the first
three decades of the fourteenth century,
preserve the formula of the legendary style
of window, while others follow that of the
mixed window. Franciscan iconography
produced a totally original creation, the
Tree of Life, a theme popularized in a
treatise written by St. Bonaventure. But
apart from these two reactions, fourteenth-century French stained glass is
characterized by its adherence to Parisian
models, all of which have disappeared,
but which are known through surviving

Church of St. Florian, Koblenz, Calvary *(left),* The Risen Christ *(right), second quarter of the fourteenth century. (Formerly in Dausenau Church, West Germany.)*

Opposite: St. Peter and St. Gereon, *Cologne, 1320–30. Hessisches Landesmuseum, Darmstadt.*

Overleaf: Details of Calvary *from the demolished church at Mutzig (Lower Rhine), c. 1310. Left,* St. Maurice *or* St. Oswald on Horseback; *right,* St. John. *Musée de l'Oeuvre Notre-Dame, Strasbourg.*

works in Normandy, the only province where this artistic activity can be traced from decade to decade.

The history of French stained glass during this period will always be as hazy as that of English stained glass during the thirteenth century.

IN ENGLAND

At the start of the fourteenth century, English stained glass still remained faithful to the formal and chromatic principles of Court art. From the 1270s onwards, the "hatchment" formula was to become the rule, since architects at the time were trying to reduce the wall area of buildings as far as possible in order to introduce more light. Bays contained numerous lancets surmounted by tympanums with tracery that was often of astonishing intricacy. Moulding spread out over the walls and vaults to a much higher degree than in France, clinging to the interior like ivy. These changes, which in architecture gave rise to what is known as the "Decorated Style" and then to the "Perpendicular Style," which made its first appearance after 1340, were to influence the development of stained glass. As in France, windows became paler and paler, forcing glaziers to find new solutions, which they did by inserting more and more panels of colourless, decorative glass at the expense of coloured ones. Using the delicate shapes of tracery and copying the drolleries in manuscripts, glaziers began to place

scenes or figures beneath tiered niches adorned with strands of leaf-work in imitation of those decorating doorways. As the century progressed, so these baldachins increased in size and became even more richly decorated, sometimes being arranged in accordance with the new Italian laws of perspective, as in the choir of Tewkesbury Abbey in Gloucestershire. The space reserved for the figure or scene was reduced accordingly, and the technique of execution became increasingly delicate and detailed, with the windows in Merton College Chapel, Oxford (1289–1311), initiating a new style of presentation which, with variants, lasted for much of the fourteenth century. As in France, both the arrangement and the draughtsmanship of the designs grew lighter. The reticulated backgrounds (known in French as *cages à mouches*) disappeared and, also as in France, the decorative repertoire became naturalistic, copying the leaves of ivy, oak, and strawberry. Seaweed as a motif was often used, as in Gloucester Cathedral, for example. The same elements also appeared in borders, side by side with heraldic motifs. The latter did not just take the form of the leopard of England, but also the fleur-de-lis of France and the rose of the Habsburgs. Heraldry occupied an important place in English stained glass during this period; it often took the place of a likeness of the donor or, if the latter were included, provided an additional element. These coats of arms involved

glaziers in very detailed work and they are one of the reasons why flashed glass developed at the end of the thirteenth century.

The quality of the actual glass underwent the same changes as in France, becoming thinner, while the colouring grew paler. The ravages of the Black Death (1348–49), however, put an end to these researches into technical improvement. English glaziers "discovered" and used silver stain at the same time as their counterparts in the Île-de-France and Normandy. The earliest English window highlighted in silver stain dates from 1309 and can be seen in York Minster. It soon became common currency and was used, for example, in the St. Catherine window in Deerhurst Church (Gloucestershire), which dates from before 1320, and in the choir of Exeter Cathedral (1310–20).

As in Normandy, the figurative style of English stained glass almost always followed mannerist conventions. The poses of the figures in the high windows in Saint-Ouen can be seen in the contemporary series—which may even be slightly earlier in date—of saints in Wells Cathedral. The differences are minimal and betray similar inspiration. However, as usual, the design of the English works is more subtle in its outline. The painters retained only the essential lines in order to endow their images with greater expressive force. The supple and elegant pose of the Deerhurst St. Catherine is proof of this. Other examples illustrate this feature

Left: Annunciation, *from Strassengel Church (Styria), fourteenth century. Victoria and Albert Museum, London. Right,* St. Stephen Preaching, *Cologne (?), c. 1300. Victoria and Albert Museum, London.*

Opposite: Angel Gabriel *(detail of an Annunciation), Alsace, first third of the fourteenth century. Musée de l'Oeuvre Notre-Dame, Strasbourg.*

just as well, such as the Virgin and Child in Eaton Bishop Church (Herefordshire). The activities of English painter-glaziers, several of whose names are known from contemporary documents, centered mainly on the great building programs of the day, as at York, where architectural work was carried out throughout the fourteenth century.

Among the finest surviving windows of the period are those in the Lady Chapel of Wells Cathedral (c. 1345), while another flourishing center was Oxford, where the earliest examples still in situ are the figures of saints in the choir of Merton College Chapel, presented by Henry de Mamesfeld, chancellor of Oxford University (1298–1311), who had no compunction in having himself portrayed more than twenty times, kneeling and holding a scroll with a Latin inscription proclaiming "Henry de Mamesfeld had me made." The Latin Chapel in Oxford Cathedral still possesses a window executed in a very delicate style between 1367 and 1369,

while from the end of the century come the windows in the narthex of New College Chapel, which are the work of an artist named Thomas of Oxford. In the area around Oxford there are several churches, most notably at Waterperry and Marsh Baldon, which also contain glass from this period. Another important contemporary center was based at Westminster, where numerous glaziers had been active since the rebuilding of the abbey in the mid thirteenth century. The modernization work on the choir of the venerable abbey at Tewkesbury (Gloucestershire) involved the installation of several windows presented by Eleanor de Clare in memory of her murdered husband. One of these represents male members of the family in armour beneath tall white niches highlighted in silver stain (c. 1360). Another example of the expertise of English glaziers during the second half of the fourteenth century is provided by the small medallion of the Angel appearing to the Shepherds, now in the Victoria and

Albert Museum in London, which presages both the realism of the fifteenth century and the fashion for roundels, which often depicted scenes of everyday life.

IN THE HOLY ROMAN EMPIRE

The art of stained glass continued to flourish in the Holy Roman Empire during the fourteenth century. It even gained momentum, since numerous churches were being built, the majority of which adopted the principles derived from the architecture of the mendicant orders, as at Esslingen in Swabia. In this geography of stained glass one must also include the regions that today make up Austria, Prussia, Poland, Bohemia, and even the Swedish island of Gotland, where some very interesting windows were created. Strasbourg continued to act as the main source of inspiration, even though work on its cathedral had finished almost thirty

León Cathedral, windows with floral decoration, fourteenth century. Only the upper panels are original.

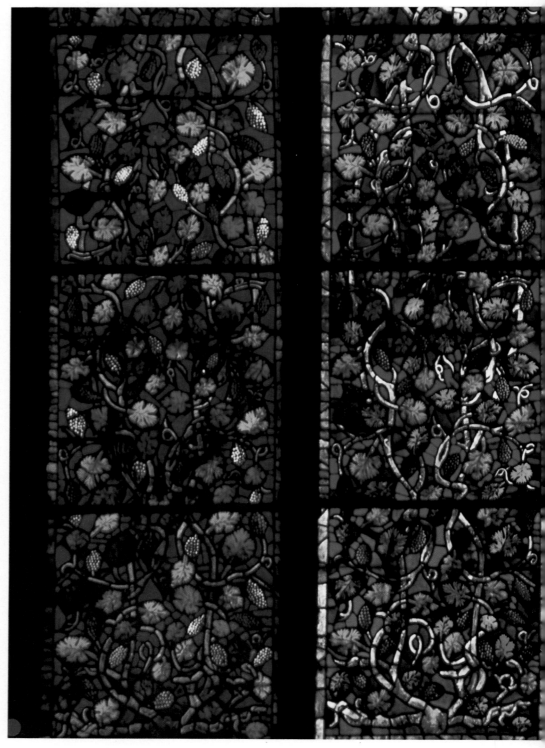

years earlier. However, a fire in the building in 1298 meant that several windows had to be replaced. Other workshops were active in churches elsewhere in the city, such as the churches of St. William and St. Thomas, and also in other Alsatian towns. Their sphere of activity even stretched beyond these confines to form a vast artistic community with the other glass artists in regions dependent upon the ecclesiastical province of Strasbourg. Like Paris, this city attracted artists who used not only the traditions of French Gothic, but also the new ideas emanating from Italy, inventing completely original stylistic formulas that were then exported to as far afield as the monasteries of Swabia. The Crucifixion window in the church at Mutzig, to the west of Strasbourg, a building that has since been destroyed, introduced a new concept with its twin-level architectonic composition. Created by a Strasbourg workshop around 1310, it is believed to be the earliest surviving window of its type. The figures, executed on a small scale and painted with great delicacy, shelter, like statuettes in a triptych, beneath small niches surmounted by immense white and yellow tabernacles. On the lower level there appear the figures of a Virgin and Child, which replace that of St. Paul, and St. Maurice, the patron of the building, on horseback, and St. Peter holding the key; on the upper level there is a Christ on the Cross surrounded by the Virgin and St. John, each occupying their own niche. The tabernacles give this composition a formal unity that is further reinforced by the regular division of the windows into rectangular panels. The colouring also accentuates this cohesive quality, with pale shades of glass used for the architectural elements, deeper ones for the background, and bright ones for the figures. Its figurative style follows the incisive and mannered graphic style of manuscripts of the region. There are other windows that could also be mentioned, a fact that underlines the degree of activity being carried on in this region during the first three decades of the thirteenth century, as well as their shared inspiration.

It was during the beginning of the fourteenth century that another type of window was created in Strasbourg, the oldest surviving example of which can be seen in the Church of St. Thomas. Two large medallions, the remains of a window dedicated to the Coronation of the Virgin and now in the north arm of the transept, spread out over the entire width of the bay, like a painting. This principle was of great importance for the evolution of Germanic stained glass right up until the end of the Middle Ages.

The different teams of glaziers turned Strasbourg Cathedral into a hive of activity during the first half of the century. They completed, among other things, a large narrative cycle covering all the lancets in the six bays of the south aisle, which illustrated, in the spirit of the *Biblia Pauperum*, a work that enjoyed great popularity in Alsace, the Childhood of the Virgin in just one window and, in the remainder, the Life of Christ, from his Childhood right up to his Second Coming on the Day of Judgement. The last window is contemporary with the splendid windows in the Chapel of St. Catherine, which is situated at the far east end of the nave. The twelve apostles, accompanied by St. Margaret and St. Mary Magdalene, hold scrolls bearing phrases from the Creed. Each figure shelters beneath soaring tabernacles, three times taller than the figures, and these white, ethereal structures stand out against red and blue backgrounds enlivened with lozenges. This group, one of the most spectacular creations in the entire history of stained

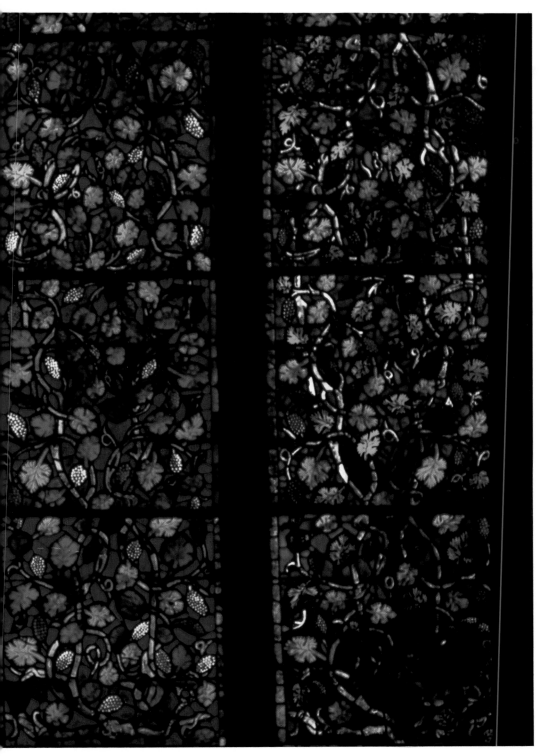

leum for this powerful family. The church was built in two sections: first the nave and then the choir in which the windows are located. Completed during the same period as the building, between 1325 and 1330, these windows pay tribute to both the spirituality of the Franciscans and the burgeoning power of the Habsburgs. From a stylistic point of view, they follow the same formal and chromatic principles as had been used for several decades by the glaziers of Alsace and the upper Rhine, but these were now transformed by an exceptional degree of graphic and pictorial mastery, a palette of extraordinary refinement, and the first-ever use in stained glass of Italian perspective. The treatment of the scenes and the figures surpasses that of any other contemporary window in the region, whether it be a narrative one or one with figures beneath ethereal tabernacles. Both the finely drawn silhouettes, with their relaxed, standing poses and their harmoniously theatrical gestures, and the calmly expressive faces possess a quality of rare elegance. The origins of the Königs-felden workshop have for a long time been the subject of controversy, but they are now thought to lie in Strasbourg.

Gothic and English styles infiltrated Cologne with comparative ease, as can be seen in the windows in the sacristy of the Church of St. Gereon, built between 1310 and 1320. The figures of saints, most of whom were patrons of the city, are arranged between bands of decorative grisaille in accordance with the "hatchment" layout, which is rare in the Holy Roman Empire. The association of decorative grisaille panels with narrative ones does not, however, follow the formulas used in France and England, sometimes being inserted between the figures and the tabernacles crowning them. This French Gothic influence can also be detected in the medallions of a Life of St. Stephen that come from a Rhenish church and can be dated to around 1300. The shape of the compartments tends to be simpler, as does the shape of the individual pieces of glass, which mirrors one of the principles of French Gothic glass during the closing decades of the thirteenth century.

In the northern reaches of the Empire the art of stained glass did not flourish until the 1340–50 period. The *opus francigenum* was exported by Strasbourg artists or disseminated by means of pattern books: the Virgin and Child in Brandenburg Cathedral, near Potsdam, represents an excellent example of penetration by the workshops of Alsace in around the 1300s. Another center was Lübeck in Lower Saxony, whose influence was felt as far afield as Scandinavia, notably in several churches on Gotland, among them the one at Lye. Local workshops often found it very hard to adapt to the delicate methods and techniques of the period around 1300,

glass, may well be the work of one of the very few master glaziers of the period whose name is known to us: John of Kirchheim.

Swabia is another center which shows the exceptional degree of expertise reached by the stained-glass workshops of this region. The art first began to prosper during the 1270s in several monasteries and country churches, and it continued its rise during the first quarter of the fourteenth century, most notably at Esslingen, to the southeast of Stuttgart. Several churches were under construction at the

time, and these were embellished with glass of an extraordinarily high formal and chromatic quality, comparable to that produced by the other workshops in Alsace and the upper Rhine. The most accomplished ensemble created by this group, however, is the one adorning the choir of the Franciscan Abbey of Königs-felden, to the southwest of Zürich. The monastery was built on the very spot where one of the first Habsburg emperors was murdered in 1308. His widow, and then his daughter, Queen Agnes of Hungary (1280–1364), turned it into a mauso-

Assisi, Lower Church of St. Francis, St. Martin Chapel, Saint, *workshop close to Simone Martini, before 1317.*

only mastering them in the second generation of craftsmen.

The beginning of the fourteenth century marked the beginning of a very active period for stained glass in eastern Europe, in the regions now forming the modern state of Austria and stretching as far as Bohemia and Poland. The mannerist, French style first appeared there at the beginning of the century, when it combined with the formal principles characteristic of the region. The surrounding areas of the narrative compartments, however, were to continue to be composed of numerous foils for several decades more, in keeping with a practice that had been followed by Germanic workshops for more than a century; but the style of figuration, the old *Zackenstil* and its numerous Byzantine elements, disappeared in the face of the new ideas of the Italian Trecento, which several painters and glaziers working for such great abbeys as the one at Klosterneuburg were among the first to adopt in Europe. This is true of the marvellous Christological and typological series created to adorn the bays in the cloister of the latter foundation, which is now in one of the chapels. Inspired by the famous ambo (now an altarpiece) created there by Nicholas of Verdun in 1181, this group foreshadows some of the trends of International Gothic art, of which Vienna was one of the main centers. The spatiality of the scenes has become Gothic: the style of the figuration, which has become very precise, owes nothing to the effects of the *Zackenstil*.

By the middle of the century the style had grown more and more refined, but it was still familiar in feel: the compositions seem almost like genre scenes. The draughtsmanship became so supple and effortless that one is made even more aware of the extraordinary expertise of these stained-glass artists. This new trend produced some brilliant works at Strassengel, near Graz (Styria), in which the scenes are each enclosed within a three-dimensional niche, like a sort of tower seen in perspective. The elegance of the silhouettes achieves a flexibility that is totally mannerist in feel. The delicacy of the ornament, particularly in the damascened backgrounds, which act as backdrops to the compositions, is further enhanced by the use of a sophisticated palette. To this group, created around 1350 and now incomplete (several panels are today in museums), can be linked others in Vienna, both in St. Stephen's

Assisi, Lower Church of St. Francis, St. Anthony Chapel, Life of St. Anthony of Padua, *workshop of Giovanni di Bonino, c. 1320.*

Cathedral and in the Church of Maria-am-Gestade. These trends persisted until the end of the century, culminating, at the turn of the fourteenth and fifteenth centuries, in the astonishing creations of the workshop responsible for the stained glass in the Herzogenkapelle, situated in the west part of St. Stephen's Cathedral in Vienna. These include the Habsburg Family window (c. 1390), which was designed along the same lines as the Jesse window. Regarded as the greatest work by this group of craftsmen working in the service of the Habsburgs, this window can now be seen in the Historical Museum of the City of Vienna. The activities of this team appear not only to have been of importance in Vienna, where it received commissions from princes and high ecclesiastical dignitaries, but also in monasteries such as the Collegiate Church (now Parish Church) of Viktring in Carinthia.

Stylistic and iconographical links can be seen between those windows and the ones commissioned by Emperor Charles IV (1316–78) for his capital, Prague, and his castle at Karlštejn in Bohemia. In these circumstances one can only lament the almost total disappearance of stained-glass windows from churches in Bohemia and Prague, which was a great artistic center during the second half of the fourteenth century, thanks to the "European" character of the Emperor Charles IV, who was on friendly terms with many of his fellow princes in Europe.

An awareness of the style of the Parléř family, a famous dynasty of Swabian architects and sculptors, is essential to an understanding of the way in which stained glass evolved in Germany after the 1360s. And yet there is not a single window that can be directly linked to one of their buildings. The originality of the Parléř style lay in the way in which it blended a delicate and supple, even precious, graphical quality with an overwhelmingly powerful sense of the plastic. This new style achieved great success among Germanic painters, and not only those involved in stained-glass painting, but also those working on panel or illuminated manuscripts. Its influence can be seen in Germanic stained glass, even though there are noticeable variations reflecting the personalities of individual workshops and artists, many of whom also painted on panel. There were two main stylistic trends: one was supple and mannered, accentuating arabesques to the detriment of outline, while the other was brusque and insistent and heralded the intensely dramatic forms of German late medieval art. Both of them, however, sought to bring a feeling of individuality to the faces and to make them more realistic, which is one of the traits of the Parléřs' art. The most important examples of this phenomenon are at Erfurt, at Rothenburg ober

der Tauber and at Ulm, all of which bear witness to the flourishing nature of stained glass at the time. All the glass, whether the Genesis window at Erfurt (c. 1370) or the large compositions in the Church of St. James at Rothenburg, followed the traditions of Bohemian pictorial art. Thirty years later, at Erfurt, the graphical power of Johann von Tiefengruben achieved an expressive force that is rare in stained glass. In southern Europe, by contrast, stained glass during the fourteenth century continued to be a peripheral art form that was not always welcomed into buildings, with murals still retaining the favour of those in charge of commissions.

IN SPAIN

There are very few Spanish buildings containing fourteenth-century stained-glass windows. There were still workshops active in León Cathedral, where their most notable creations are the roses in the tympanum of the aisle windows, which contain representations of Virtues and Vices. It is hard to date these medallions in their present state. Their colouring is still dark, but in their draughtsmanship they echo the forms characteristic of International Gothic. Greater originality is shown by the windows beneath, which are adorned with large-scale vegetal motifs painted on strongly coloured glass. Heavily restored during the nineteenth century, they differ very little from French or even Germanic decorative windows.

During the fourteenth century, Catalonia was the main center of building activity in Christian Spain, but architectural techniques were on the whole very different from those of Gothic France. Stained glass was still a "minor" art, very few examples of which have survived, apart from a few panels in the cathedrals of Vich and Gerona.

IN ITALY

The situation regarding stained glass in Italy was quite different from that prevailing in Spain because the Italians invented new stylistic techniques for the medium. These no longer relied on Germanic or French traditions, as had been the case at Assisi in the previous century. The art of Giotto plays an essential part in understanding this development. The earliest fourteenth-century stained-glass windows in Italy are those in the Lower Church at Assisi, which was altered at the beginning of the century, when chapels were added to the earlier building and stained glass was inserted in the new bays. These windows do not all follow the same style. Some, like the one in the St. John Chapel, still reflect the mannered quality of Cimabue and retain borders as a final concession to Germanic stained glass,

while others, like the one in the St. Magdalene Chapel, are strongly influenced by the plastic qualities of Giotto. In fact, several of the latter artist's pupils worked on the frescoes of the Lower Church around 1305. The window dedicated to Mary Magdalene was probably influenced by the wall paintings.

Simone Martini was undoubtedly the author of the figures in the windows in the St. Martin Chapel, which he decorated with frescoes in the 1350s. The windows, which comprise six lancets, reveal an archaic composition reminiscent of Germanic stained glass. The figures of the saints, three in each lancet, are contained within multifoil or circular frames. The decoration blends archaic motifs, such as a running frieze of palmettes, with new ones, such as friezes of flat leaves based on the ivy. The style of the figures, however, follows that used by Simone Martini, with a brilliant, pale palette which endows them with astonishing vigour. In the middle of the century, artists were summoned from Umbria to work on the Upper Church at Assisi, and this is one of the most original aspects of Italian stained glass, which we already mentioned in the context of the thirteenth century: the way that mural or conventional painters often provided cartoons for stained-glass windows, contrary to what happened in France and England.

The situation was the same in Florence. The oldest medallions in the Church of Santa Croce, in the roses adorning the tympanums of the apse windows, were perhaps created by glass painters from the circle of Pacino di Buonaguida and Taddeo Gaddi. Later in date are the figures in the Bardi Chapel, the cartoons for which were the work of the Master of Figline. There are signs of Giotto's influence. The style of the figures, monumental in feel, is very linear, but this is countered by a wealth of elaborate decoration. Taddeo Gaddi was also responsible for the window in the Baroncelli Chapel, again in Santa Croce, whose frescoes were created by Maso di Bianco, and it is worth noting that there is a certain link between Gaddi's windows and the ones by Simone Martini at Assisi. The style is just as grandiose as that shown by the figures adorning the bays of the apse in Santa Croce. Almost sculptural in appearance, they possess that great feeling of tranquillity characteristic of the work of Agnolo Gaddi.

In Santa Maria Novella, the Virgin and Child beneath an architectural baldachin is less noteworthy than the beautiful rose in the west front portraying the Coronation of the Virgin. This window, recently restored, is the work of Andrea da Firenze and recalls, both in its subject matter and its treatment, the rose window at Siena. The central medallion portrays the actual event, which is surrounded by a choir of

angelic musicians forming a sort of living garland whose pose and configuration both display astonishing originality. Like the Siena rose, the one in Santa Maria Novella pays tribute to the work of the cartoonist by its brilliant execution. In the oratory of Or San Michele, by contrast, the narrative compositions relating to the Life of the Virgin and the Childhood of Christ must have been of extraordinarily high quality, but their present appearance is so altered that it is hard to assess their style. They doubtless blended features characteristic of the International Gothic style with a Florentine strength of outline. At the turn of the century, the great Mariotto di Nardo window in the Church of St. Dominic at Perugia showed its adherence to this European style in the supple movement of the figures, the richness of the landscape, and the subtlety of the colouring. It is to panel painting, which had achieved such a high degree of development at this period, that these must be compared.

Thus, although stained glass during the fourteenth century lost its earlier role as a prime moving force in art, it nevertheless underwent a series of transformations which produced works that are just as remarkable.

Church of Santa Maria Novella, Florence, Coronation of the Virgin, *rose window in façade, work of Andrea di Buonaiuto, 1365.*

5
The Fifteenth Century: Master Glaziers in the Service of Princes

Stained glass continued to thrive in Europe during the fifteenth century, but a great many windows from the period have been lost, particularly in France and Flanders, making any analysis of them a difficult task. It tended to draw even closer to conventional painting, whose visual effects it was often able to surpass thanks to the intrinsic qualities of its backing medium, glass, and also to the exceptional expertise of the artists involved. During the opening decades of the century the International Gothic style reigned supreme, but after 1440–50 the Flemish style of the van Eyck brothers became fashionable and stained-glass artists, like other painters, strove to emulate their vigorous forms and strongly contrasting colours. It took varying lengths of time before this reaction was felt in Europe; its influence was spread by Flemish craftsmen being summoned to work on projects far from their homeland and by means of cartoons drawn on paper, which were easily transportable.

GENERAL CHARACTERISTICS

The very nature of the glazier's profession seems to have changed during the fifteenth century. The majority of artists now began to lose their anonymity. Although the names of earlier glaziers are known, it is difficult to actually attribute any windows to them. From the fifteenth century onwards, however, such knowledge becomes possible, as, for example, in the two rose windows created during the mid fifteenth century by André Robin, painter to King René of Anjou, which are still in their original position in the transept of Angers Cathedral. The activities of some glaziers can be followed almost year by year, like those of the Alsatian Peter Hemmel.

Several workshops began to devote themselves exclusively to maintenance

Tournai Cathedral, transept, south arm; detail, Bishop Anselm Returns to Tournai After a Journey to Rome, *end of fifteenth century.*

Overleaf: Bourges Cathedral, Jacques Coeur Chapel, choir, north side, Annunciation, *1448–50.*

projects and ceased to produce original works, responsibility for which was entrusted to senior artists summoned to carry out specific commissions.

Many glass painters were quite prepared to move to new towns, as had already happened in the previous century, or even to emigrate still farther afield. In this context one should mention Arnoult of Nijmegen, who worked in Tournai before moving to Rouen during the opening years of the sixteenth century, where he remained for twelve years, and the Fleming Guillaume Spicre, who was employed by the Duke of Burgundy between 1454 and 1468, while others, such as Laurent Girardin and Jean Prévost, who were attached to the chapter of St. John in Lyon, worked for cathedral chapters, creating new windows and also accepting responsibility for maintenance work. Such duties were the subject of contracts that laid down the rights and obligations of both parties. Glaziers were paid for restoration work either by the year or by the day or, in the case of new windows, generally by the panel. The glass and lead were as a rule provided by the employer, as were the glaziers' working premises.

The profession was held in considerable esteem. King Charles V exempted it from taxes at the end of the fourteenth century, a measure that was renewed on several occasions during the following century. The statues promulgated by Charles VIII in favour of the glaziers of Lyon underline their preferential treatment vis-à-vis other craft associations. There were a large number of glaziers at the time. In Bruges during the mid fifteenth century no fewer than eighty names appear on the registers of the Guild of St. Luke, the brotherhood to which that city's painters belonged. There were just as many in Paris, Lyon, and Strasbourg, banded together in corporations which each had its own rules. Behind every "master" or painter there was also a large team composed of skilled craftsmen and apprentices, whose training normally lasted for five years.

During the fifteenth century famous artists often provided cartoons for windows, especially now that paper had

become the usual medium for such works. This innovation meant that the designs could easily be taken from one place to another and could also be reproduced more easily. The same models were used on several occasions, and there were workshops specializing in this process, notably the one run by the Gesuati brothers in Florence. Engraving on copper, which was widely practiced at the time, became the favourite inspiration of glaziers, particularly in the Germanic countries.

As in the preceding century, patronage not only favoured the rapid development of the craft, but also allowed numerous painter-glaziers to move from project to project and to familiarize others with their particular style, which the latter would then adopt. This process was hastened by patrons who, as a result of judicious dynastic marriages, owned lands in very disparate regions. They often kept the same painters in their service, who accompanied them whenever they changed their place of residence. Another important element was the rise in middle-class patronage. Rich merchants were growing in economic importance and a large number of them, such as the "silversmith" Jacques Coeur in Bourges, found in artistic commissions a means of highlighting their power. But, as in the past, trade and craft associations continued to donate windows, such as the drapers of Semur-en-Auxois, in Burgundy, who in around 1460 had themselves depicted going about their daily work: steeping cloth in a vat and cutting it with the aid of large shears.

Secular stained glass enjoyed considerable growth, not only in castles, but also in communal buildings such as town halls. Sometimes glaziers even took part in temporary structures erected for the solemn entry of kings or princes into their town. Only a few examples of secular stained glass have survived, such as the galleass, a boat painted on clear glass, bearing the arms of Jacques Coeur, which is a vestige of the decoration from his town house in Bourges.

Workshops everywhere gave full rein to their technical prowess. Being familiar with all the possibilities of silver stain, painters began to explore the potential of

engraving on glass, using Venetian glass, which was marbled in different shades. As for the actual painting process, that had attained new heights thanks to the use of different brushes to achieve the desired effect. These craftmasters knew how to control pictorial effects by varying the dilution of the vitreous paint and by adding vitrifiable ingredients which made them less variable. They also knew how to create modelled effects with a brush, wipe them with a pad, rework them with a fitch, and lighten them in order to reproduce the effects obtained in drawing or painting on panel. They also began to employ other types of paints better suited to the stylistic subtleties they were seeking. One of the constant features of fifteenth-century stained glass was the search for inspiration in other areas of art, but without ever indulging in slavish imitation.

During the early decades of the century, this monumental art continued to follow International Gothic trends. Windows still retained the same general arrangement as before. The figures or scenes, standing out against dark backgrounds, were sheltered beneath colourless architectural canopies whose vertical elements, portrayed in perspective, began to take up more and more space. In the middle of the century, certain workshops started to adopt the spatial innovations emanating from Flanders. The composition of windows altered once again. The scenes, however many lancets they covered, now formed a single entity enclosed within a vast architectural setting.

The tympanums still contained not only small scenes, but, more commonly, angels, sometimes holding the armorial bearings of the window's donor or donors, sometimes playing musical instruments or perhaps holding candles and censers, but always forming a sort of celestial apotheosis to the scene or figures depicted beneath. The juxtaposition of the reality portrayed in the scenes and the heavenly paradise contained in these tympanums very accurately reflects the dichotomous mentality of the period, as Johan Huizinga so effectively analyzed in his work *The Waning of the Middle Ages*, the first English edition of which appeared in 1924.

The iconographical language also developed. Under the influence of Flemish painting, the subject matter changed, striving to become more "real," as in the themes of Christ's Childhood and Passion, which now included familiar details. Landscape became one of the essential elements, and stained glass rapidly adopted it in place of the damascened background, which now disappeared. The events of the Passion were injected with a feeling of pathos that characterizes the art of this period, which was haunted by the ideas of Death and the End of the World; the tale of the Apocalypse, for example, began to reappear in windows. New themes, such as that of the Apostles' Creed, which was widely treated in stained glass, first in the Sainte-Chapelle at Bourges (c. 1400–5) and then in the one at Riom (c. 1460). This subject brought prophets and apostles together in order to stress the continuity between the old and the new. The Jesse Tree, which was less fashionable, was revived not only as a means of glorifying Christ, but also, and more especially, the Virgin. Religious theater and its mysteries influenced the conception and the actual composition of certain images, which now imitated stage settings by presenting the characters on different planes.

HISTORY

The history of stained glass in Europe during the fifteenth century has still to be written, but would such an enterprise be possible? So many works of the period have disappeared, victims of time and man. In France, for example, many key works have vanished, especially in Paris. The activities of the Flemish workshops can be traced only with difficulty through the few works that have survived in Flanders. In Italy, painters and sculptors continued to supply cartoons, whereas the Spanish relied on foreign artists, either Germanic or French. In order to create a comprehensive panorama of stained glass during this period it would be necessary to understand the wide variety of links that existed between the different workshops within a single region, their relationship with their fellows in other centers, and also the way in which they interacted with artists working in other media, such as painting on panel. This subject has so far only been touched upon.

FRANCE

There are several famous series, created at the turn of the fourteenth and fifteenth centuries, which give us an idea of what Parisian stained glass may have been like during the first decades of the fifteenth century, all contemporary windows in Paris having been destroyed. These take the form of the "royal" windows adorning several bays in the choir of Évreux Cathedral. Originally, this group of commemorative windows was more important than it is today. The royal personages, whose identity is still the subject of controversy despite extensive research, belong to the Évreux-Navarre family and include Charles VI (1380–1422) and Pierre de Mortain (1366–1412). In accordance with accepted practice, each royal figure is presented to the Virgin by a saint, who stands in another lancet. Even though the elegance of the draughtsmanship perpetuates the International Gothic style, certain formal innovations can be detected. The figures are placed on pedestals portrayed in perspective, and their faces are depicted with an unusual degree of realism. These characteristics are matched by a rich palette containing a harmonious balance between pale and dark glass. These windows, created between 1395 and 1400, were probably made by Parisian masters working in the service of King Charles VI. They attest to the flourishing nature of the workshops of Paris, where nothing survives today. Other windows were installed in the choir of this cathedral during the first half of the century, among them the so-called "Three Marys" window (c. 1450), which celebrated the liberation of Burgundy (1450) and the presentation to the cathedral of the relics of St. Mary Cleophas and of St. Mary Salome.

One has to travel to Bourges, which Duke Jean de Berry, brother to King Charles V, turned into a sumptuous capital city, in order to appreciate the extraordinary degree of perfection attained by fifteenth-century stained glass. From the very beginning of the century come the remnants of stained glass from the Sainte-Chapelle, which was demolished during the second half of the eighteenth century. It proved possible to salvage some of these windows, which were reused during the nineteenth century in several windows in the cathedral crypt, where they will soon be replaced following restoration work. The group originally illustrated the theme of the Apostles' Creed, in which prophets and apostles are united in a sort of dialogue. The figures are sometimes placed inside, and sometimes at the entry of the white architectural niches, with the prophets wearing turbans and caps and the apostles bareheaded in accordance with tradition. They are beautifully executed. The paint is softly applied and the light yet firm lines delicately emphasize the modelling, which was achieved through the use of fitches and conventional brushes. The faces have an elaborately worked quality which contrasts with the sculptural breadth of the heavily draped robes. By their graphic subtlety and their meticulous use of colour, these figures display a close relationship with those appearing in illuminated manuscripts by the workshop of André Beauneveu, a painter and sculptor in the employ of the Duke de Berry. In the wake of this series came several windows presented to Bourges Cathedral by important dignitaries of the Berry entourage: the ones donated by canon Pierre Trousseau in the north of the choir and, in the south, by Simon Aligret, the duke's physician. Like the figures from the Sainte-Chapelle, the donors of these

Sainte-Chapelle, Paris, interior of west front, rose window, Apocalypse, *c. 1485.*

windows and their accompanying saints stand out against dark, damascened backgrounds between white architectural elements that take up more and more space, to the detriment of the actual "portraits," but in accordance with a chromatic principle that lasted for much of the fifteenth century.

The new ideas derived from the van Eyck school of painting can be seen on both an iconographical and a stylistic level in the famous Annunciation window presented to the cathedral by Jacques Coeur, probably in 1448. The patron saints of the silversmith and his wife, St. James and St. Catherine, stand in the lancets at either side of the Annunciation. Although the figures each appear in a separate lancet, the composition makes no allowances for this division. A large

portico with three arches, their vaulting decorated with fleur-de-lis, unites the group. The central scene, the Annunciation, appears in a double bay, while St. James stands under an arch to the left and St. Catherine stands under one to the right. The artist was also familiar with the new Flemish ideas on iconography, as can be seen in the actual layout of the window, in the presence of the small figures adorning the architectural elements and in the richness of the costumes. The angel Gabriel wears a large red cape decorated with large yellow leaves and with a gold orphrey that is also adorned with small figures of apostles. The Virgin, St. Catherine, and even St. James wear equally sumptuous clothes of somewhat overwhelming heaviness. The symbolism of the window is fully expressed in its

Toledo Cathedral, interior of west front, rose window, end of fifteenth century.
Opposite: Toledo Cathedral, transept, south arm; detail, Astrology and Fame, *end of fifteenth century.*

Overleaf: Christ Among the Doctors; *detail showing the doctors; work of Master Johann, c. 1406, from the Abbey Church of Rein (Styria). Hessisches Landesmuseum, Darmstadt.*

brilliant colours, in the white windows opening out in the background of the portico, rather like symbolic openings, and in its taste for elaborate detail. The high standard of its execution is reflected in the extraordinarily poetic quality that emanates from it. All the technical possibilities of the medium have been exploited with admirable skill. The modelling has

Opposite: Arrest of Christ; *detail, by Master Johann, c. 1406, from the Abbey Church of Rein (Styria), Hessisches Landesmuseum, Darmstadt.*

Below left: St. Martin; *below right,* St. George, *c. 1440, from Partenheim parish church (Hesse). Hessisches Landesmuseum, Darmstadt.*

been worked with a brush, reworked with a fitch, and then heightened by meticulous abrasion with a stylus or other sharp instrument to convey the strength or, in the case of the angel Gabriel, the youthfulness of the faces. The same technical quality reappears in other, later windows in the cathedral dating from the middle of the century, such as the Fradet window (1462–64), which is traditional in both composition and style. The lancets of the window in the chapel founded by Pierre de Beaucaire, a canon of the cathedral, portray the four most important doctors of the Church (St. Ambrose, St. Augustine, St. Gregory, and St. Jerome) beneath architectural canopies that still stand out against damascened backgrounds, with a Last Judgement in the tympanum. In this window, however, the colour is brighter than in the preceding ones and landscape puts in a timid appearance in the background of the architectural elements sheltering the figures. There is a similar style to

be found in the Sainte-Chapelle at Riom, another building erected on the initiative of the Duke de Berry shortly before his death in 1412, in the Apostles' Creed series that dates from the third quarter of the century. There is little else to remind us of the activities of the glass artists of Berry and the neighbouring provinces.

The situation is the same at Lyon, where little survives of the considerable output recorded by contemporary archive documents in this metropolitan city that stood at the artistic crossroads between Italy and northern France. Only Lyon Cathedral has retained a few panels, and these consist solely of elements of tracery preserved in several bays in the side chapels of the nave, one of which takes the form of an Annunciation accompanied by angels. The latter, completed during the middle of the century, betray the influence of the van Eycks in both their graphic outline and their treatment, which shows how this stylistic trend had already infiltrated the city well

before the activities of the Master of Moulins and his circle, who worked not only in Lyonnais, but also in neighbouring regions, where they were summoned by rich patrons. Although this master's links with Lyon are now acknowledged, the works that can definitely be attributed to him are still very few in number, whether they be the glass presented by Cardinal Charles de Bourbon, who died in 1488, for the windows of the chevet of the collegiate church (now Moulins Cathedral) or the recently discovered fragments from the windows in the chapel that he had built at the south side of the nave of Lyon Cathedral.

Dijon, which after the accession to the throne of Philip the Bold in 1364 had become an artistic capital, continued to play this role during the fifteenth century. But, in the realms of stained glass, many works have either disappeared or are known only from fragments, as is so often the case in France. This is true of the glass

Below left: Female Donor of the Mérode Family Presented by an Angel; detail, c. 1450, from St. Catherine's Church, Cologne (?). Hessisches Landesmuseum, Darmstadt. Below right: St. George and the Dragon; detail, from Neckarstein parish church. Hessisches Landesmuseum, Darmstadt. Opposite: St. Catherine, by Peter Hemmel, 1480, from the Abbey Church of Nonnberg, Salzburg. Hessisches Landesmuseum, Darmstadt.

Overleaf: Left, Adam in the Garden of Eden; detail of a panel by Peter Hemmel c. 1470, from the choir of the destroyed Church of Saint-Pierre-le-Vieux, Strasbourg. Musée de l'Oeuvre Notre-Dame, Strasbourg. Right, Descent into Limbo; detail, by Peter Hemmel, from the destroyed Church of Saint-Pierre-le-Vieux, c. 1480.

in the Sainte-Chapelle in Dijon, which was built at the beginning of the century and shortly afterwards became the seat of the Order of the Golden Fleece. Only a few pieces of this are now preserved in museums in France and elsewhere. The princes of Burgundy employed mainly Flemish glaziers in their service, and these influenced the output of local workshops, which soon adopted the realism and vigorous shapes of Flemish art.

A large number of workshops were active in the west of France. At Le Mans Cathedral, a local team, working in the tradition prevailing at the beginning of the century, created the stained glass in the north rose of the transept, which had just been built. This window, whose subjects are, in the upper half, the Coronation of the Virgin and, in the lower half, the Last Judgement, can be dated to the 1440s. The large window on which it rests contains, in addition to an Apostles' Creed, likenesses of saints, including St. Louis, and of the donors, members of the Anjou family.

This group is not homogeneous, with certain figures having been taken from lateral windows in the transept. The execution of the latter displays a graphical firmness that is lacking in the style of the rose, which would suggest a slightly later date. And yet the style of the principal workshop is reflected in the two rose windows in the transept of Angers Cathedral and in the figures of a Creed in Quimper Cathedral. The iconography of the two Angers roses, the work of a stained-glass artist named André Robin, is typical of the end of the Middle Ages. The north one illustrates the theme of Christ appearing at the end of the world, complete with representations of the signs heralding this terrible event, and the Works of the Months, while the south one displays a more classic theme, that of the Glorification of Christ. The palette is very pale, a little darker in the south rose, and the draughtsmanship sometimes recalls the mannered art of the beginning of the century, but the pictorial treatment has

already become much stronger in parts, presaging the formal development of stained-glass painting in France from the second half of the century onwards. The beautifully limpid windows in Notre-Dame-la-Riche in Tours, which date from around 1460, may possibly be based on cartoons by the painter Fouquet, though this hypothesis is still the subject of considerable controversy.

A large number of windows from the second part of the fifteenth century have survived in Normandy, but their styles differ widely. Some still adhere to the traditions of the beginning of the century, while others already mark a return to colour. Both trends can be seen in the Church of Saint-Maclou at Rouen, as they can at the Church of Caudebec-en-Caux, situated on the Seine between Rouen and Le Havre. Rouen was also a very important center of production and a great many of the windows installed at the time in outlying churches were made by the workshops established in this artistically

and ecclesiastically important city.

During the second part of the century Paris regained its position as an artistic capital. As far as stained glass is concerned, the earliest signs of this revival can be seen in the Church of Saint-Séverin, in the figures of saints, executed in a rather angular style, which are shown sheltered beneath white niches in accordance with the prevailing fashion. Then, from the end of the century, come the brightly coloured figures in the high windows of the choir. In the wake of this trend, which was a mixture of influences derived from Germanic engravings and Flemish paintings, we find the Apocalypse rose in the west front of the Saint-Chapelle. A work of extraordinary technical virtuosity, this window exploits all the opportunities offered by stained glass at the time to create a fantastic universe in keeping with its eschatological subject.

FLANDERS

During the fifteenth century, stained glass occupied a very privileged position in Flanders. Numerous artists were commissioned by patrons to work on projects throughout Europe and also to supply cartoons. And yet very little of this immense output still remains in situ. The oldest surviving windows are those in St. Martin's Church at Hal in Brabant, which depict large figures set in architectural niches. More characteristic of Flemish painting, however, are the scenes devoted to the Book of Genesis, now in a window in the church's sacristy, which owe a great debt to the art of the painter Melchior Broederlam. But we have to wait until the third quarter of the century to understand what the van Eyck style meant for Flemish stained glass. The magnificent Coronation of the Virgin by the Holy Trinity in the Collegiate Church of Saint-Gommaire at Lierre allies a feeling of monumental authority to a pictorial style close to that of Rogier van der Weyden. The richness of the decoration and the subtle use of colour accentuate the work's feeling of unreality. In the Church of Saint-Pierre and Saint-Guidon at Anderlecht, near Brussels, the window depicting the Virgin recalls the art of Hugo van der Goes, underlining once again the close links that existed between painting on panel and painting on glass.

In the rounded bays at the end of the arms of the transepts in Tournai Cathedral there are some reassembled windows, unfortunately heavily restored during the nineteenth century, which came originally from the ambulatory and which illustrate episodes from the city's history during the Middle Ages. The series in the southern arm recalls the struggles during the sixth century between the brothers Sigebert, King of Austrasia, and Chilperic, King of Neustria, who fled to Tournai; the other one, facing it, shows the Bishop of Tournai returning to his episcopal seat in the twelfth century after a journey to the Pope in Rome. The two series, completed between the end of the fifteenth and beginning of the sixteenth century, were the work of several painters, one of whom was later to enjoy a brilliant career at Rouen. His name was Arnoult of Nijmegen and he lived in France between 1500 and 1512, making an invaluable contribution to the advancement of stained glass at Rouen.

ENGLAND

The English followed the same principles as those used by the Franco-Flemish masters. Despite such difficulties as the Wars of the Roses, a considerable amount of stained glass was produced right up until 1485. The majority of workshops were established in urban centers, from whence they radiated out into the countryside, obtaining numerous commissions for castles and rural churches. In some of these cities, such as York, for example, painter-glaziers banded together to form powerful guilds. This northern English "school," which was already famous during the fourteenth century, remained very active in York itself, where it created works for All Saints Church and St. Martin's Church, and also carried out commissions in areas such as Worcestershire, in Great Malvern Priory Church, for example. In the east, Norwich fulfilled the same role as York in the north, with its workshops producing glass for both Norfolk and Suffolk, while at Oxford, where the stained-glass tradition had been firmly established since the thirteenth century, work was still carried on, notably in All Souls College Chapel.

English glaziers had to adapt the Franco-Flemish modes of stained glass to fit in with the complex shapes of the bays of churches built in the Perpendicular style, which was the prevailing architectural style of the day, filling the pierced tracery with scenes or choirs of angels, as in France. Heraldry was still widely used and took the place of the scenes of donors that had become such a common feature of Continental windows. Colouring for a long time remained pale, due to the use of pale lozenges, sometimes decorated with leaves, flowers, animals, and armorial bearings, as a background for the figures or scenes. This type of window enjoyed a great vogue in England during the fifteenth century.

During the second half of the century architectural settings disappeared and figures began to be portrayed against a background of landscapes, as in the window in St. John's Chapel in Ludlow Church, Shropshire. By way of contrast, another window in the same chapel retains white architectural settings and damascened backgrounds. At the end of the century, as in France, the tradition of windows with white architectural elements continued, but the full-colour window was revived in, for example, the Beauchamp family chapel in St. Mary's Church, Warwick, to the southeast of Birmingham, whose stained glass was created by John Pruddle, an artist who also worked at Westminster Abbey in the service of Henry VI.

THE HOLY ROMAN EMPIRE

The fifteenth century marked Germanic stained glass's greatest period of expansion, when its influence spread well beyond the frontiers of the Empire through glass artists being summoned to work on projects elsewhere in Europe, such as Seville Cathedral around 1480. It achieved an expressive force different from that of any other country, often arriving at an intense degree of realism. Collaboration between glaziers and engravers was a constant feature that transformed the whole evolution of stained glass in the Empire. Engraving, rather than conventional painting, soon became the main source of inspiration for stained-glass artists and this dominance altered the whole technical development of stained glass, which became increasingly loaded down with ornamentation, for which glaziers used all the technical resources at their disposal, notably that of glass-engraving. Glaziers maintained such close links with each other that in the absence of archive documents such as contracts it is often difficult to make any definite attributions. In fact, these artists were able to work on different materials and in different media, creating works of just as high a caliber on wood, paper, copper, or glass. Furthermore, they were trained in workshops that taught different artistic techniques such as stained glass and engraving.

One of the most prolific centers during the first half of the century was Ulm, thanks to the Acker family. In around 1430, the father, Jacob Acker, worked on several windows in the chapel founded by the Besserer family, using cartoons by the painter Lucas Moser, author of the famous altarpiece at Tiefenbronn in Swabia. Their collaboration still retains the imprint of the International Gothic style, even though there is a certain hardness apparent in the faces. Jacob's son, Hans, was summoned to Berne where he executed a series of windows for the cathedral choir around 1440. Their influence extended to all regions of the upper Rhine and also to

Head of Weeping Woman, *fragment from the workshop of Peter Hemmel, from the demolished Church of Sainte-Madeleine, Strasbourg, 1480–81.*

Opposite: Adoration of the Magi, *workshop of Peter Hemmel, 1480–90. Musée de l'Oeuvre Notre-Dame, Strasbourg.*

Below: Church of St. Lawrence, Nürnberg, choir, south side, Rieterfenster; details of window showing scenes from the Old Testament, presented by the Rieter family, 1479.

backgrounds, some of them French, some Flemish, and some even Italian.

From the middle of the century, Strasbourg stained glass was dominated by the figure of Peter Hemmel. Born in the small Alsatian village of Andlau around 1420, he became a resident of Strasbourg and a master glazier by marrying the widow of a

two windows for the Church of Sainte-Madeleine, Strasbourg, the remains of which, rescued from a fire in 1904, are today preserved in the Musée de l'Oeuvre Notre-Dame; they include one particularly fine section portraying the head of a woman crying. He was then charged with numerous commissions in Freiburg im

Lorraine, in the Church of Saint-Marcel at Zetting, near Sarreguemines.

As in the past, the workshops of Alsace were extremely active and followed several different stylistic trends. In the St. Catherine window in the Church of St. George at Sélestat, between Colmar and Strasbourg, a local artist, Hans Tieffenthal, who also worked in Basle and Strasbourg and perhaps in Burgundy, remained faithful to the mannerist formulas of International Gothic as expressed in the regions of the upper Rhine (c. 1435–40). Hans Hirtz, by contrast, also called the "Painter of the Karlsruhe Passion," was active in Strasbourg between 1420 and 1460 approximately. He is thought to have been responsible for the Life of the Virgin in St. William's Church, the style of which bears the imprint of the realism of Rogier van der Weyden. As always, Strasbourg acted as a center for the exchange of artistic ideas between glass artists of very different

glazier whose work he took over. Later on, in 1475–76, he was obliged to assume the duties of a municipal magistrate. He died at the beginning of the sixteenth century. Little is known of his earliest works. From the years around 1465 up until the end of the century he obtained numerous commissions for churches, not only in Alsace, but also in Lorraine and the Rhineland as far as Salzburg. He was summoned by princes and even kings to provide windows, which shows how famous he was. At Strasbourg, only the St. Catherine window (1472) in St. William's Church is still in place. Earlier he had worked in the Church of Saint-Pierre-le-Vieux, whose panel depicting Adam in Paradise (c. 1470) is now on display in the Musée de l'Oeuvre Notre-Dame in Strasbourg. Because of the large number of commissions, he collaborated with four other Alsatian stained-glass artists, while at the same time continuing to work with his children. In 1478–80 he completed

Breisgau Cathedral, the Church of Our Lady in Munich, St. Lawrence's Church in Nürnberg and Ulm Cathedral, to name just the most important. The windows were made in his workshop in Strasbourg and then transported to their destination. Relying heavily for inspiration on engravings and wood carvings, which were then in fashion, Peter Hemmel and his associates were closely acquainted with all the technical possibilities offered by stained glass, which they exploited to the full in order to translate the effects of Flemish realism. In their art they were the forerunners of the great masters of the Renaissance.

There was also a great deal of activity among glaziers in other towns of the Empire. In the north, the workshops of Lübeck penetrated as far north as Scandinavia, most notably at Vika in Dalarna, Sweden. Production in the Rhineland, strongly influenced by Flemish painting, was centered on Cologne in particular. At

Below left: Exodus from Egypt. *Below right:* Moses and Joshua. *Details from* Rieterfenster, *Church of St. Lawrence, Nürnberg, 1479.*

Opposite: Church of St. Lawrence, Nürnberg, choir, south side, Rieterfenster, *window showing scenes from the Old Testament, presented by the Rieter family, 1479.*

the end of the century, realism asserted itself very forcefully in the window presented by the Rieter family to St. Lawrence's Church in Nürnberg in 1479. The lower register of this window is devoted to representations of the donors, while the remaining six portray the history of Moses and His People. The scenes, arranged in rectangular compartments, are accompanied by explanatory inscriptions; the figures still stand out against damascened backgrounds, but landscape elements appear in some scenes; the style is lively and full of movement, with the almost familiar quality characteristic of Flemish art, whereas the white architectural elements have become less obtrusive, forming a single frame around the scene. Following the splendid works produced by the court workshop at the beginning of the century, Austrian stained glass found it hard to move with the times, as can be seen, for example, in the chapel of Wiener Neustadt Castle, on the Danube, to the west of Vienna. In Switzerland, the fashion

for roundels, small medallions depicting sacred or profane subjects set into white windows, spread rapidly and was transmitted to regions as far north as Flanders. Painters were quick to adopt this style of stained glass, which became increasingly popular during the sixteenth century.

SPAIN

Although the art of stained glass enjoyed a certain vogue in Spain during the fifteenth century, it was entrusted to foreign masters, most frequently Flemish, French, and Germanic, whose names we know from the contracts they signed with their Spanish employers, generally cathedral chapters. They came principally from towns well known for stained glass, like Nicolas Colin, a native of Troyes, who was active in Barcelona at the end of the century, and Thierry de Mes (Metz?), who worked in Saragossa. During the middle of the century there were also several Flemings and Alsatians living and

working in Toledo and Seville.

Even though there were a few local artists, stained glass still continued to be a peripheral art form in Spain, even in León Cathedral, where a whole series of glass artists had been working since the second half of the thirteenth century.

At the beginning of the century, the other centers of production were still Barcelona, in Catalonia, and Burgos, in Castile, where a large number of foreigners had settled. Almost nothing, however, remains of the numerous windows created in Burgos at the time, particularly in the cathedral. A great deal of building was carried out in Catalonia, which was to the advantage of stained glass. From the beginning of the century comes the window in the St. Andrew Chapel in the Cathedral of St. Eulalia, the style of which owes a great debt to the art of Luis Borrassá, who created the altarpiece in the chapel. Only slightly later in date are the windows in the chapter hall of the monastery of Santa Maria de Pedralbes, on the

Milan Cathedral, nave, south side. Below left: Story of St. Eligius *by Niccolò da Varallo, 1480; detail showing* The Investiture of the Saint as Bishop. *Below right:* Life of St. John the Evangelist *by Cristoforo de Mottis, 1478; detail showing* The Meeting with Craton.

stained-glass windows in the fourteenth century. Archbishop Sancho de Rojas (1415–22) summoned a glazier of French extraction, Juan Dolfin, who worked there until 1427, creating the majority of the windows in the choir and transept. Subsequently, a successor to Rojas, Alonso de Carrillo (1447–82), called upon

Alsatian glaziers, the artistic heirs to Peter Hemmel, who worked in Seville Cathedral around 1480.

ITALY

As in the preceding century, in Italy it was painters or sculptors who supplied the

outskirts of Barcelona, and also the one in the apse of Seo d'Urgel Cathedral, to the northeast of the city. The rose in Barcelona's Church of Santa María del Mar only dates from 1460. Its subject is the Coronation of the Virgin and it is the work of Antonio Llonye or Lunyi, who also worked in Piedmont and at Toulouse.

It was in Toledo Cathedral, however, that Spanish stained glass enjoyed its greatest moment during the fifteenth century. Begun in 1227, the city's Gothic cathedral had already been decorated with

a number of French and Germanic masters who, drawing on their own experiences, gave Spanish stained glass its own identity and breathed new life into the art. The most celebrated glaziers of the day were Pedro Bonifacio, who had worked in Barcelona, and, most important of all, Enrique Alemán, who was active in Toledo between 1485 and 1492. At the end of the century, when Ferdinand and Isabella achieved the unification of Spain, a brilliant new era opened up for Spanish stained glass, marked by the presence of

cartoons, as in the case of the large window in the apse of St. Dominic's Church at Perugia, the design for which is attributed to the Florentine Mariotto di Nardo. This work, dating from around 1410, is the first example of Italian stained glass making systematic use of silver stain, almost a century after it was first used by French and English workshops. In the lower register, as well as the arms of the family who had donated the window, there appear four scenes of the life of St. James, which display the same degree of formal

Milan Cahtedral south aisle, Life of Christ; *detail of* Christ's Entry into Jerusalem, showing Zacchaeus in the tree, 1470.

independence found in contemporary paintings on panel, but in the following registers there is a return to the Gothic formula of superimposed saints beneath architectural canopies. As in northern European windows, the elevations of these white architectural structures are based on Gothic designs, but the figures follow the formulas of International Gothic.

During the same period, it was Ghiberti who received the commission for the cartoons for the three rose windows in the west front of Florence Cathedral. The one in the center, which is the most important of the group, has the Assumption of the Virgin for its subject. It was completed around 1405 by a glazier of Germanic origins, Niccolò Tedesco, and still adheres to the Gothic formulas of the Trecento. Ghiberti is thought to have provided at least twenty cartoons, seventeen of which are mentioned in contemporary documents, such as the ones portraying figures of saints and prophets for the windows in the apse and the arms of the transept. Between 1443 and 1445 he supplied the beautiful compositions portraying the Presentation in the Temple, Christ on the Mount of Olives, and also the Ascension, destined for three of the eight lunettes in the dome and executed by a local glazier, Bernardo di Francesco. The other cartoons for this series were commissioned from Paolo Uccello, Andrea del Castagno, and Donatello, who created exceptional works that truly reflect the spirit of the Renaissance. Work on Donatello's Coronation of the Virgin was begun in 1438 by a glazier from Pisa. Despite the present poor condition of this rose, it can be seen that the composition, which displays a remarkable degree of formal authority, brings new life to a centuries-old subject by means of its sculptural use of line combined with great purity of colour, with the white robe of the Virgin contrasting with the bright red mantle of Christ.

Originally, Paolo Uccello supplied three compositions, but only two have survived: a Nativity drawn in 1443 and a Resurrection completed in the following year. The Annunciation was lost during the nineteenth century. In the Resurrection, the figure of Christ, standing on his tomb, surrounded by a bright mandorla and standing out against a blue ground, radiates a remarkable feeling of formal power that is even further enhanced by the almost Baroque arrangement of the folds

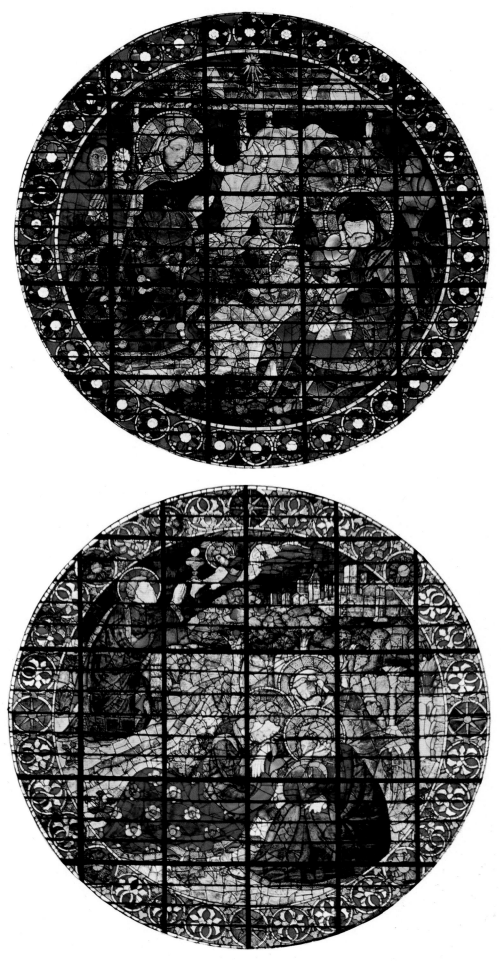

*Florence Cathedral, lunettes in the dome.
Above,* Nativity *by Paolo Uccello, 1443; below,*
Christ in the Garden of Gethsemane *by
Lorenzo Ghiberti and Bernardo di Francesco,
1443–44.*

of his shroud. Andrea del Castagno's
Deposition was also composed in 1444,
but it took several years to complete
because the painter returned to the work
on numerous occasions, modifying it and
trying to translate his pictorial art onto
glass in as faithful a way as possible.
Castagno's behaviour highlights the difficulties encountered by these occasional
cartoonists in reproducing their styles on a
backing medium with which they were
less familiar.

The same practice was often repeated in
Tuscany during the fifteenth century. Fra
Filippo Lippi, for example, provided
cartoons for the Virgin and Child in Prato
Cathedral. Alessio Baldovinetti also tried
his hand as a cartoonist, creating, among
other things, a number of Old Testament
scenes for windows in Pisa Cathedral (c.
1460). While working on the frescoes in
the apse of Santa Maria Novella in Florence, Ghirlandaio was commissioned to
create cartoons for the three windows in
the apse dedicated to the Life of the Virgin
(before 1450). The formal style of this
painter can also be seen in other windows,
such as those in Santa Maria delle Carceri
in Prato. Some workshops, such as those
of the Gesuati order in Florence, reused
designs by painters and either modified
them to fit in with the dimensions of new
windows or exploited them in a completely different way, sometimes stripping
them of all stylistic originality. This is
what happened in Bologna, where stained
glass was dominated by the figure of the
Dominican Jacob of Ulm, who created a
large number of windows for the bays in
the chapels of the Cathedral of San Petro-
nio, achieving ever greater feats of technical prowess. The world of the Renaissance
finally penetrated Bolognese stained glass
in the person of the Ferrarese painter
Lorenzo Cossa, who is thought to have
provided the cartoon for the rose in the
façade of San Giovanni in Monte. Illustrating the episode of St. John the Evangelist writing on the island of Patmos,
seated on the ground, in a landscape
containing a seven-branched candelabra,
this rose succeeds in translating the
painter's energetic and plastic style
through its brilliant technical execution
and sharply contrasting colours.

The situation in northern Italy seems to
have been completely different, but the
only important windows to have survived
are those in Milan Cathedral. Begun in
1386–87, this ambitious but eclectic structure received its first stained glass in 1404,
of which only a few fragments have

Church of Notre-Dame, Semur-en-Auxois (Côte-d'Or), nave, north side, Drapers *(donors), c. 1460.*

survived, scattered through several windows in the building. This program had to be halted for several decades and was not resumed until the 1460s. The resumption of work allowed for stained glass to be fitted throughout the cathedral, an enterprise that lasted up until the middle of the sixteenth century. The windows in the apse were dedicated to the illustration of the Old and New Testaments and, in the axial bay, the Apocalypse. The side windows were donated, in a way that was unique in Italy, by Milanese guilds, who chose to represent the lives of their patron saints: the goldsmiths, for example, chose St. Eligius, while the notaries chose St. John the Evangelist. But these windows have suffered such disastrous restorations, particularly during the nineteenth century, that today it is difficult to assess which sections are original.

Many workshops participated in the project. A single composition was selected for all the windows, whose scenes are similarly arranged in rectangular panels, a layout that had already been used at the beginning of the century in the scenes of the Life of St. James in the lower register of the great window in the Church of St. Dominic in Perugia. In Milan, several panels are often needed to illustrate a single episode (two for the Annunciation, six for the Crucifixion), but each one contains an integral scene, together with the antique architectural elements, portrayed in perspective, which enclose it. Cristoforo de Mottis, a Milanese fresco artist, was the author of the Life of St. John the Evangelist, which is now divided between two windows in the right side of the nave (1476). The style is familiar and supple and the colouration is softened by the whiteness of the architectural elements which, again portrayed in perspective, give a rhythmical unity to the compositions. In 1479, Niccolò Varallo signed a contract with the apothecaries' guild for a window dedicated to St. John the Damascene, and the following year he signed another with the goldsmiths for the Life of St. Eligius. Although there is a similarity with the compositions created by de Mottis, the pictorial technique is harder and more metallic, quite unlike the delicate, affected style of Vincenzo Foppa, another Lombard, who was responsible for the New Testament window and who is also thought to have worked in the Certosa at Pavia. These artists, and many others like them, gave considerable impetus to Milanese stained glass over a period that lasted several decades.

6
From the Sixteenth to the Eighteenth Century: Triumph and Decline of Stained Glass

The position of stained glass in sixteenth-century Europe is extremely complex. Up until the middle of the century it had continued to thrive under the domination of Flemish influences, but from the middle of the century, and even earlier in England, the religious crisis affecting Europe, with all its political and social consequences, led not only to the destruction of a great many early windows but also to a dearth of commissions.

In England, the Reformation resulted in the loss of a great deal of stained glass, with an edict of Edward VI in 1547 decreeing that all monuments to Roman Catholicism were to be demolished. Like architecture, stained glass fell victim to this drastic proscription, which was renewed a century later, when royal commissioners were dispatched to supervise the destruction. In France, 1562 saw the loss of numerous works of art, including the large quantities of stained glass destroyed by the Protestants when they occupied the cities of Le Mans, Lyon, and Poitiers. Windows had such heavy damage inflicted on them at the time that it often proved impossible to restore them. Where repairs were possible, people generally just made a single window out of all the different panels that they had managed to salvage. In the Low Countries, the Calvinists behaved in a similar fashion, destroying everything that had any connection with Roman Catholicism.

When those countries which chose the Reformation, such as England or the Low Countries, subsequently abandoned historiated religious stained glass, their glaziers often diverted their energies to lay commissions for armorial glass to adorn churches, town halls, and private houses. In countries that remained faithful to Rome, such as Spain, Italy, and France, the Counter-Reformation profoundly altered religious thinking. There was no longer the same place for stained glass as there had been in Gothic buildings, particularly since architecture, in its return to antique forms, no longer had any need for it.

From around 1500, the spirit of the Renaissance penetrated other European centers besides Italy and, as at Rouen, altered the formal and stylistic development of stained glass. To begin with, workshops merely adopted its decorative conventions, replacing angels with putti, for example, and arranging their scenes on plinths decorated with vases, swags, and bucraniums. They then enclosed them in broad porticoes with entablatures and coffered ceilings portrayed in accordance with the laws of perspective. But this new aesthetic led to an almost complete break between the window and its containing bay. The latter often continued to reflect the Flamboyant style so that, for the first time in the history of stained glass, windows no longer matched their architectural settings. The sixteenth century adopted "the principle of the unified bay" (L. Grodecki), in which the scene, like a painting, extended over the full width of its composition, ignoring the way in which the mullions divided it into several lancets. This new type of window also involved an increase in the size of the glass elements, while the actual method of cutting the glass altered.

The sixteenth century was, like the fourteenth, a period in which technical invention flourished. First, a diamond was used to cut the glass instead of a red-hot iron rod, which meant that larger and also more intricately shaped pieces could now be obtained. The use of the diamond spread rapidly throughout Europe, since this new tool made it easier to create inserts and to achieve contrasts between the large segments used for clothing, for example, and the small ones used for embroidery and braiding. This newly mastered skill allowed for delicate cutting that corresponded with the modelled effects being sought by Renaissance artists. The way in which the glass was inserted into the lead armatures also changed, because the rods altered in size, their gauge becoming thinner and their claws thicker than before so as to get a better grip on the new, very thin glass. The range of colours also changed, with new and more varied stains being used than in the past. These stains differed considerably from region to re-

gion and even from one glassworks to another. The use of overlaid glass became commonplace since that allowed for a greater number of subsequent engraving processes. The most important innovations, however, concerned the application of the paint. As well as the traditional copper- and iron-oxide-based paints, glaziers could now use paints that were applied to the glass like enamel paints. One of the first of these new pigments was sanguine, known to French glaziers by the name "Jean Cousin," after the Sens artist active during the first half of the sixteenth century. This hematite-based paint, red in colour, was used principally to enhance the flesh tones of faces and to redden lips, but glass artists linked closely to the School of Fontainebleau used it to paint scenes like the profane series dedicated to the loves of Cupid and Psyche, originally in the château of Écouen and now in the château of Chantilly. The use of enamels and vitrifiable colours spread rapidly, especially since it allowed for the application of several colours to a single piece of glass and even for the shading effects that were so highly prized at the time. The first dated example of its use in France goes back to 1543, in a window in the choir of Montfort l'Amaury Church dedicated to the Childhood of Christ. In Mesnil-Aubry, near Écouen, to the north of Paris, one of the windows in the chevet presented by Anne de Montmorency contains a combination of sanguine and blue enamels, the first time that the latter had been used (c. 1555). Unlike silver stain and sanguine, which permeate the glass and alter its colouring, enamels adhere less deeply. This procedure makes the application of paint much easier, but workshops soon forgot how to master either its application or its firing, which was carried out for either too long or too short a time. By the end of the sixteenth century and the beginning of the seventeenth, a great many glaziers had lost much of their skill and stained glass began to enter a period of "rest."

The innovative characteristics of the Renaissance appeared towards the end of the fifteenth century, but the Gothic style was to last for several decades longer,

Conches Church (Eure), nave, south side, Nativity, sixteenth century.

affected to varying degrees by Germanic, Flemish, and Italian influences. Compositions on the whole followed the principle of a single scene per bay and were still surrounded by antique classical structures between which elements of landscape gradually emerged. Where they persisted, Gothic niches embraced the whole window, instead of having one figure in each lancet. The legendary window become fashionable once again, generally composed of juxtaposed rectangular scenes in accordance with a Flemish formula dating back to the fifteenth century.

Iconography also drew inspiration from the Renaissance, as in the Chariot window, a work by the Leprince workshop of Beauvais for the Church of St. Vincent in Rouen, now in the new church dedicated to St. Joan of Arc (1515). It portrays the Triumph of the Virgin who, through the birth of her Son, purged original sin and put an end to the reign of Satan. The scenes are depicted in the form of classical triumphs in accordance with an iconographical formula very popular during the Renaissance.

Stained glass reflected little of the deep spiritual crisis affecting Europe at the time, despite the fact that it derived its inspiration from engravings and paintings by artists engaged in this religious drama. Even though there is a certain feeling of pathos in the works of such men as the German Baldung Grien and the Frenchman Mathieu Bléville, the majority of artists hid it in a mass of colour and movement. A familiarity with the works of such artists as Dürer in Germany and Marco Antonio in Italy is necessary to understand the thematic inspiration of a great many windows of this period, and we know that Breton craftsmen ordered engravings from a specialist press at Antwerp run by C. Plantin. In the Collegiate Church of Brou, near Bourg-en-Bresse, the Flemish overseer, Loys van Boghem, called upon a painter in Brussels, perhaps Nicolas Rombouts, to supply him with paper cartoons for several windows which he then had completed on site by three craftsmen (1525–30), one of whom was the Lyonnais Antoine Noisin. The five windows in the chevet form a heraldic ensemble which surrounds the donors, Margaret of Austria and Maximilian the Fair, accompanied by their patron saints and kneeling before large scenes portraying the posthumous apparitions of Christ. The heraldic windows follow the same style of composition adopted in 1524 by the painter Nicolas Rombouts for windows in the Cathedral of Saint-Gudule in Brussels. Windows of this type were widely used in Europe from the sixteenth to the eighteenth century, especially in Protestant countries, where they were often accompanied by historical subjects and sometimes even by portrayals of contemporary events.

The fashion for small stained-glass panels hung in front of windows, initiated in Switzerland, soon became more and more commonplace. Known as *Kabinettscheiben*, many included heraldic motifs and also celebrated significant events in the life of a particular man or family. These panels were produced by a number of Swiss workshops, such as the one run by Tobias Stimmer at Schaffhausen in the sixteenth century or by the Spenglers at Constance in the seventeenth. France and Italy followed this fashion only spasmodically, whereas in the Germanic countries and in Holland, as well as in England, it has enjoyed considerable popularity right up until the present day.

As in the past, glaziers were frequently on the move, either to learn their craft or to change their place of residence. In this way France played host to several master glaziers, among them the Flemish Arnoult of Nijmegen, already mentioned in the previous chapter, who dominated stained-glass production in Rouen during the first three decades of the century.

FRANCE

Nearly two thirds of old French stained glass dates from the sixteenth century, which is clear proof of the little-known fact that the art flourished during this period in France, particularly bearing in mind that output declined rapidly after 1560. In addition to such well-known masters as the Parisian Nicolas Beaurain, who worked for the architect Philibert Delorme on the Sainte-Chapelle at Vincennes (after 1550), Mathieu Bléville, a native of Picardy who moved to Champagne, or the Leprince dynasty at Beauvais, there was a whole host of other workshops creating windows of uneven quality, some of them even mediocre. And yet stained glass should be regarded as the most privileged means of pictorial expression in Renaissance France.

The workshops of Paris were very active throughout the first half of the sixteenth century. From the 1540s onwards, the mannerist style of the School of Fontainebleau inspired a large number of glass artists, not only in Paris, but throughout France. These craftsmen did not just work on civil and religious buildings in the capital, but also in the surrounding provinces. The painter Jean Chastelain, who executed two windows for the Church of Saint-Germain-l'Auxerrois, was probably also the author of the windows in the chevet of the Church of Saint-Aspais at Melun (c. 1530).

Others, by contrast, such as the Master

of Montmorency, who was active around 1530, were truly creative, even though certain features of their work reflect the influences of Flemish art. Paradoxically, since the beginning of the century, the Dutchman Arnoult of Nijmegen had imposed an Italianate style on the stained glass of Rouen which was to influence Norman windows for several decades, even after the arrival of another, even more gifted master, glazier Engrand Leprince. Member of a Beauvais dynasty of glass artists, of which he is the most famous representative, Engrand Leprince had by 1525 created the splendid Jesse Tree in St. Stephen's Church in Beauvais, the work to which he owes his reputation. He also received commissions for other buildings in the city, including the cathedral.

Church of St. Joan of Arc, Rouen, Life of St. Peter; *detail showing the head of the saint, c. 1530, from the Church of St. Vincent (now demolished).*

Overleaf: Left, Church of Notre-Dame-en-Vaux, Châlons-sur-Marne, St. James at the Battle of Clavijo *by Mathieu Bléville, 1525; right, Church of the Trinity, Vendôme, choir, south side; detail,* Miracle of the Fish, *sixteenth century.*

The situation in Champagne was different. To the north, particularly in Reims and Châlons-sur-Marne, a number of painters were active, many of whom were of Flemish origin, as well as Mathieu Bléville, a native of Picardy, who was responsible for the window depicting

St. James at the Battle of Clavijo (1525), a work rich in both colour and movement. To the south, at Troyes, a city in which evidence of the stained-glass tradition goes back to the twelfth century, there were numerous workshops involved in a sort of mass-production process, repeatedly using the same cartoons, the majority of whose prototypes date back to the end of the fifteenth century. Their output generally took the form of legendary windows, with juxtaposed scenes, executed in a familiar and very accessible style that included copious inscriptions identifying the various subjects. Their most original work was the set of windows in the nave of Troyes Cathedral completed at the turn of the fifteenth and sixteenth centuries. The activities of these workshops spread beyond the confines of the region. Some worked in Sens Cathedral and others in Champagne and Burgundy, but the actual windows were made at Troyes and then transported to their final destination. From 1535 onwards, coloured windows were gradually replaced by windows in white grisaille with silver-stain highlights.

In Lorraine, production was dominated by the figure of Valentin Bousch, records of whose activities go back to 1514. He first worked in the Church of Saint-Nicolas-de-Port, near Nancy, a popular place of pilgrimage, and then in Metz Cathedral, whose official glass artist he became in 1520, a post that he occupied until his death in 1541. He was also employed on other buildings in the region. His greatest work is the large window in the south arm of the cathedral transept, which he completed in 1526–27. Bousch's style owes many of its stylistic traits to Germanic art, notably that of Baldung Grien, an artist whom he probably knew.

Franche-Comté has preserved only one important group, that of Saint-Julien-en-Surans in Jura, executed at the beginning of the sixteenth century by a Lyonnais workshop which also worked in Aosta Cathedral. The fame of Lyonnais glass artists spread even beyond the provinces bordering their home town; one of them was summoned to Saint-Nicolas-de-Port in Lorraine, for example. In Lyon itself, however, very few works have survived from the period preceding the Renaissance, except at L'Arbresle, near Roanne. The group that best recaptures the skill of the craftsmen of Lyon is the one in the church at Brou, which we have already mentioned. Based on cartoons by a Flemish artist, these windows are not only inspired by the art of Flanders, but also contain elements derived from Italian art, while still retaining certain Gothic characteristics. This amalgam of different traditions and influences very well convey the spirit of French stained glass during the opening decades of the century. In Bur-

Opposite: Arezzo Cathedral (Italy); detail of Expulsion of the Merchants from the Temple *by Guillaume de Marcillat, sixteenth century.*

Above: Oxford Cathedral; detail, Jonah Before the City of Nineveh *by Abraham van Linge, seventeenth century.*

gundy, one thinks particularly of the group in the church at Saint-Florentin, executed by craftsmen from Troyes, and the Jesse Tree in Autun Cathedral (1515), which remains within the Flemish sphere of influence.

The glass artist Jean Lécuyer exerted a decisive influence on stained glass in Berry during the first half of the sixteenth century. It was he who was responsible for two of the century's most beautiful windows: the one in Bourges Cathedral's Tuillier Chapel, named after its donors, and the one depicting the Life of

St. Claude in the Church of Saint-Bonnet. They are balanced works, both in their composition and in their pictorial execution, with pale colouring and numerous Italianate influences. An appreciation of the latter influences is essential to our understanding of the way in which stained glass developed in the Loire region and in Touraine as far as Maine, where the Courtois dynasty held sway at La Ferté-Bernard, a small town near Le Mans.

Brittany contained a large number of workshops, some of them rather amateurish, open to influences of every type, which they tried to interpret with varying degrees of success. As was the case throughout France, from the middle of the century the innovations introduced by the School of Fontainebleau transformed the development of Breton stained glass.

There were numerous centers of production in the south of France, generally influenced by Italian art, but their output has suffered heavy losses. The group of windows in the choir of Auch Cathedral, inspired by the decorative repertoire of northern Italy, differs from the stained glass of the other regions by virtue of its violent colouring and expressive force. Created by a glazier called Arnaut de Moles around 1510, the windows bear witness to the existence of traditions other than those of northern France and underline the variety of trends influencing French stained glass during the period.

FLANDERS

The sixteenth century marked the heyday of Flemish stained glass. Commissions remained plentiful despite the religious wars, but the most outstanding feature is the way in which Flemish glass artists provided cartoons to craftsmen in other regions or, like Arnoult of Nijmegen, moved to towns in other countries and worked on projects there. The stained glass of Flanders is characterized by the same realistic treatment of subject matter that occurs in contemporary painting. Landscapes often appear in the background between the architectural elements on which the coats of arms of the donors are depicted. The range of colours is brilliant and is accentuated by the judicious use of silver-stain highlights, but costumes are executed with almost too great an attention to detail and the glass loses much of its translucency. The Flemings later blended the new ideas emanating from Italy with their own traditions, a trend that can be seen in the works of Bernaert van Orley, who trained in Rome under Raphael. The two windows that he completed in 1537 for the Cathedral of Saint-Gudule in Brussels show how well he had learned from his experiences in Italy. Beneath a vast temple weighed down with garlands and friezes there kneel

the Holy Roman Emperor Charles V and his wife Isabella in the north bay and, in the south bay, Louis of Hungary and his wife Maria, the sister of Charles V, with the former kneeling before God and the latter before the Holy Trinity. The execution displays extraordinary virtuosity, combining every sort of engraving process and silver-stain highlight with a perfectly mastered pictorial technique. The compositions are astonishingly rich, but also astonishingly formal. Less than twenty years separate these stiffly formal windows from the lively compositions by Nicolas Rombouts in 1519 for the chevet of the Collegiate Church of Saint-Gommaire at Lierre in Belgium.

Secular stained glass, which enjoyed considerable growth at the time, faced the same difficulties: as a rule, the greater the technical skill the more conventional and unexciting the stained glass became. And yet the windows completed between 1555 and 1603 in the Church of Gouda in the Netherlands, the earliest of which were commissioned by Catholics and portrayed, among other things, the Life and Passion of Christ, while the later ones were commissioned by Protestants, are all still of very high quality. The oldest ones, technically much less complicated than those of van Orley, were the work of two local craftsmen, the brothers Dirck and Wouter Crabeth, and they create a striking impression by virtue of their monumental authority, their elegant line, which betrays strong Italian influences, and their brilliant colouring. The full-scale cartoons and sketches that have survived attest to the extraordinary attention to detail that went into these windows. In 1572, Gouda rebelled against King Philip II of Spain and certain scenes deemed to be too far removed from Calvinist doctrine were destroyed.

In these regions the vogue for small heraldic panels, some of which included subjects taken from everyday life, grew increasingly widespread and gave rise to what was almost a full-scale industry. Painted in enamel on white glass, these panels are like translucent miniatures, but they exploit all the possibilities offered by a technique that was becoming increasingly sophisticated.

ENGLAND

Dirck Vellert provided several cartoons for important series of windows destined for King's College Chapel, Cambridge, the building of which was completed in 1515. To an even greater extent than the Sainte-Chapelle in Paris, built almost three centuries earlier, this great chapel, still Gothic in style, is like a glass cage in which the tall, broad windows, executed in two stages (between 1515 and 1517 and between 1526 and 1531), almost com-

pletely replace the walls. Glass artists, nearly all of Germanic or Flemish origin, were summoned to work on the project and it was these craftsmen who virtually monopolized the craft in England, gaining acceptance for the new ideas of the Italian Renaissance and changing the face of stained glass in England. Evidence of this stranglehold by Flemish craftsmen can be seen in most English windows of the period, such as the one portraying the miracles of St. Nicholas in Hillesden Church in Buckinghamshire. Roundels, which became very popular in England, also reflected the same trends. From 1534 onwards, when Henry VIII broke with the Papacy, destruction in Catholic buildings was widespread. Religious stained glass was banned and glaziers consequently turned to secular commissions, especially heraldic windows and the small panels depicting profane subjects that had proved so popular in Switzerland, and the Low Countries.

THE HOLY ROMAN EMPIRE

The advance of stained glass in the Holy Roman Empire was slowed down by the advent of the Reformation. And yet, during the opening decades of the century the great workshops of Cologne and Nürnberg continued their activities, often exploiting the cartoons of such great painters as Hans Holbein, Albrecht Dürer, and Hans Baldung Grien. An appreciation of the role of Albrecht Dürer is vital in understanding the development not only of Germanic stained glass, but also of stained glass throughout Europe during the sixteenth century. Not only did he personally draw several cartoons, among them the ones for a window in the Schmidtmayer Chapel in the Church of St. Lawrence in Nürnberg, but, more important, he also executed engravings which acted as a source of inspiration for countless glaziers. He also trained a large number of pupils, who in turn became celebrated cartoonists, such as Hans von Kulmbach, and Hans Baldung Grien, who drew the cartoons for the windows in the choir of Freiburg Cathedral, which were executed by a younger associate of the Alsatian Peter Hemmel. A section of these windows is now preserved in the city's Augustinermuseum.

It was through Dürer that Renaissance influences penetrated Germanic stained glass, which, as in the past, retained a taste for formal and even pictorial pathos. As in

Bourges Cathedral, north side, Baptismal Chapel, The Apostles Round the Tomb of the Virgin; above, in the tympanum, The Assumption of the Virgin; below, the donors, the Maréchal de Montigny and his wife Gabrielle de Crevant, 1619.

Wragby Church, Yorkshire, Swiss windows of the seventeenth and eighteenth centuries; bottom row (from left to right), Tobias Curses His Blind Father, Beheading of St. John the Baptist; *top row (from left to right),* Crucifixion, Deposition.

Switzerland, stained glass became a complementary element of decoration in middle-class homes and town houses. The small panels decorated with armorial devices and allegorical subjects also proliferated, exploiting, as elsewhere, the opportunities offered by the technique of enamelling.

SPAIN

The accession to the throne of the Catholic kings marks the golden age of Spanish stained glass. Master glaziers, more often than not foreigners, were summoned to work on such great projects as Seville Cathedral, an undertaking that lasted for more than a hundred years and employed several generations of artists, who worked on it from the end of the fifteenth century to the end of the sixteenth. In Old Castile, the influence of Burgos continued to permeate Spain, attracting a large number of foreign craftsmen and master glaziers, some of whom stayed for a short time and others who settled

permanently in the city. During the opening decades of the sixteenth century the Burgos workshops still obeyed the conventions of Gothic art, but the foreigners gradually prevailed upon them to adopt the new ideas of the Italian Renaissance or even to absorb their own traditions, mainly those of Flemish art. From 1520–25 onwards, Spanish stained glass was dominated by the figure of Arnao de Flandes, who settled in Burgos. He was founder of a whole dynasty of glaziers, two members of which, his sons Arnao de Flandes and Arnao de Vergara worked mainly in Andalusia, most notably in the cathedrals of Seville and Granada. Like the Alsatian Peter Hemmel during the fif-

York Minster, transept, south arm, King Solomon *by William Peckitt, eighteenth century.*

teenth century, they ran their workshop as a commercial enterprise, employing glass artists from different artistic backgrounds to cope with the large numbers of commissions. In addition to this family of glaziers, we know the names of other craftsmen active in Andalusia during the second half of the century, men such as Carlos de Brujas, who created the splendid Resurrection window in Seville Cathedral (1558), and Jean de Campin, author of several windows in Granada Cathedral between 1554 and 1561. In many cases, several painters were summoned to work in a single building, as happened at Segovia Cathedral from the 1540s onwards. The foreman laid down the program to be carried out and then allotted various tasks to the different masters. He even arranged for some windows to be brought from Antwerp, not only to finish the project more quickly, but also to save money, since stained glass imported from Flanders was cheaper at the time than locally produced glass.

The situation in Catalonia was different. The glaziers were mainly local men because the tradition of stained glass was firmly established in the region. The Fontanet family, who came originally from the province of Lérida, received the majority of commissions issued during the first half of the century.

ITALY

From the beginning of the century, Italian stained glass lost the position that it had enjoyed in earlier centuries. No longer was it a vital complement to architecture, whose formal concepts and means of lighting had changed. Coloured stained glass was banished from the majority of buildings in favour of clear glass, which fitted in better with the architectural effects being sought at the time. And

141

yet, at the beginning of the century a French glass artist, Guillaume de Marcillat, who was possibly a native of Berry, settled in Italy following a dispute in his home country. A highly experienced glazier, as we are told by his pupil Vasari, who also wrote his life, Marcillat received a commission for two windows dedicated to the Life of the Virgin in the axial Chapel of Santa Maria del Popolo in Rome, which he completed between 1508 and 1510. Vasari writes that these windows brought him "great fame and an easier life." He then created further windows for the church before travelling to Cortona at the request of a cardinal. In this town he executed several windows, of which only a few panels now survive in an American and an English museum. During the same period, around 1515, he visited Arezzo, where he was granted several commissions, then, after a further stay in Rome, he returned to Arezzo and supervised the creation of five historiated windows in the south aisle of the cathedral. Completed between 1519 and 1525, these portray, in the chronological order of their execution, the Baptism of Christ, the Calling of St. Matthew, the Raising of Lazarus, Jesus Expelling the Merchants from the Temple, and the Woman taken in Adultery. Displaying extraordinary technical skill, as Vasari explains, they exploit the innate qualities of stained glass to the full, while at the same time mirroring the effects obtained in conventional painting as closely as possible. Marcillat, who was also a painter and, more especially, a fresco artist, succeeded where many other glaziers had failed because of his talent and his continual thirst for technical knowledge. He died shortly after the completion of this series in 1529, but he had, nonetheless, been able to supervise other works at Arezzo and also in other buildings in the region, the majority of which have not survived. Marcillat had several pupils, including Pastorino, to whom, according to Vasari, "he left his glass, his tools, and his drawings." It was, in fact, Pastorino who supervised the creation of the window in the west front of Siena Cathedral in 1549.

Work was resumed in Milan Cathedral in 1539 after a long interval, and a few years later, in 1544, an overseer was appointed, a glazier from Cologne called Konrad Much, which became Italianized to "de Mochis." Formulas from beyond the Alps and from northern Europe displaced the ones characteristic of Italian stained glass, which had in any case been almost totally superseded in Milan Cathedral. In 1572, the project's overseer was a Fleming, Valère van Diependaele, member of a family of master glaziers originating in Louvain. From now on, Italian stained glass became the domain of Flemish artists.

THE SEVENTEENTH AND EIGHTEENTH CENTURIES

From the second half of the sixteenth century the art of stained glass went into a rapid decline. The causes of this were mainly religious or economic, or sometimes a combination of the two. Bernard Palissy tells of the wretched way in which French glass artists pushed their carts from village to village. Production ground to a halt almost everywhere, apart from a few towns: in France, at Paris, Bourges, and Troyes (thanks to the Gontier family); in England, at Oxford, where, around 1630, Abraham and Bernard de Linge used enamels to paint religious subjects in several windows of the cathedral and various college chapels; in Spain, at Burgos and a number of other cities, where a few glaziers, often foreigners, continued to work. In the Flemish and Germanic countries, the fashion for heraldic panels accompanied by religious or everyday subjects became astonishingly widespread. There were family workshops which devoted themselves exclusively to the production of this sort of stained glass, such as the Lincks, a Swiss family of specialists who settled in Strasbourg. Between 1626 and 1631 they made more than two hundred panels for the Carthusian monastery at Molsheim, almost all of which are now lost. For most of the time, however, craftsmen were limited to carrying out restoration work of variable quality, patching up existing windows and painting straight onto glass without any firing. The traditional technical recipes were almost completely forgotten, despite the work entitled *Arte Vetraria*, published by Neri in Florence in 1612. Some workshops even had trouble obtaining coloured glass because glassworks no longer bothered to produce it. Faced with difficulties of this sort, glaziers settled for white windows with coloured borders enlivened by religious or vegetal motifs. Colour was no longer fashionable; often, in fact, the authorities had old stained glass removed and replaced with white windows. In 1678, for example, the monks of the Celestine monastery at Lyon sold all the fifteenth-century glass in their chapel and installed colourless windows.

Stained glass, nevertheless, still had its enthusiasts. In the mid eighteenth century, an English enthusiast, Horace Walpole, formed a number of collections in his house at Strawberry Hill, near London, including one of stained glass. His example was subsequently followed by other members of the English aristocracy, who began seeking out old stained glass both in England and on the Continent. In fact, the first public sales of stained glass were held in London. What is more, during the 1770s certain glaziers began to try to rediscover the processes used by the old master craftsmen. Among them was Pierre le Vieil, a famous master glazier in Paris active from the 1730s onwards. A friend of the Encyclopedists, in 1768 he wrote a learned work for the French Academy of Sciences entitled *L'Art de la peinture sur verre et de la vitrerie*, which was published in 1774, two years after his death. Beginning with a historical introduction, it explained the difficulties of preserving old stained glass that was darkening the interiors of buildings. Several English artists began to produce stained glass, such as the Price brothers in Oxford. William Peckitt, originally an engraver and gilder, created several windows for such major churches as York Minster, where he executed a number of large figures for the bays of the south transept.

Other painters supplied cartoons, like the American Benjamin West, who created cartoons for windows in Salisbury Cathedral. Even Sir Joshua Reynolds designed one, representing the Nativity, which was executed by a craftsman from Dublin in 1778. The window, which can still be seen in New College Chapel, Oxford, bears no relation to traditional stained glass: it is painted in enamels on large plates of glass held together by broad lead rods.

Several artists tried to rediscover the secrets of such old techniques as flashing. In this context there is the rather sad story of the Frenchman Jean-Adolphe Dannecker, who lived in Strasbourg. Dannecker, who had made his money from gingerbread and who also held several important civic posts in his hometown, became obsessed with the idea of rediscovering the secrets of traditional stained-glass manufacture and lost his fortune in the process. And yet he did succeed in producing several windows, among them a Virgin and Child which he made for a high window in Strasbourg Cathedral in 1756 and which can today be seen in the Musée de l'Oeuvre Notre-Dame. A few years later, in 1764, he addressed a petition to the superintendent of the King's Buildings to reestablish the art of stained glass, the recipes for which he thought he had rediscovered. The reply, which came from the famous engraver Charles Nicolas Cochin, was unequivocal: "In truth, use is no longer made of it [stained glass] because neither in apartments nor even churches do people want anything that might diminish the light. Thus, in the event of it being proved that it [the art] had been lost and that it had been rediscovered, people would not know what use to make of it."

The ovens were going out and the secrets of the workshops seemed to have been lost forever.

Church of St. John and St. Paul, Venice, Warrior Saint by Girolamo Mocetto, sixteenth century.

7

The Nineteenth-Century Revival

In France, at the beginning of the nineteenth century, stained glass seemed destined to disappear. Coloured glass was hard to find and the traditional techniques were forgotten. Following the reopening of religious buildings to worship in 1801, the restoration of the numerous stained-glass windows that had deteriorated during the Revolution was often entrusted to ordinary glaziers and even roofers, as at Lyon. In England, Belgium, and the Germanic countries, craftsmen endlessly repeated the same types of armorial panels. During the opening decades of the century, however, the Romantics and a number of intellectuals, most notably in England, became increasingly interested in the Middle Ages. This "rediscovery" of the Middle Ages or, rather, of Gothic art, which was fostered by architects such as the Englishman A. W. N. Pugin or writers such as Goethe, himself a collector of old stained glass, was accompanied by enthusiastic research into medieval art. These investigations were naturally to the advantage of stained glass, but it was necessary to "rediscover" the manufacturing processes not only of stained glass, but also of ordinary glass, especially the coloured varieties. The chemist Alexandre Brongniart, director of the Sèvres factory, when embarking on a series of experiments to rediscover the methods used in making medieval glass, blithely wrote in 1802 that "The art of painting on glass is not lost at all: we possess all the means of carrying it out." And yet it took more than twenty years to discover these methods, particularly since the first joint attempts carried out in England and France did not produce the anticipated results. It was not until 1826 that Gustave Bontemps, a chemical engineer and director of the Choisy-le-Roi glassworks, was the first man in Europe to manufacture red glass stained in the body. In addition, some essential operations, such as the firing of pieces of glass bearing grisaille painting and their insertion into a lead armature, were very poorly mastered in both France

Decorative window with letters of the alphabet by William Morris, c. 1870. Private collection.

and England, where glass painting was still carried out in enamels on large sheets of glass. The first quarter of the century should be regarded as an experimental period in which practitioners of the art of stained glass received their training. Several chemists, following in Bontemps's footsteps, took part in these experiments, but the stained glass made in France and England was still very different from that created during the Middle Ages, as can be seen in the window portraying the Crucified Christ installed in 1816 in the Church of Saint-Roch in Paris. Still in place in a bay in a south chapel of the nave, this window, the work of a chemist, continues the practice of using large sheets of glass painted in enamels, although a few pieces are held together by clearly visible lead rods, which was a novelty at the time. In 1826 a call went out for English craftsmen still working in this tradition to create windows for several Parisian churches that had been "despoiled during the Revolution": three at Sainte-Élisabeth illustrating theological virtues, based on cartoons executed in the previous century by Sir Joshua Reynolds for New College Chapel in Oxford, and one, a Marriage of the Virgin, for Saint-Étienne-du-Mont. They were still far from rediscovering the procedures used during the Middle Ages, whereas there were German workshops which had already succeeded in reproducing them. The latter had managed to manufacture glass stained in the body, they knew how to paint using traditional vitreous paints, they knew how to fire it correctly, and they also knew how to insert it into lead armatures as in the Middle Ages.

THE SÈVRES WORKSHOP

By opening a stained-glass workshop in 1828 at the Sèvres factory, Brongniart no doubt thought that he would speed up the process of rediscovering the medieval recipes. He made no headway, however, despite a report on stained-glass techniques that he published the following year. Sèvres, which enjoyed the official patronage of King Louis-Philippe, continued, for the most part, to paint in enamels on poor-quality glass, despite Brong-

niart's incessant reiterations that his painters were capable of emulating the old processes.

The Sèvres workshop, which remained active up until 1854, occupies its own special place in the development of French stained glass during the first half of the nineteenth century. It provided considerable impetus thanks to the personality of its director, Brongniart, an indefatigable researcher. Many commissions were placed by the king and his family, more often than not for the chapels of their private residences, as in the case of the chapel at the château of Carheil, near Nantes. Some works were presented by the king to towns or institutions. In 1844, for example, he gave three windows to the Cathedral of Saint-Flour in Auvergne which portray the town's medieval past and whose cartoons were the work of the architect Viollet-le-Duc. In fact, Sèvres recruited the services of such famous painters as Devéria, Ingres, and Delacroix to provide cartoons, but these artists were generally commissioned to provide only a part of the windows, either the borders or the central section. Ingres, for example, was responsible for the central sections in the Royal Chapel at Dreux, where he created twelve figures of male and female saints that Viollet-le-Duc had to adapt to the building's windows by adding architectural elements. The workshop also specialized in copying paintings, which they transferred onto glass. In 1842, Louis-Philippe commissioned eleven windows for the Royal Chapel in the château of Amboise whose central figures were taken from Spanish and Italian paintings in the Louvre. The borders, however, were conceived and designed by Viollet-le-Duc and were inspired by French sculptures from the end of the Middle Ages. This sort of disparity recurred in a large number of windows made at Sèvres and was severely censured by contemporary critics. Nowadays, however, people tend to regard this trait as one of the workshop's most original characteristics. Work was strictly regimented. Each craftsman or painter had his task far too strictly circumscribed for a skill as artistic as that of the master glass-artist. Despite Brongniart's best efforts, Sèvres

Lady with Fruit by William Morris, c. 1870. Private collection.

Opposite: Window with coat of arms, English, c. 1845. Private collection.

final work, including Jean-Baptiste Lassus, the architect in charge of the building's restoration, the elder Didron, who was responsible for the iconography, Louis Steinheil *père*, who designed and executed the cartoon, and Reboulleau, a chemist "converted" to stained glass. Its treatment copied that of the Gothic windows in the Sainte-Chapelle in Paris. By favouring the Parisian style prevailing at the time of St. Louis, this work determined the course taken by French "archaeological" stained glass for several decades. Fifty years later, in 1889, the younger Didron, nephew of the man responsible for the iconography at Saint-Germain, was able to write in a retrospective article on stained glass during the nineteenth century: "In order to demonstrate more readily the excellence and superiority of the style adopted, people copied that of the windows in the Sainte-Chapelle. . . . The appearance of this window was a milestone for the specialized world of those interested in the renaissance of stained glass." Today, however, it has to be recognized that archaeological stained glass drew inspiration from periods other than the Middle Ages. As early as 1840, for example, the Clermont-Ferrand glazier Thévenot had used Renaissance models for several windows in the north chapels of the nave of Bayeux Cathedral.

THE REVIVAL

In England, Thomas Willement was a great pioneering figure. A specialist in the still fashionable heraldic panels, he also created windows for religious buildings. Unlike French stained-glass artists, he did not draw inspiration from thirteenth-century Gothic glass, very little of which survives in England, but from glass of the fourteenth century, the period when English stained glass was flourishing.

From the 1830s onwards, stained glass became a favourite subject for experimentation in England, where it combined a large number of different trends orchestrated by the famous architect Augustus Pugin, himself a prolific cartoonist of stained-glass windows, on which he collaborated with numerous craftsmen, most notably his associate John Hardman. The renaissance of stained glass gained not only from the constant growth of interest in medieval art, but also from the favourable religious mood prevailing in the country. Stained glass came to be regarded as the equivalent of a catechism. From its first issues in 1841, the journal of the

was rapidly overtaken by provincial workshops such as the one set up at Le Mans by Antoine Lusson.

ARCHAEOLOGICAL STAINED GLASS IN FRANCE

Between 1830 and 1840 several workshops, then known as "manufactories," were opened, like the one belonging to Thibaud and Thévenot at Clermont-Ferrand in 1831. During that same year the publication of Victor Hugo's work on Notre-Dame Cathedral in Paris had the effect of focusing the French public's attention on the Middle Ages. Already scholars, architects, and churchmen were

doing their best to encourage the involvement of the civil and religious authorities, emphasizing the problems of conserving medieval buildings. The year 1834 saw the foundation of the famous French Archaeological Society, whose members met several times a year to study monuments, generally medieval ones. In stained-glass workshops craftsmen strove to relearn the traditional techniques of applying paints and creating lead armatures, basing their work on medieval models. At the end of the decade, in 1839, the first "archaeological" window in France was installed in the axial bay of the chevet of the Church of Saint-Germain-l'Auxerrois in Paris. The combined efforts of five people were needed to produce the

*Coats of arms: Left, from a Belgian window,
c. 1890; right, from an English window, c. 1880.
Private collection.*

famous Cambridge Camden Society, *The Ecclesiologist*, emphasized the vital role that should be played by stained glass not only as a means of decorating a building, but also as a purveyor of symbolic messages. At this date English stained glass, although in a stage of full development, was still technically mediocre. Charles Winston, a highly regarded master glazier, tried to remedy this state of affairs by having fragments of medieval glass subjected to chemical analysis in order to manufacture identical pieces that could be used for both restoration and original works. In the famous 1851 International Exhibition at the Crystal Palace in London, work by some thirty master glaziers of different nationalities was displayed. The English glass seemed less interesting than that produced elsewhere in Europe. There was no hint of the stylistic originality that it was to acquire in the ensuing years through William Morris.

THE NAZARENES AND STAINED GLASS

The ten years between 1840 and 1850 represent a significant stage in the revival of European stained glass. New workshops were founded, including those by Giuseppe Bertini in Milan and Jean-Baptiste Capronnier in Brussels. In Germany, Munich continued to be an important creative center as a result of its links with the Nazarene painters, whose works, often known through lithographs, were a favourite source of inspiration for many European glaziers. In 1809 a group of young painters in Vienna founded an association known as the Brotherhood of St. Luke. Their goal was to rediscover the creative spirit of the medieval and Renaissance artists and to oppose their contemporaries, whom they regarded as being corrupt on several levels. The following year the group settled in Rome in a

deconsecrated monastery and lived in almost monastic poverty, hoping to rediscover the creative and religious world of Dürer, who had also worked in Italy, and of Raphael and Perugino. The Nazarenes, whose leaders were the painters Friedrich Overbeck and Peter Cornelius, tried to instill their works with a strong religious feeling. Their colours remained intentionally medieval and were flatly applied. This decision, which was both aesthetic and spiritual, corresponded with the goals of a number of European master glass painters, not only English, but also French. Such well-known paintings by Overbeck as *The Death of Joseph* and *Christ Suffering the Children to Come unto Him* were popularized through stained glass. The English Pre-Raphaelite movement, which took up the essential elements of Nazarene doctrine, evoked a ready response among both stained-glass artists and their cartoonists, such as Dante

The Fox and the Stork (based on the fable by Aesop) by Walter Crane, c. 1900. Private collection.

Gabriel Rossetti. In France, two pupils of Overbeck, the brothers Karl and Friedrich Kuckelbecker, who had previously been painters in the Munich workshop, settled in Le Mans during the 1850s and even commissioned cartoons from their German friends, like the artist Johann de Rodhen. At Lyon, the artist Claudius Lavergne followed the Nazarenes' example in 1840 by founding the Society of St. John the Evangelist, the motto of which was: "To learn like Overbeck and his companions to make use of one's art to do good."

THE MAJOR RESTORATION PROJECTS

Practitioners of the art began to reap the benefits of their researches. In 1845, for example, Gustave Bontemps succeeded in making layered glass, a technique which allowed for engraving. Several master glaziers also published works on the technique and history of stained glass. In 1843 Count Charles de l'Escalopier had translated the treatise of the monk Theophilus into French in a work that aroused great interest in France and throughout Europe. Large restoration projects were inaugurated in France under the auspices of the Service des Édifices Diocésains in the case of cathedrals and the Service des Monuments Historiques in the case of other protected buildings. These undertakings, often harshly judged by modern authorities, were in fact carried out with great care. Life-size tracings were taken of the windows before removing them, as happened at both Le Mans and Bourges Cathedral. During the course of the work, inspections were carried out on site, when meetings were held attended by, in addition to the architect and master glazier, archaeologists such as the Jesuit priests Cahier and Martin, authors of an indispensable work on the thirteenth-century windows of Bourges Cathedral which was published between 1841 and 1844. It would take too long to quote the names of all the churchmen actively involved in these works, but mention should be made of Cardinal de Bonald, Archbishop of Lyon from 1839, who was originally in charge of "Christian archaeology" in the seminaries, and Abbé Tournesac at Le Mans who, being an architect, was able to give advice to numerous clergymen and also put them in touch with master glaziers. Some, such as Abbé Texier in Limousin, even published articles on the history of stained glass. Stained-glass artists frequently moved in these learned circles: Émile Thibaud belonged to

numerous archaeological societies in Clermont-Ferrand, where he met the prelates who were his potential clients. In nineteenth-century France commissions were frequently obtained as a result of this sort of social connection.

The practice of restoration enabled those involved to make great technical progress, but these men often had no compunction in radically altering an old window in order to give it a coherence it no longer possessed, thereby irrevocably destroying its original composition and iconographical meaning. This blinkered attitude is frequently the underlying reason for the poor condition of many early windows, especially since restoration was not carried out along the same strictly scientific lines as today. The cleaning of corroded and discoloured glass was often performed using hydrofluoric acid, a method recommended by the famous French chemist Chevreul, and abraded

with metal scrapers. We now know that such methods make glass very fragile and vulnerable, but in the nineteenth century people were unaware of these unfortunate consequences. Restorers were also quick to remove panels which in their opinion were beyond redemption.

Old stained glass undergoing restoration also often inspired advocates of the "archaeological" window. In 1845 Thévenot adapted the iconography and style of several windows in the chevet of Bourges Cathedral when creating his own windows in the ambulatory of the Romanesque Church of Notre-Dame-du-Port in his hometown of Clermont-Ferrand. There are also countless other examples of this phenomenon. The formal derivation of "archaeological" windows is often discernible, but there was rarely any slavish copying. Nineteenth-century glaziers frequently altered the arrangement of medieval motifs, creating a

layout which differs radically from that found in early works. This sort of adaptation, which also affected iconography, often gave rise to some very interesting windows that were in keeping with the neo-Gothic or neo-Romanesque buildings for which they were destined. This is particularly true of windows created during the 1840–60 period, very few of which have survived. This type of window subsequently became the subject of mass production.

As well as gaining firsthand knowledge of earlier works, French craftsmen were also able to avail themselves of reviews such as *Annales archéologiques*. Founded in 1844 by Adolphe Didron the elder, this review assembled doctrinal articles in which the art of stained glass was regarded as a moral art, a craft endowed with lofty spiritual values, which pleased both churchmen and master glaziers alike.

"It is from mosaics that one should act, and not from paintings," wrote the elder Didron in 1844 in *Annales archéologiques*. People paid such attention to his pronouncements that the restoration of the Gothic windows in the Sainte-Chapelle, begun in 1846, became a matter of national interest and not just the concern of the intelligentsia. Louis-Philippe himself was taking a personal interest in the project before 1848. The work, entrusted to Antoine Lusson and Maréchal de Metz with the collaboration of the archaeologist François de Guilhermy, and with Louis-Auguste Steinheil supplying the cartoons, coincided with the new familiarity with the stained glass of the time of St. Louis, the style of which so often acted as a point of reference for French master glaziers. The latter, particularly those entrusted with important restoration work, excelled in the interpretation of medieval glass. Henri Gérente was one of its finest cartoonists, but he died prematurely in 1849, just after winning the competition to restore the windows of the Sainte-Chapelle. His brother Alfred, a sculptor by training, took over his workshop and became one of the master glaziers appointed by the architect Viollet-le-Duc, completing as many restorations as original works and working on such buildings as the Abbey Church of Saint-Denis (1849–58) and Notre-Dame Cathedral in Paris (1861–65). Nicolas Coffetier, often associated with the cartoonist Louis

Steinheil, was just as frequently employed by Viollet-le-Duc.

In the provinces, Antoine Lusson had settled at Le Mans and in 1844 was one of the first glaziers to complete an archaeological window, based on a cartoon by Henri Gérente, for the Church of Notre-Dame-de-la-Couture in Le Mans. Thomas Lobin, who set up shop in Tours in 1850, was destined to become one of the most respected painter-glaziers in western France. These craftsmen and many others

imitated every type of medieval window: the legendary type, with its superimposed compartments, and that of the large figure beneath an architectural canopy, a formula that they both used and abused. The clear grisaille window, less expensive to produce, was often chosen, with its architectural inspiration often derived from the styles prevailing at the end of the thirteenth century or the beginning of the fourteenth. After 1870, however, because of the great rise in commissions, the

Opposite: Decorative stained-glass windows for private houses. Above left, water plants and birds, c. 1870; above right, wildflowers, c. 1920. Below left, checkerboard pattern, c. 1860–70; below right, pelican with heraldic motif, c. 1860. Private collections.

Right: Church of Saint-Vincent de Paul, Paris; detail of Baptism of Christ *by Maréchal de Metz, 1844.*

Bouvines Church, northeastern France; detail of Battle of Bouvines *in 1214 by Lucien Magne, showing Philip II surrounded by soldiers, 1867. Bouvines (Nord).*

manufacture of this type of window became so industrialized that it lost all creative character.

While this trend was taking its course, certain other craftsmen began to express interest in the stained-glass "painting," which covered a whole bay with a single composition and ignored the divisions created by the lancets. Since 1830 the Sèvres workshop had adopted the custom of transferring paintings like Proud'hon's *Assumption of the Virgin* onto glass, but Charles Maréchal de Metz, a master glazier from Lorraine, was one of the first to make systematic use of this type of composition. Despite the misgivings of medievalists, this former pupil of Dela-

croix, who was also a brilliant technician, succeeded in giving this type of window a new lease on life during the 1845–50 period. At the same time, in Lyon, certain local master glaziers became strongly attracted to the stained-glass "painting" as a means of interpreting their mystical universe. In this respect, Claudius Lavergne is a classic example. A pupil of Ingres and closely linked to the Nazarenes, he was one of the most passionate advocates of the stained-glass "painting," which responded to his spiritual ideal. And yet, this type of window gradually became just as academic as the archaeological type, even though it called for a much more sophisticated technique than the

latter, which was far easier to produce. Material analysis of a stained-glass "painting" reveals the multiple use of engraving processes, paint applied in several firings and based on different-coloured paints and the addition of silver stain, enamel, and sanguine highlights in order to achieve, as during the Renaissance, the effects of a painting on glass. It was therefore another form of "archaeological" window, even though its historical points of reference were totally different; critics of the day regarded it as being more "modern," but its inspiration was just as historical.

The development of religious stained glass in nineteenth-century France was

Collegiate Church of Notre-Dame-du-Mur, Morlaix (Brittany); detail of Procession in Honour of the Virgin *by Jean-Louis Nicolas, showing Breton women at prayer, 1862.*

characterized by the existence of these two separate trends, a rivalry that culminated in 1894 in the competition held at Orléans Cathedral for the creation of a series of windows devoted to the story of Joan of Arc. The supporters of the different movements once again came into conflict just as stained glass was beginning to break loose from the formalism which, with a few rare exceptions, had characterized it for much of the nineteenth century.

In defense of the creators of stained glass, it should be said that commissions had become so numerous that they were in many cases obliged to resort to mass-production techniques. In 1840 there were no more than some forty workshops in the whole of France, whereas by the end of the Second Empire this figure had risen to more than two hundred. In addition to these workshops there were also "factories" employing up to fifty workmen, each with his own well-defined task. There were draughtsmen responsible for creating the sketches and also cutters, painters, burners, who were in charge of the ovens, now fired by gas, and finally the men who mounted the glass in lead rods and those who fitted the pieces together. The output of the Maréchal de Metz workshop between 1837, the date of its foundation, and 1867, when it was handed over to Charles Champigneulle, has recently been assessed at almost 12,000 windows for 1,600 buildings, which makes a total of around 57,000 square meters (68,172 square yards) of glass. This overload of work led to a lack of creative dynamism, a criticism still levelled at nineteenth-century glass. Craftsmen were even obliged to resort to industrial manufacturing processes that were prejudicial to the artistic nature of the craft, such as the printing of paints onto glass.

WILLIAM MORRIS AND HIS ASSOCIATES

It was in 1861 that William Morris and his associates, who included the painter Edward Burne-Jones, founded a firm in Holborn, London, devoted to decoration and the graphic arts, called Morris and Co. Ltd., an enterprise which exerted a lasting influence on the development of religious and secular stained glass in both England and on the Continent up until the First World War. Morris, a committed Socialist, and Burne-Jones had known each other since their student days and were both passionate admirers of the Pre-Raphaelite poet and painter Dante Gabriel Rossetti, who worked with them from 1861 to 1864. Another Pre-Raphaelite

painter, Ford Madox Brown, an architect, Philip Webb, and Charles J. Faulkner and Peter P. Marshall were the other members. Founded on egalitarian principles, this artistic company dealt in not only stained glass, but also furniture, wallpaper, and wall hangings. Stained glass was just one of the media that attracted the group's talents. They saw the decoration of a house or any other building as an organic whole. This attitude was to have important repercussions in the realm of secular stained glass after 1860. They were, like all their artistic contemporaries, great purists and concentrated predominantly on medieval art, particularly of the fourteenth and fifteenth centuries, but

later, under the influence of Rossetti and the art critic John Ruskin, they developed an interest in the Italian Renaissance. One thinks, for example, of the St. George series based on cartoons by Rossetti (1862), now in the Victoria and Albert Museum, London, which may have been inspired by Pisanello's frescoes in the Church of San Zeno in Verona.

Philip Webb was in charge of adapting the cartoons to their windows, while at the same time acting as a decorative designer. Morris selected the glass and the glass artists were entrusted with the task of transcribing the cartoons. When compared with the sort of academic works that were so commonplace in contemporary

France, it is easy to understand why the windows produced by Morris and Co. were greeted with such enthusiasm. In them, stained glass rediscovered its role as an art of light and colour, while new life was breathed into its graphical element by the adoption of the sinuous lines of Pre-Raphaelite painting. Its decorative repertoire was also revised; the stylized foliage often placed by Morris in the background of his compositions from 1861 onwards leads into Art Nouveau. Although the earliest windows created by the group are still steeped in medievalism, their later ones freed themselves from the medievalist straitjacket and acquired an original and defiantly modern quality. In 1875 the partnership dissolved. Morris and Burne-Jones continued their researches independently. The former devoted more and more of his energies to textiles, while the latter remained faithful to stained glass, which evolved into shapes that became more and more supple.

The success of Morris and Co. gave a considerable boost to religious and secular glass in England, with its effects being felt both in the colonies and in the United States. Stained glass invaded the home, giving rise to compositions with ever more eclectic subject matter. Some was purely decorative, whereas some portrayed flowers and animals. Much of the latter is now no longer in its original setting but is preserved in museums or private collections. A large number of artists followed the example set by Morris and his associates and began to act as not only cartoonists, but also designers of textiles, mosaics, and furniture. Some of them, active during the same period as Morris and Burne-Jones, played a significant role in the decorative arts: figures such as Henry G. A. Holiday, who during his long career collaborated with a large number of different workshops. The Scotsman Daniel Cottier, who lived in Edinburgh, opened branches in New York and Sydney in 1873 and played an important part in influencing the development of secular stained glass in America. Charles Eamer Kempe, whose first windows adorn Bombay Cathedral (1869), was a very prolific artist who often drew on English fifteenth-century glass for his inspiration. Nathaniel H. J. Westlake, the first historian to have studied medieval stained glass on a European basis, supplied numerous cartoons to various workshops. At the end of the century, Walter Crane, like his predecessors, continued to produce cartoons for churches and houses alike. President of

Opposite: Spring *by Eugène Grasset, Paris, 1884. Musée des Arts décoratifs, Paris.*

Right: "Tiffany" window by Giovanni Beltrami for the casino at Terme di San Pellegrino, Bergamo, 1907.

the Century Guild of Arts, a group of artists founded in 1882 and now acknowledged as having played a major part in the development of the art in England, he returned to a highly painted form of stained glass, often created by means of overlays, a process that was to become more and more common among members of this group at the turn of the century.

Other artists outside London were to follow the example set by these painters and cartoonists, who often formed themselves into groups like the Arts and Crafts Movement. In Glasgow, which at the end of the nineteenth century was one of the richest cities in the British Empire, a group headed by James Guthrie carried out a great deal of work. In the company of Andrew Webbs, a pupil of Cottier, Guthrie founded a firm specializing in secular stained glass, for which a large number of the cartoons were designed by the famous architect Charles Rennie Mackintosh, one of the originators of Art Nouveau.

THE UNIVERSAL EXHIBITIONS AND SECULAR STAINED GLASS

The Universal Exhibitions which were held with almost clockwork regularity throughout the second half of the nineteenth century (thirteen between 1851 and 1900) allowed stained-glass artists to compare their works with those of other countries. One section or "class," to use the contemporary term, was reserved for them in the section devoted to Fine Arts. Stained glass was also often used as part of the pavilions' architecture. Competitions were also held during these exhibitions, with prizes awarded to the best exhibits. Glaziers had a chance to assess the technical advances made by their fellow artists, while cartoonists were on the look-out for changes in taste and new fashions. Art critics became involved and produced their own eulogies. In 1867, for example, Japanese art, which had already been seen at the 1862 Exhibition in London, took Paris and the rest of France by storm. The flora and fauna of Japanese prints inspired glass painters everywhere, even the most mediocre ones, and were endlessly copied and recopied in the panels of glass screens surrounding the stairwells of blocks of flats. The 1893 Exhibition in Chicago was to allow the Oriental art dealer and collector Samuel Bing, who had been commissioned by the French Government to investigate American art, to discover the talent of the American glass

157

painter Louis Comfort Tiffany, who had founded his own factory in Corona, New York, in 1879. This event marked the beginning of a very productive partnership, since in 1895 Bing displayed a number of Tiffany stained-glass windows in Paris, based on cartoons by Toulouse-Lautrec, Bonnard, Vuillard, Vallotton, and Sérusier. In the same way, the association of glass and iron was enthusiastically hailed at the 1889 Exhibition in Paris: it was an idea that led to such astonishing creations as the dome of the Galeries Lafayette in Paris, which is adorned with a stained-glass window by Jacques Gruber (1908).

Thanks to the first Universal Exhibitions, particularly the one held in Paris in 1855, secular stained glass developed rapidly in France. During the middle of the century, the Parisian Prosper Lafaye was alone in drawing inspiration from sixteenth- and seventeenth-century Swiss windows. It was not until the second half of the century that stained glass first appeared in public buildings and then in private houses, as part of the decoration of rooms and even furniture. Maréchal de Metz was one of the first to realize the interest that existed in this sort of stained glass.

The opening years of the Third Republic were the period in which secular stained glass really took off in France, when it became a purely decorative art form, rather like wallpaper. This fashion "rejuvenated" stained glass, which was certainly in need of an injection of fresh ideas. Glaziers took full advantage of this fashion, especially since the new structures based on iron girders allowed for very daring combinations of glass and architecture. It was against this background that there appeared such innovations as Eugène Grasset's *Spring*, executed by the Parisian glazier Félix Gaudin in 1884. In this work, now in the Musée des Arts décoratifs in Paris, Grasset, a Swiss artist who had settled in France, succeeded in creating a glass poster of which he was to produce countless versions. By simplifying his use of line he managed to give a new autonomy to the composition, which contains a balanced blend of different inspirations: the young girl, whose appearance recalls the art of both Botticelli and the Pre-Raphaelites, walks through a Japanese-influenced landscape.

Stained glass soon penetrated every area of French architecture, from town halls to prefectures and from schools to universities. Stained glass also invaded railway stations, department stores, banks and savings banks, as in the one at Puy-en-Velay, where several windows created by a local master glazier in the bank's boardroom glorify the virtues of work and saving. In cafés, brasseries, and even brothels, stained-glass artists gave full rein to their imagination and created windows peopled by sinuous female figures adorned with jewels and flowers, wandering among beds of flowers, particularly irises. Many of these windows have since disappeared, however, victims of the changing tastes of the 1920s. The same is also true of the numerous windows that adorned pavilions in the Universal Exhibitions. Few have been saved and it is often necessary to refer to catalogues to find out about them. Stained glass became so fashionable in France that at the turn of the century substitute materials appeared, such as *vitrauphanie*, a sort of transparent paper to be applied to windows in imiation of stained glass. Once again, the future of stained glass seemed to be in jeopardy.

ART NOUVEAU

It was four European architects, the Catalan Antonio Gaudí, the Scotsman Charles Rennie Mackintosh, the Frenchman Hector Guimard, and the Belgian Victor Horta, who revived the spirit of stained glass during the 1890s and allowed it to regain its monumental authority. These four creative geniuses also exercised a determining influence on the formation of Art Nouveau, which originated in Europe. Stained glass played an essential role in its development because the theorists of Art Nouveau regarded architecture as an organic entity, in which decoration and furniture are just as important as the actual building. They thus abolished the distinction between architecture, hitherto regarded as a major art, and its decoration, especially stained glass, which had been previously treated as a minor one. In addition, they wanted to make art participate in the struggle of the workers, which often explains its iconographical renewal, particularly noticeable in stained glass. This trend developed in different ways, however, depending on the country or the individual artist adopting it. In Germany it was called *Jugendstil*, in Holland *Nieuwe Kunst*, in Italy *Stile Liberty*, and in England and France *Art Nouveau*. Although all these movements had the same basic goals, they did not express themselves in the same stylistic fashion. One of the principal aims was a return to the observation and imitation of Nature. Flora therefore became the characteristic decorative motif of Art Nouveau. In stained glass this choice ended up by changing its very conception, particularly since master glaziers were now beginning to use overlay techniques and also to employ American and opalescent glass. But there are considerable differences between the almost abstract spareness of Mackintosh's windows in Glasgow, and the decorative extravagance of Horta's windows in Brussels.

In the crypt of Santa María de Cervello, the unfinished chapel of the Güell colony in Barcelona, Gaudí recreated the light of Romanesque glass in rose windows in the shapes of flowers that often contain a cross design at the center. But he also anticipated the future development of stained glass by using simple, clear shapes and uncluttered surfaces with the merest hint of silver stain which presage the experimental work of Matisse. In this chapel, built between 1898 and 1914, the Catalan architect has succeeded in restoring to stained glass the light-bearing role that it had been deprived of for so long.

There were other attempts in Europe to combat the complacent academicism into which the arts had fallen, but stained glass did not always play an essential role in this process. In Germany, the Jugendstil

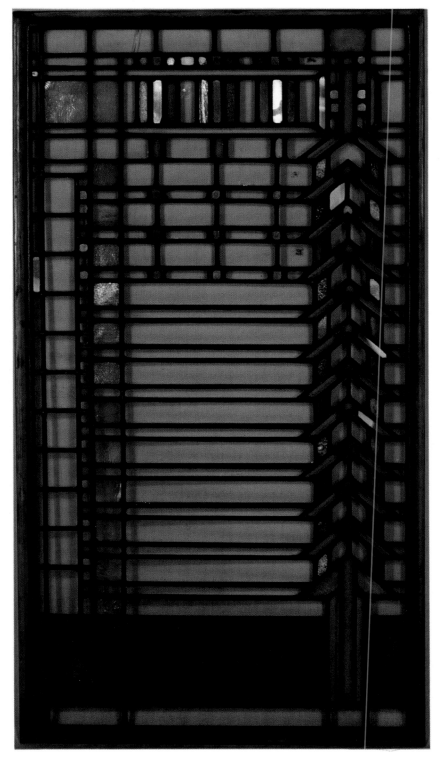

movement, which was both pacifist and anticlerical, made a very definite impression on secular stained glass, which now became an experimental arena for a number of glaziers. After a period in which the majority of these craftsmen used flora as an indispensable element of their decorative repertoire, glass evolved towards linear forms under the influence of the architect and designer Peter Behrens. In Austria, nineteen artists, among them Gustav Klimt, left the official association of artists in 1897 to found the Sezession, a term which was later used by Austrians to designate Art Nouveau. Like

Gaudí and Mackintosh, these artists wanted no more of the historicism that was obscuring their artistic personalities. They wanted to rediscover the regenerative function of art and they started an arts review with the evocative title of *Ver Sacrum* (Sacred Spring). They found their inspiration in a return to a pagan antiquity peopled by gods and goddesses. By adopting the shape of the pediment of an ancient temple for his monumental figure of the Eternal Father, which formed the central section of his cartoon for a window in the Church of St. Leopold at Amsteinhof, not far from Vienna, the painter Kolo Moser,

one of the founders of the Wiener Werkstätte (Vienna Workshops), a sort of craft cooperative, was fully applying the precepts laid down by the Sezession group. The Pole Josef Mehoffer, who was summoned to Switzerland at the end of the century to create the windows in the nave of Fribourg Cathedral, also relied on popular elements for his inspiration. In the Franciscan Church at Kraków, Stanislaw Wyspianski surpassed the works of German painters by the freeness of his compositions and by his unrestrained use of colour (1897–1902).

It was in France, however, that stained

glass gave Art Nouveau a new and unique dimension. When Gauguin wrote at the end of the century, "Stained-glass windows, a beautiful form of regenerative painting..." he can scarcely have been thinking of the Symbolists or the Nabis or even of himself, despite the fact that he had personally created a few stained-glass windows, the best-preserved of which is the one in the villa at Cap-Ferrat on the Côte d'Azur, which was formerly the home of the English writer Somerset Maugham. The latter artists, with the exception of Maurice Denis, missed their chance to exploit an art form that was perfectly suited to their temperament. It was artists of the Nancy School, faithful to the tenets of Art Nouveau, who were to breathe new life into French stained glass during the 1890s. Since 1870, Nancy had become a prosperous city, attracting numerous artists from Alsace who had chosen to live in France. Jacques Gruber, the greatest master glazier of this school, was one of these artists. In 1893 he worked with the brothers Auguste and Antonin Daum, who created objects by superimposing several layers of coloured glass on white glass, a process perfected by Émile Gallé. Gruber's originality lay in the way in which he adapted this technique, which was intended for three-dimensional shapes such as vases and bowls, to the flat surfaces of stained glass. An incomparable technician, Gruber also used acid-etched layered glass, American relief glass, and dichroic glass, the colours of which change according to the angle of viewing. A combination of iridescent materials, accompanied by the sinuous lines characteristic of Art Nouveau and a highly sophisticated system of lead mounts, allowed Gruber to inject a new feeling of excitement into secular stained glass, which up until then had been of little

Opposite: Hunter *by Lindo Grassi, stained-glass screen, 1915. Private collection.*

Right: Cornfield *by Teodoro Wolf-Ferrari, 1912. Private collection.*

interest to glaziers. Gruber also strove constantly to adapt his work to its architectural environment, taking advantage of the new opportunities provided by metal-based structures. And yet he drew inspiration from the same sources as his artistic contemporaries. He roamed the forests of Lorraine in search of inspiration, translating what he saw there—the mushrooms, thistles, jonquils, insects, birds—into a sinuous and elemental graphic style influenced by Japanese art.

In 1920 he began to renew his technique, giving it a new stylistic purity that can be seen in his *Basket of Fruit* created in 1922. He subsequently transformed his conception of light, adopting a geometric cut characteristic of the 1925 period and using glass with machine-made relief and colourless tones. Gruber, with the exception of Fernand Léger, was the only master glazier interested in the life of the working man.

Italy was also affected by the Art Nouveau phenomenon, where it was called the Stile Liberty after the famous Englishman A. L. Liberty, founder of the shop specializing in interior decoration whose products were highly prized by the Italians. The large exhibition held in Turin in 1902, devoted to Art Nouveau, persuaded Italian architects and decorators to change stylistic direction, particularly those in the north. However, the hearts of Italian artists were not really in the new movement. In the realm of stained glass, for example, the allegorical and floral windows created by the Milanese Giovanni Beltrami between 1905 and 1907 for the casino at Terme di San Pellegrino, the famous Italian spa, bear witness to this fact. They are decorative works, competent enough, but without much originality.

We should now look back and recall the extraordinary flowering of American stained glass that occurred during the closing decades of the nineteenth century and the opening ones of the twentieth, a period dominated by two astonishing personalities, John La Farge and Louis Comfort Tiffany, the former born in 1836 and the latter in 1848. John La Farge, who had once, during a trip to Europe, been a pupil in the workshop of Thomas Couture, came late to stained glass, via religious wall-painting. In 1876 he enjoyed great success as a result of his decoration of Trinity Church in Boston. Two years later, Louis Comfort Tiffany created a sensation among Europeans at the 1878 Universal Exhibition in Paris. The latter discovered for the first time a quality of glass they had never seen before: iridescent and opalescent. Tiffany used it to make vases, lamps, and stained-glass panels. Later on he was to perfect his manufacturing technique and obtain a glass, called Favrile, which consisted of several layers of glass pressed together. At the 1889 Universal Exhibition, John La Farge showed a stained-glass window that was enthusiastically received.

In 1889, Tiffany had joined up with the French dealer Samuel Bing, who sent him cartoons by famous painters to reproduce in glass. It was during this period that the fame of the American artist reached its height. The following year, first in Paris and then in London, Tiffany exhibited his *Four Seasons*, which is regarded as his greatest work. Each season is represented by a symbolic landscape whose particular mood is conveyed by iridescent tones of opalescent glass. Like many artists attracted to Art Nouveau, his favourite subjects were birds, namely peacocks, which he depicted in luxuriant natural settings, like the gardens of the millionaires who were his constant clients. Tiffany achieved immediate success with his secular stained glass and was obliged to engage a whole army of painters and craftsmen in his studio, especially since he also created furniture. But he retained constant and strict control over all stained-glass cartoons, which were his favourite means of artistic expression; these always had to be shown to him before being submitted to a client. On the other hand, Tiffany encountered considerable difficulties in gaining acceptance for his landscape windows in the many religious buildings that were being erected in America at the time. Like the Europeans, Americans preferred exemplary subjects taken from the Bible or the Gospels. It took him many years to convince people of the symbolic and religious value of a landscape, and even then he was not always successful. One of the most important windows of this type is the one in the First Presbyterian Church at Far Rockway, Long Island, New York, which portrays an immense tree in a marshy landscape (c. 1905).

THE BIRTH OF ABSTRACT STAINED GLASS

At the same time as Art Nouveau stained glass was producing its most striking works in an almost exclusively decorative style, Frank Lloyd Wright and others were already preaching a functional brand of architecture in which decoration was reduced to its barest minimum. This Chicago architect did not, however, totally banish stained glass from his buildings, but subjected it to a geometricality that was taken up by the artists of the Bauhaus. Paul Klee, who taught at the Bauhaus, also ran a stained-glass workshop there for a time, subsequently taken over by the painter Josef Albers from 1923 and 1933. Abstraction first appeared in stained glass before the 1930s, when the decoration of the Café de l'Aubette in Strasbourg's Place Kléber was entrusted to Theo van Doesburg who, together with Piet Mondrian, was one of the founders of the Dutch *de Stijl* group and author in 1924 of a manifesto on Elementarism, in which he extolled the virtues of the oblique. He enrolled the services of Jean Arp and his wife, Sophie Taeuber, to help create this group of stained glass in 1926, the majority of which is now lost. This enterprise was not, however, followed by any further abstract experiments in France until the 1950s. By contrast, the German Expressionist style, whose cause was often furthered by painters teaching in art schools, produced some very worthwhile Cubist works, such as those of the Dutchman Johann Thorn Prikker, who died in 1932. His pupils Anton Weidling and Heinrich Campendonk kept his monumental tradition alive and also worked on the restoration of German churches in the aftermath of the Second World War, the former dying in 1965 and the latter in 1957. Ewald Dülberg recalled his early days as an engraver when he worked as a stained-glass painter. His best-known works, *The Wise Virgins* and *The Foolish Virgins*, now in Strasbourg's Museé d'Art moderne are characterized by an austerely Expressionist style.

After the First World War, French glaziers devoted most of their energies to the vital work of restoring glass damaged during the hostilities. It was also during this period that Jacques le Chevallier encouraged the development of workshops devoted to ecclesiastical art, in which painters and craftsmen were brought together. But these collaborations were not very fruitful. The International Exhibition of 1937 did not achieve the hoped-for success, despite the fact that the Pontifical Pavilion, then the Marian Pavilion, contained a display of figurative windows intended to replace the nineteenth-century ones, which were now out of favour, in the nave of Notre-Dame in Paris. Lively polemics greeted these works, many of which were very old-fashioned in their treatment. It was not until 1939, when an exhibition dedicated to the decorative arts was held in the Petit-Palais on the initiative of Jean Hébert-Stevens, that the public became aware of the first tentative works of Jean Bazaine, Roger Bissière, and Francis Gruber. But this encounter was never followed up. Shortly afterwards, the Second World War broke out, postponing for many years, for those who did not perish in the conflict, their hopes of achieving self-expression through stained glass.

Opposite: Basket of Fruit by Jacques Gruber, Nancy School, 1922. Private collection.

8
From 1945 to the Present Day: Contemporary Trends

In 1945 a large number of churches in Europe, particularly in France and Germany, had been either partially or totally destroyed. In many cases the structure was still standing, but the stained glass had been blown out. In France, for example, although old windows were protected during the conflict and removed to safekeeping, nineteenth-century ones were left in place. In Lyon Cathedral, there was a very fine group of nineteenth-century windows, almost all of which were destroyed in 1944. They have since been replaced by contemporary works. Following the restoration of various buildings during the 1950s, the main focus has been on filling bays with new glass. This long-term project has still not been completed in France. One thinks, for example, of the Church of the Holy Sepulcher at Abbeville or the Cathedral of Saint-Dié in the Vosges. However, mindful of past mistakes and of the direction in which modern art is evolving, painter-glaziers and also those in charge of commissions, who are often architects attached to the Service des Monuments Historiques, have taken a different course from that adopted during the last century. Since the 1920s and '30s, a large number of artists have acknowledged that even if nineteenth-century glaziers did discover the traditional techniques, what use did they make of them? The result was often an academic style of painting completely bereft of any emotional content because it ignored the fundamental relationship between light and colour. As a result of being little more than an exercise in technical prowess, as far as its method of execution was concerned, and in repetition, as far as the iconography, most artists agreed that stained glass had become an almost moribund art. The painter Maurice Denis had tried another approach, inspired by the work of Fra Angelico. He thought that he

could replace creative brilliance with deep faith, but he rarely succeeded in creating any feeling of true emotion, except in one of his first secular commissions, *Les Chemins de la Vie* (The Paths of Life), completed in 1895 for the home of Baron Cochin. It can now be seen in the Priory Museum at Saint-Germain-en-Laye. Maurice Denis was looking in the wrong direction, but between the wars he persuaded a large number of artists, including Georges Desvallières, Jean Hébert-Stevens, and Pauline Peugniez, to work in the Atelier d'Art Sacré, founded in 1919. The same spirit motivated the painters who founded two other workshops dedicated to sacred art, L'Arche and Les Artisans de l'Autel ("The Ark" and "Craftsmen of the Altar"), the latter under the leadership of Louis Barillet and Jacques Le Chevallier. During this period, however, most architects, with a few exceptions such as Auguste Perret at Notre-Dame-du-Raincy (1923), did not always allow artists to give full rein to their inspiration.

Too many of them once more confused stained glass and decorative arts, while others, notably members of the clergy, saw stained glass purely as a vehicle for the catechism. Caught between these two extremes, stained glass could not breathe and its works became either doomed to failure or continued in the old, academic style. There were, nonetheless, certain brilliant exceptions: Marguerite Huré at Voreppe Seminary, near Grenoble, the Swiss artists Alexandre Cingria and Hans Stocker (the former enriched his works with all sorts of plain and mirrored glass, while the latter's greatest work is to be seen in St. Anthony's Church in Basel), Louis Barillet, who often worked in partnership with the architect Mallet-Stevens, Jacques Gruber, in whose workshop his two sons began working (his successor, Jean-Jacques, and Francis, the painter), and Jacques Le Chevallier. For most of the time, however, even when architecture was using new materials such as reinforced concrete, artists remained hesitant about the use of stained glass, never rediscovering the emotional dimension that is its true vocation.

In order for it to recover this role, it was

necessary for stained glass to be rescued from the straitjacket into which academicism had forced it and for artists to understand, assuming that they were willing, that the road to the renewal of stained glass lay through painting, which was undergoing a period of radical change. The master glazier Jean Hébert-Stevens strove to achieve this goal as early as 1927, when he used the cartoons of Georges Desvallières for the windows of the Ossuaire de Douaumont, near Verdun. In order to be successful, however, his attempts had to be followed by other craftsmen and to evoke an enthusiastic response not only among artists, but also among the clergy. This was, in fact, to happen, thanks to the Dominican fathers Marie-Alain Couturier and Raymond Régamey, who in 1937 took charge of the review *Art Sacré*, founded two years earlier.

Father Couturier wrote as follows in this publication in 1938: "... The first duty of stained glass must be to protect and defend, and that immediately implies certain characteristics of an artistic nature: first, unity and peace, through stained-glass windows that appear peaceful and pacifist (even before one knows what they represent); to think twice before adopting jarring lines, violent and gaudy harmonies, discordant forces ... The second duty of stained glass is to enrich inner light with its own richness... All this is a matter of realities that are properly plastic, properly aesthetic. I have spoken of harmony, of softness, of peace, which are the architectural qualities of the monuments themselves. I have spoken of the discomposure or the composure of the imagination and the senses, which are organs governing aesthetic feeling ... Now, that is achieved with colours, shapes, and lines. It is therefore governed not by principles, but by taste and sensibility, commodities which are definitely not that common" (*Art Sacré*, December 1938, p. 344 sq.). This statement, almost a manifesto, caused an outcry among both artists and clergy even after the Second World War, fuelled by the disagreements between supporters of figurative and of abstract stained glass, a polemic that is now happily a thing of the past. Thanks to

Opposite: Vase *by Georges Rouault, 1949. Private collection.*

Overleaf: Old Testament windows *by Marc Chagall (right, detail), created in the Simon-Marcq workshop in Reims for Metz Cathedral, 1963.*

The Holy Tunic *by Fernand Léger, 1951.*
Modern Religious Art Collection, Vatican
Museum.

the activities of Father Couturier, a new conception of stained glass was emerging. But this did not bear fruit until after the Second World War, despite the exhibition at the Petit-Palais in Paris in 1939, which, on the initiative of Jean Hébert-Stevens, presented stained-glass windows based on cartoons by painters such as Rouault.

After his return from the United States, where he had spent part of the war, Father Couturier was summoned by another churchman, Canon Devémy, then convalescing in a sanatorium in Savoie, to carry out the stained-glass decoration of the chapel of Notre-Dame-de-Toute-Grâce at Plateau d'Assy in Haute-Savoie, built by the architect Maurice Novarina between 1937 and 1946. The windows in the crypt had been created and installed in 1938 by Marguerite Huré. During this period the painter Georges Rouault was preparing cartoons for some windows in the church, one of which, *Le Christ aux outrages* (The Mocking of Christ), executed by Paul Bony, had been presented in 1939 at the Petit-Palais exhibition. Rouault's talent allowed him to bring a new dimension to stained glass, in which the eternal conflict between the opaque and the transparent hides a highly spiri-

tualized universe, even by means of the simple bouquet of flowers which, at Assy, symbolizes hope in Jesus Christ. Rouault provided five cartoons for this building, all completed by Paul Bony and installed before 1950. Father Couturier subsequently called on the services of other painters—Jean Berçot, Jean Bazaine, and Maurice Brianchon—and himself created several cartoons, again executed by Paul Bony, who in 1948 also installed one of his own creations, a representation of St. Peter. In fact, Father Couturier had assembled too many artists with conflicting talents; Assy Church lost its exemplary character and became nothing more than a showcase for stained glass in the 1950s. After Father Couturier's death in 1954, Marc Chagall was requested to provide his first stained-glass cartoons for windows in the baptistery, again executed by Paul Bony and put into place in 1957.

The Assy experience was of benefit, however, because it encouraged other projects. In 1947, for example, Canon Lucien Ledeur, who was in charge of sacred art in Franche-Comté, had invited Alfred Manessier to design some nonfigurative windows for the old church at Les Bréseux in Franche-Comté. This was the

first time in France that anyone had risked inserting abstract windows in an old building. The gamble paid off. Thanks to his experience as a painter, Manessier knew precisely how to endow stained glass with fresh chromatic and formal parameters, and it resulted in his services being widely requested by numerous architects for works in both old and new buildings in France and elsewhere in Europe. Nowadays Manessier is just as much at home using traditional stained-glass techniques, as in the large window in the Chapel of the Holy Sepulcher at Fribourg Cathedral (1976), as he is using that of glass *dalles*, or slabs, as in the Church of Alby-sur-Chéran in Savoy (1978).

In 1951, Canon Ledeur summoned Fernand Léger to the Church of the Sacred Heart at Audincourt. This building, erected by Novarina, takes the form of a single nave brought to life by a vast fresco of glass *dalles*. Léger was able to endow this vast composition with a monumental force which truly reflects his immense talent, proving that it is not necessary to be a believer to work on behalf of the sacred.

Between 1948 and 1951, Henri Matisse devoted almost all his energies to the

Right: Window by Alfred Manessier for the crypt of Essen Monastery, West Germany. Created in the Loire workshop, Chartres.

building and decoration of the Rosary Chapel at the Dominican Monastery in Vence, near Nice. The windows, for which he created the cartoons, reflect his paper cut-out technique. They take the form of simple yet powerfully executed shapes, the intensity of whose colours creates a very moving impression. In his secular glass, such as that created for the Time-Life Building in New York (1952), now in the city's Museum of Modern Art, Matisse followed the same aesthetic path.

With Assy, Audincourt, Les Bréseux, and Vence, stained glass had recovered its monumental authority. In 1955, at Ronchamp Church, near Belfort, Le Corbusier opted for a poetic style comparable to that found in Romanesque glass. The windows in the south front are like loopholes, driven through a thick wall, where the light floods in through white and coloured glass sometimes painted with symbols.

Just as these experiments were being carried out, the 1953 exhibition of early stained glass organized at the Pavillon de Marsan in Paris, on the initiative of Jean Verrier, who was then inspector general of historic monuments, and supervised by Louis Grodecki, author of its remarkable

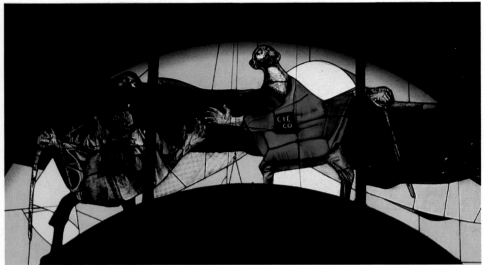

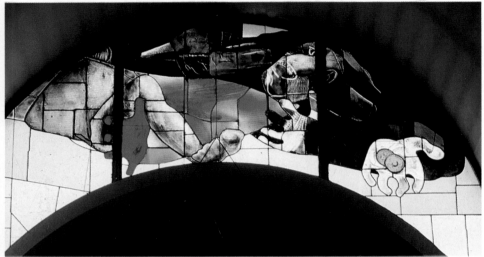

Windows by Richino (Enrico) Castiglioni for Prospiano Abbey, Varese. Left: The Tree of Knowledge; top, Pietà; above, The Crime, 1965. Made in the Lindo and Alessandro Grassi workshop.

catalogue, encouraged stained-glass craftsmen not only to make comparative studies, but also to ask a number of vital questions. They realized that their illustrious and often anonymous predecessors had encountered the same difficulties in tackling the problems of glass and light. A few of the architects attached to the Service des Monuments Historiques, whose task it was to replace works destroyed during the war with new glass, grasped the enormous benefits to be derived from stained glass. This is what happened with the architect Robert Renard, who, aided by Jacques Dupont, immediately put Jacques Villon to work in Metz Cathedral on the Chapel of the Holy Sacrament, situated off the north side of the nave (1956–57). Thanks to his powers of expression, Villon succeeded in upgrading a rather mediocre chapel by means of a series of five Christological windows executed by Charles Marcq. Renard then proceeded to call on Roger Bissière to supply nonfigurative cartoons for the Gothic tympanums above the portals of the south tower, which were also brought to life by Charles Marcq (1958). The following year, Marc Chagall agreed to

Detail of Life of St. Stephen *by Aligi Sassu, 1960, Church of St. Stephen, Viggiù, Varese. Made in the Lindo and Alessandro Grassi workshop.*

paint the cartoons for the ambulatory windows, which he dedicated to Jacob and the Angel, Moses and David and, finally, the Garden of Eden. Assisted by the brilliant skills of Brigitte Simon and Charles Marcq in the Reims workshop, which was responsible for carrying out his great international commissions, Chagall succeeded in involving us in his own private world: one that is both biblical and ethereal. But we should not be mistaken: Chagall's window is a very "artful" work, a window that exploits all the resources of engraving and painting on glass, while at the same time retaining a great deal of freedom. Ten years later, in 1969, Chagall was to return to this building, when he worked on the windows in the north arm

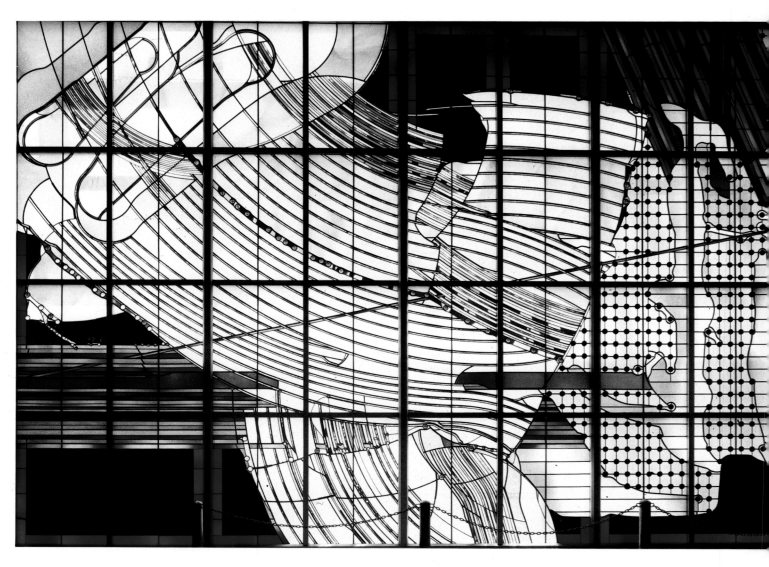

Water and Light by Ludwig Schaffrath, 1981–82; window for Omiya Railway Station, Japan.

of the triforium, creating *Le Grand Bouquet*, a vast, soaring frieze that stands out against mellow white glass. Windows by Chagall adorn numerous buildings throughout the world: in France, in the Chapel of the Virgin at Reims Cathedral (1974), where he attained a strictly formal and chromatic quality; in Germany, in the Church of St. Stephen at Mainz (1978–79); in Switzerland, in the Fraumünster Church at Zürich (1969); in England, in the small church at Tudeley in Kent (1967); in Israel, in the synagogue of the Hadassah Medical Center, in which he paid tribute to the Twelve Tribes of Israel (1962); in the United States, where, in the United Nations Headquarters in New York, he created a window dedicated to Peace, in memory of the U.N. Secretary-General Dag Hammarskjöld (1966).

Metz Cathedral was not the only French building to benefit from this new state of affairs. In 1953–54, Georges Braque installed a group of three symbolic windows in the small chapel dedicated to St. Dominic at Varengeville on the Normandy coast not far from Dieppe. His greatest work, however, is the all-blue Jesse Tree, based on his own sketches, which he created for the axial windows of the village's parish church in 1955. This was finally installed in 1960 thanks to the engraver Raoul Ubac, who supplied a cartoon, of as high a standard as Braque's, for the neighbouring window. Now that the settlement problems affecting the building have been solved by means of major underpinning works, a further series of stained glass has been planned, but what can one place opposite two such accomplished works, two such major creations of contemporary stained glass?

Still in Normandy, at the Château des Reux, Calvados, in an old chapel converted into a music room, the Expressionist style of Francis Bott has created a skillful balance between light and painting (1954). It is not possible, however, to name all the artists who, between 1950 and 1970, worked in either old or contemporary buildings. Many commissions emanated from religious communities, both in France and in other countries. Jean Bazaine, who had begun working in stained glass before the war, took five years to complete the group of eight windows in the chevet of the Church of Saint-Séverin in Paris (1965–70). Exe-

cuted by Bernard Allain, they symbolize by means of swirling compositions the purifying effects of water, the fountain of Life. Jean Le Moal has worked mainly in Brittany. In 1956 he created a number of nonfigurative cartoons for the Church of Notre-Dame at Rennes, but his greatest achievement is his group of windows for the choir and transept of the ancient cathedral of Saint-Malo, where he breathed new life into the severe and somber granite of its architecture (1968). Still active, Le Moal has recently completed some windows for Nantes Cathedral. In the basilica of Charleville-Mézières, René Dürrbach treated the windows like vast tapestries, giving a new feeling of animation, by means of swirling lines and violent colours, to an architectural structure that was sorely in need of it. Joseph Sima and Vieira da Silva complement each other's works in the old Church of St. James at Reims. The former designed the cartoons for the windows in the upper choir in bright colours, while the latter produced small-scale works, intended to be viewed from close quarters and very highly painted, in the side chapels to the north and south of the choir. Special

mention should be made of Jean-Luc Perrot, who was one of the first artists to try to enhance the plastic qualities of stained glass, which is one of the major preoccupations of several modern master glaziers. He began working in accordance with traditional technique and created some powerful abstract compositions for the church at Gy in Haute-Saône (1952) and the Trinquetaille Baptistery at Arles (1953). The following year he carried out technical research into glass in a large French firm. This research bore fruit in 1957 with the installation in the Church of St. Joan of Arc at Belfort, of glass *dalles* set into a surface of some 18 square meters (59 sq. feet). Very somber in colour, these lights are of different thicknesses. In this way Perrot rejoined the ranks of the old Romanesque master glaziers, who knew how to exploit these variations, while at the same time trying to adapt them to the needs of contemporary architecture. Perrot's work is now of great contemporary relevance and may well be taken up again. In 1955, in the Church of Notre-Dame-des-Pauvres at Issy-les-Moulineaux, a suburb to the south of Paris, Léon Zack created a wall of glass in

which the daring, but patiently elaborated lead armature gives the work an astonishing vitality.

"Not everyone who wants to should tackle stained glass," wrote François Mathey in 1958 in the chapter devoted to contemporary stained glass in his collective work *Le Vitrail français*. How right he was in cautioning stained-glass artists against themselves at a time when many of them were on the verge of falling into the yawning chasm of nonfigurative art. In the domain of stained glass, the result was sometimes disastrous, even farcical, because glass artists often yielded to the facile. We all know buildings in which we close our eyes when faced by the stained glass for fear that we might otherwise deface it. Some craftsmen, on the other hand, did succeed in instilling painterly qualities into their works, but they were few in number. Jean-Jacques Gruber used his familiarity with traditional techniques and his unparallelled knowledge to achieve a supple and elaborate effect, as in his window for the Breton Church of Pont-Croix, which was one of his last works (1978). Gruber's skill at creating panels to accompany old windows was unrivalled, as can be seen in his two lancets beneath the early thirteenth-century rose windows in the north arm of the transept of Strasbourg Cathedral. Jacques Le Chevallier created a mood of monumental authority in the high windows of the nave of Notre-Dame in Paris, a group completed in 1965. Charles Marcq and Brigitte Simon, while transcribing a large number of cartoons by painters, are themselves also creators. The former favours windows with trompe-l'oeil architecture standing out against blue skies, as in the Flamboyant chapel of the Bourbons at Lyon Cathedral (1974). In her latest works, the windows in the north arm of Reims Cathedral, the latter seems to translate the skies of the Champagne district that she knows so well (1980).

GERMANY

Prior to the 1950s there were already glass artists active in Germany, where so many churches had been destroyed. Anton Wendling, who had already settled in Aachen (Aix-la-Chapelle) before the war, displayed an eclectic quality during the latter years of his life. He conceived some abstract windows in the choir of Aachen Cathedral in 1949, then a wall of figurative and symbolic glass in the city's Church of St. Sebastian in 1954. Georg Meistermann is another link with the prewar period. His first windows, executed in 1938 for the Church of St. Engelbert at Solingen in the Ruhr, subsequently destroyed in a bombing raid, were already nonfigurative. In the stained glass in Cologne's Church of St. Maria-im-Kapitol, completed and installed in windows of the transept in 1965 by the Rhenish Oidtmann workshop, a famous establishment in Germany, Meistermann's talent reached its zenith. His works achieve monumental authority through a lively graphical quality; paint is only used in counterpoint, solely as a means of suggesting. This approach gives his compositions a formal freedom that has rarely been equalled. Although in his earliest windows Wilhelm Buschulte was still linked to Expressionism, in recent years he has freed himself from these restraints and, after an Abstract period, now either creates windows completely in vitreous paints, as in the St. Anne Chapel in Hildesheim Cathedral (1977–80), or adopts a figurative style, as in the Church of St. Heribert in Cologne (1977–80). Famous outside Germany as a result of his teaching activities, Ludwig Schaffrath in 1962 introduced windows at Aachen Cathedral which possess a rhythmical quality derived from the lines created by their lead rods. Schaffrath subsequently specialized in the creation of great walls of light, producing long, undulating compositions like the one in the railway station at Omiya in Japan (1981–82). Another important work by this artist is the glass wall stamped with large letters created in 1979 for the playground of the Anne Frank School at Aachen. These walls of glass suited the spare, sometimes stark architecture of recent years and ensured that German artists and their teams of craftsmen received numerous commissions both at home and abroad. Among the other stained-glass painters and cartoonists who best represent the great flowering of the art in West Germany, mention should be made of Paul Weigmann, Maria Katzgrau, and Johannes Schreiter. Some glass artists, such as Klaus Kilian and Dieter Hartmann, are seeking a new approach to their art and are reestablishing links with the French tradition at a time when there are signs of a revival of Expressionism.

ENGLAND

The situation in England is less brilliant, despite figures such as Patrick Reyntiens, who created windows after cartoons by the painter John Piper (1955–62). The same partnership was responsible for the nonfigurative windows in the lantern tower of Liverpool Cathedral. Of the younger generation, Brian Clarke has chosen the path of Neo-Constructivism, while Tim Lewis is training a number of young people at his workshop in Swansea, South Wales. The Irish stained-glass artist Evie Hone, who died in 1955, was also highly regarded in England, where in 1949 she created the great windows in Eton College Chapel depicting the Last Supper and the Crucifixion, the style of which is strongly influenced by Rouault. In the Commonwealth countries of New Zealand and Australia, there is particular interest in secular stained glass. The leading lights of the Australian movement are Leonard French and David Wright, both of whom draw inspiration from French master glaziers.

The trend towards commissioning cartoons from painters became widespread in Europe around the 1960s, even in Italy, where stained glass continued to be a marginal art form. In Switzerland, on the other hand, a certain affinity has developed during the postwar period between Swiss artists and those from elsewhere in Europe, particularly France, who were frequently summoned to execute works in Swiss religious foundations: Estève at Berlincourt, Fernand Léger at Courfaivre and Bissière at Cornol. The activities of Pierre Fasel, founder of the Musée du Vitrail at Romont, a small town between Lausanne and Fribourg, have ensured the persistence of a climate favourable to stained glass through his early and more recent exhibitions.

In some countries the tradition of secular stained glass still lives on. Unfortunately this is not the case in France, despite the efforts of a certain number of practitioners, such as Mireille and Jacques Juteau and Gérard Hermet, who are still searching for new openings, especially in schools. In the United States, by contrast, the boom in secular stained glass had the effect of renewing the whole spirit of the art, most notably in California, where a new "pro-stained-glass movement" developed out of the efforts of such artists as Harold Cummings and Roger Darricarrere. The American master glaziers, of which there are a great number, are today trying to work with glass in tandem with other materials. For many decades American output had been dominated by Charles J. Connick and Robert Sowers, who prevented stained glass from freeing itself from the chromatic traditions prevailing during the nineteenth century. And yet Sowers did produce a few major compositions, among them the windows in the chapel of Stephens College at Columbia, Missouri, a commission placed with him in 1957 by the architect, Eeo Saarinen. In 1962, he also received a commission for the large window that adorns the American Airlines building at John F. Kennedy International Airport, New York City.

The glass *dalle* or "slab," the first of which was created in 1927 by the Parisian master glazier Jean Gaudin, enjoyed a considerable success when combined with the reinforced-concrete architecture of the 1950s. It also gained from the rebuilding of numerous religious buildings in Europe during the postwar period. After years of hesitant and tentative experiments, dotted with a few spectacular successes such as Léger's "fresco" in the Church of the Sacred Heart at Audincourt or Le Moal's works in the crypt of the same building, this technique has almost won over its critics and is now even used in old buildings, thanks to artists such as Henri Guérin. It has now become the favourite medium of expression for artists like Job Guével and his family who, by making their own glass and reaping the benefit of years of research into this new technique, have succeeded in creating works of great sensitivity. Others handle this type of glass with as much facility as the Chartres artist Gabriel Loire, who introduced this technique to the United States in 1955 in the First Presbyterian Church at Stamford, Connecticut. One of his last works was the Children's Tower in the Modern Art Museum at Hakone, near Tokyo,

The Tower of Children *or* Symphony of Fortune *by Gabriel Loire. Hakone Open-Air Museum, Japan.*

Overleaf: Left, abstract window by Anzolo Fuga, 1970; right, Flowers of Villa Taranto, *1970, made in the Lindo and Alessandro Grassi workshop. Private collection.*

where he used the *dalle* to introduce us to the magical world of childhood, which he enlivened with flowers, birds, and even clowns. Nowadays this technique has its own masterpieces scattered throughout the world. What is more, it is still developing, thanks to the introduction of new materials, notably resins, which are used instead of cement to bind the pieces of glass together.

The technique of pieces of glass stuck onto a larger plate has attracted a number of disciples during recent years, especially in Europe, but France still appears to be reluctant to adopt this new form of assemblage.

Traditional stained glass still has its enthusiasts in France, even more so since a number of misunderstandings have been cleared up. In 1965, Paul Virilio, a stained-glass artist who became a sociologist, wrote: "It is, in fact, freedom and invention that stained glass, once it had become a manufactured object, needed in the first place, and it was painters who opened up windows onto an area that regained its poetic quality . . . But it is to the abstract-art generation that stained glass owes the

emergence of a language, that is to say, a coherent striving towards a new expressiveness" (Introduction to the catalogue of the exhibition "A Thousand Years of the Art of Stained Glass," at the Musée de l'Ancienne Douane, Strasbourg, 1965). The collaboration between painters and craftsmen still continues today: Charles Marcq recently created three windows, based on cartoons by Joan Miró, for the interior of the west front of the Church of Saint-Frambourg, now the Fondation Cziffra, at Senlis. Soulages, Hontaï, and the American Sam Francis are preparing cartoons for windows in Nevers Cathedral. Jean-Pierre Raynaud has achieved a stroke of genius in the Abbey Church of Noirlac, near Bourges, by reinterpreting the Cistercian style of grisaille window in a defiantly modern way. This need to create a space that is both coherent and "colourless" is presently exercising the minds of a great many artists. Gérard Lardeur has put forward one solution, a good deal more radical than that proposed by Jean-Pierre Raynaud, in his splendid grey and black "lattice" windows in Cambrai Cathedral. The son of a master glazier, Lardeur treats

stained glass like sculpture, an art that he has for a long time practiced. He urges us to look at stained glass through new eyes, as do other French glass artists capable of adapting themselves to the constantly changing and often unexpected requirements of this difficult yet fascinating art: figures such as Jeannette Weiss-Gruber, Sylvie Gaudin, Didier Alliou, and many others. The latest research in France, however, can be seen in the creations of three young craftsmen: Jean Mauret, who splinters light into a multitude of pieces; Jean-Dominique Fleury, who favours large sheets of glass that he covers with vitreous paints in oblique rhythms; and Gilles Roosval, the latest arrival on the scene, who is trying to cancel out the effects created by the lead rods through strictly controlled painted effects. Despite their different techniques, these three painters have all succeeded in creating new and eye-catching forms of transparency. They show that stained glass is an art that still possesses an ability to surprise. It may no longer retain the same privileged position that it occupied during the Middle Ages, but it can still arouse strong emotions.

The Techniques of Stained Glass
A Few Words from the Middle Ages on
Stained Glass
Collections of Stained Glass
Glossary
Bibliography

9

The Techniques of Stained Glass

The execution of a stained-glass window is a lengthy process involving several stages, but the methods of its manufacture have varied little since the Middle Ages. The latter are known to us thanks to the work of the Rhenish monk Theophilus. His work is still of contemporary relevance, even though over the centuries this artistic technique has been further enriched with new recipes and processes. In addition to the traditional technique, contemporary architecture has allowed for the development of the glass *dalle*, a slab set in concrete, cement, or even resin.

□ THE MANUFACTURE OF GLASS

Before describing the various stages in the creation of stained glass let us examine the actual material from which it is made. Today, as during the Middle Ages, the glass for stained-glass windows is always blown, but in Theophilus's time its manufacture was empirical, meaning that it was dictated by experience. Theophilus recommended a mixture made from two parts of wood ash (to provide potassium) to one part of river sand (which took the place of silica). The result was a silica-free glass, which therefore lacked toughness. What is more, this type of glass degrades easily under the action of atmospheric humidity, which is one of the reasons for the deterioration of medieval windows and the darkening of their glass.

There were two methods of manufacturing stained glass in use from the twelfth century onwards. Theophilus describes only one in his treatise, that of the "muff" (A), because the region in which he lived produced a large number of glass vessels (bottles, vases, goblets, etc.). The other process, that of the "sheet" or "crown" (B), was widely used in France from the twelfth century.

The glass was, and still is, always coloured in the body by the addition of metal oxides. In the Middle Ages, the most frequently used stains were oxides of iron, copper, and manganese. The procedures were a very hit-or-miss affair and Theophilus explains that some colours appear spontaneously in the overfiring of white glass because the basic paste, made of wood ash and river sand, was not completely free of impurities. The latter produced unforeseeable mishaps which are no

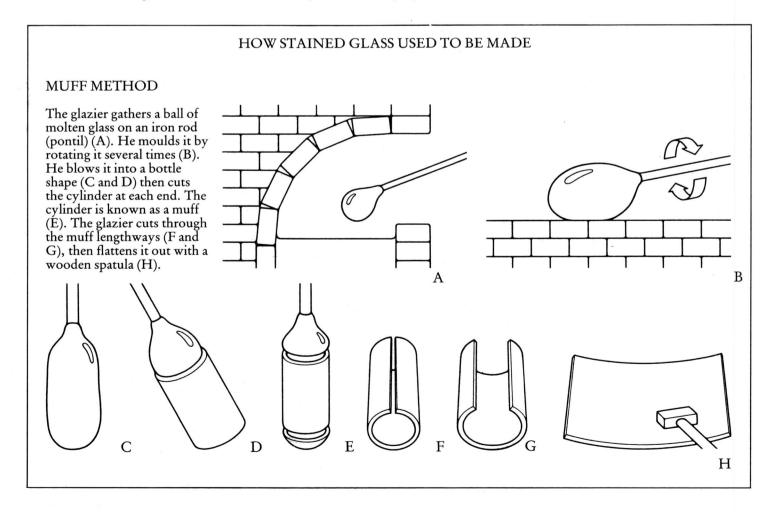

HOW STAINED GLASS USED TO BE MADE

MUFF METHOD

The glazier gathers a ball of molten glass on an iron rod (pontil) (A). He moulds it by rotating it several times (B). He blows it into a bottle shape (C and D) then cuts the cylinder at each end. The cylinder is known as a muff (E). The glazier cuts through the muff lengthways (F and G), then flattens it out with a wooden spatula (H).

longer possible; the proportions are now composed of pure materials. Copper oxide could therefore produce several colours: yellow, green, or blue. Some stains were extracts of minerals such as cobalt, which provided the blues, unaltered until today, of the three Romanesque windows in the west front of Chartres Cathedral.

Red glass alone was made in a different way, because its colouring only allowed for a small amount of light to pass through. The ball of molten glass, known as the parison or gather, was dipped at the moment of blowing in a crucible filled with nothing but melted red colouring matter, which gave a glass with a gradual range of shades.

The use of "flashed" or "plated" glass, meaning glass that is composed of several layers, at least two of which are of different colours, began at the end of the thirteenth century to allow for the technique of abrasion or etching. Using this technique the surface colour is abraded, most commonly by the action of hydrofluoric acid on the glass, revealing the underlying colour. Modern glass artists frequently use this type of glass.

The American types of glass, generally called "Tiffany glass," which were perfected in the United States and England at the end of the nineteenth century, became very fashionable on the Continent and were often used by the Nancy School.

After 1920, a large number of stained-glass artists used glass with machine-made relief, which was mass-produced at the time.

THE MAKING OF A STAINED-GLASS WINDOW

□ DESIGN

This represents the preliminary step in the creation of a stained-glass window. The design must give an idea of the completed work and is a sort of "declaration of intent" for the approval of the architect or the client. Generally executed on a scale of 1:10, it has to include the design of the iron armatures that divide the window into panels, as well as its graphical and chromatic composition.

□ COLOUR

Colouration is an essential element in the creation of a window. It is the operation that allows the stained-glass artist to establish a colour scheme in keeping with the situation and function of the windows within the building for which it is intended. The colours are selected from a colour chart that contains all the shades of glass at the artist's disposal.

□ CARTOON

A working drawing or "cartoon" is then made to exactly the same dimensions as the final work. The cartoon has to be very carefully executed and match the precise measurements of the panels that will divide the bay.

□ CUTLINE

The artist places a piece of tracing paper over the cartoon and traces the line of the lead cames, thus delineating the shapes that will decide the cut of the glass. This drawing is then transferred to stronger paper by means of carbon; this is the traced cutline. Before the tracing is taken off the cartoon all the panels are numbered, so that each section will have its correct place during the process of making the window. Once that operation has been carried out, the different drawings are separated. The cartoon is then pinned to the wall and acts as a reference guide throughout the period of the window's creation.

□ TEMPLATE

This stage consists of preparing the paper templates that will later be cut out in glass. The outlines of the panels are cut with a knife, and the constituent pieces with double-bladed pattern shears. When

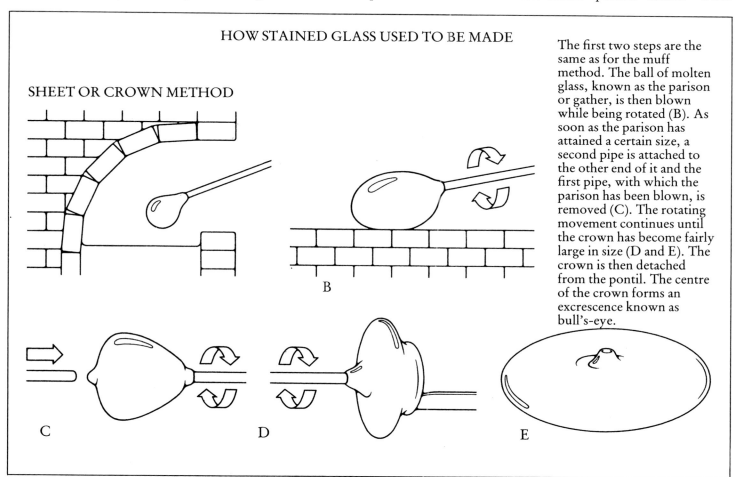

HOW STAINED GLASS USED TO BE MADE

SHEET OR CROWN METHOD

B

C

D

E

The first two steps are the same as for the muff method. The ball of molten glass, known as the parison or gather, is then blown while being rotated (B). As soon as the parison has attained a certain size, a second pipe is attached to the other end of it and the first pipe, with which the parison has been blown, is removed (C). The rotating movement continues until the crown has become fairly large in size (D and E). The crown is then detached from the pontil. The centre of the crown forms an excrescence known as bull's-eye.

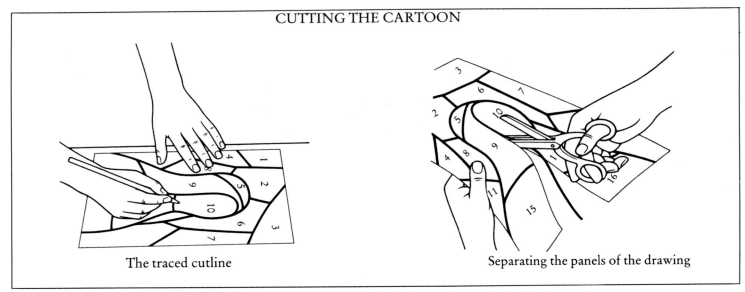

CUTTING THE CARTOON

The traced cutline

Separating the panels of the drawing

the cutting is carried out, a thin strip of paper one millimeter (0.039 inches) wide is left. This corresponds to the width of the lead came. Each piece cut out in this way is called a "template."

□ CUTTING

Since the Renaissance, glass has been cut using a diamond; previously, master glaziers and their assistants had used a red-hot rod. The glass cutter follows the outline of the template, which is held in position on the sheet of glass by hand. The diamond does not, however, score the glass very deeply. The piece of glass then has to be detached by applying pressure to the sheet with the fingers and tapping with a small knapping or chipping hammer. Grozing pliers or grozers are used to correct any possible irregularities. A small hand grindstone or a file is then rubbed over the edges to avoid any splitting. The cut-out glass must always be accompanied

by its template. It is now placed on a frame.

□ PAINTING

If the artist so desires, or if the design demands it, the next step is the application of paint, which has the effect of modifying and modulating the translucence of the glass. But before that step, the painter creates a provisional setting using wax. First of all, he assembles the panel, then he introduces the melted wax between the pieces. The painter can then proceed with the painting in one of two ways. He can either place the panel vertically in front of a window, which allows him to stand back to do his painting, or he can paint the glass by placing the panel on a transparent table and resting his forearm on a miniature bench.

He uses a black or brown material called vitreous paint. This paint is a powder of iron or copper oxide to which a flux is

added. It is extended by means of vinegar and diluted with gum arabic or spirit-based thinner.

This preparation should have a different consistency, depending on the effects to be achieved. It is also applied by means of different brushes, each of which has a specific use.

There are brushes used for lines (see page 183: 1, 2, and 3), others for matting, the process whereby paint is applied in broad sweeps so as to achieve either regular shading or a gradation of shades, depending on the effect being sought (4 and 5). Stippling involves "ruffling" the surface of the glass with small strokes of a bristle brush (fitch) (6, 7). The next step, if details are to be picked or scratched out, involves working on the dry paint with the aid of etching needles (8), or the handles of brushes. Some of the shaded areas will also be reinforced by means of brushwork.

Nowadays there are different colours of paint, unlike the situation during the

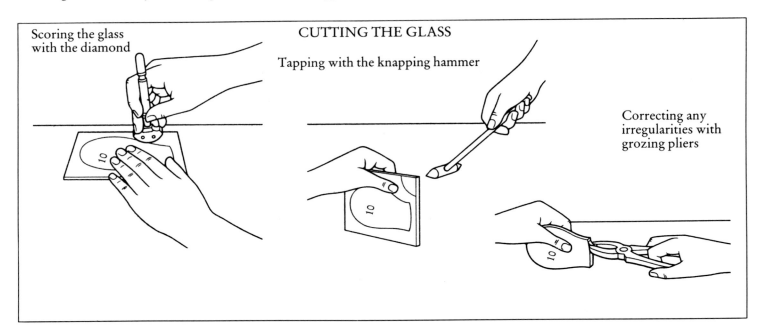

CUTTING THE GLASS

Scoring the glass with the diamond

Tapping with the knapping hammer

Correcting any irregularities with grozing pliers

Middle Ages. They are generally water-based and fixed by means of gum arabic.

Each artist has his own methods of applying paint. It is this work which represents part of his talent.

The modern painter on glass has other means at his disposal when applying paint:

□ SILVER STAIN

Since the 1300s artists have enriched their palette with a yellow transparent stain, which is neither a paint nor an enamel, but a silver nitrate, finely ground with gamboge gum and thinned with water. It has the great advantage of changing the colour of a piece of glass without the glazier having to resort to a cut. White glass becomes yellow and other glasses change in accordance with the laws of complementary colours: blue, for example, turns green. Silver stain is generally applied to the outside of the glass with a badger-hair blender so as to obtain a flat tone which, depending on the consistency of the preparation, can range from pale to orange yellow.

□ JEAN COUSIN

This pigment bears the name of a painter active at Sens during the sixteenth century and was used from this period onwards. It is used for flesh tones. Hard to work with and rarely used nowadays, it takes the form of an iron-oxide-based powder mixed with a flux.

□ ENAMELS

The great period of enamel paints stretches from the seventeenth to the nineteenth century. Their application calls for a long apprenticeship and their results are often uncertain because the firing time varies according to the quality of glass. The enamels used for stained glass are metal-oxide-based.

□ ETCHING (ABRASION)

Etching can be carried out before the glass is painted and it can give a stained-glass window a much richer effect. Since the introduction at the end of the thirteenth century of flashed glass, which consists of layers of different coloured glass, glaziers have used the technique of etching or abrading. This process, the aim of which is to reveal the colour of the glass beneath, was originally carried out by means of emery or metal files. Craftsmen nowadays use mechanical devices such as drills and grinding wheels, but they mainly use hydrofluoric acid (52 to 60 per cent), a dangerous technique, but one that produce remarkable effects, as, for example, in the stained-glass windows of Jacques Gruber and the Nancy School. Glaziers using this acid have to take strict

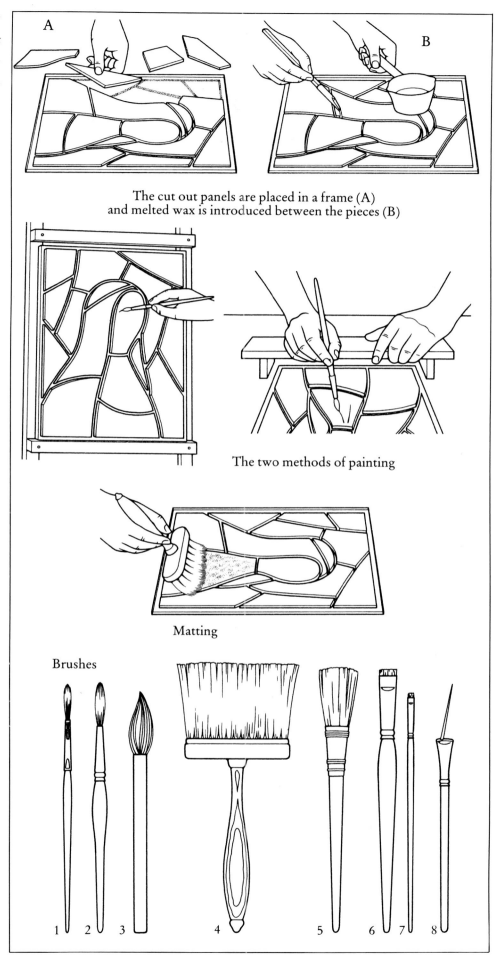

The cut out panels are placed in a frame (A) and melted wax is introduced between the pieces (B)

The two methods of painting

Matting

Brushes

1   2   3   4   5   6   7   8

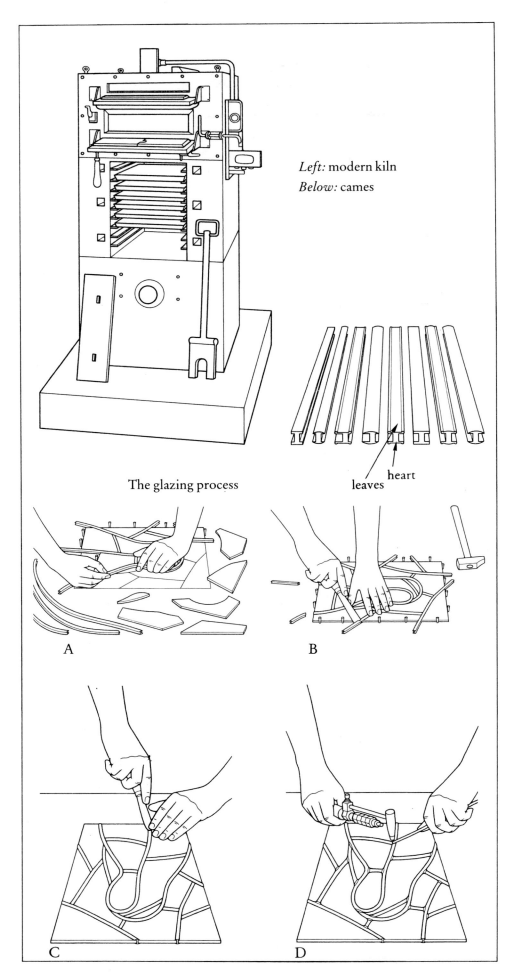

Left: modern kiln
Below: cames

heart

leaves

The glazing process

A

B

C

D

precautions and work in specially adapted and well-ventilated surroundings. The areas of glass that are to remain untreated are masked with an acid-resistant paste or contact paper. Abrading by means of sandblasting, often used in making frosted glass, can sometimes be used.

□ FIRING

Vitreous paints, silver stain, sanguine (the so-called "Jean Cousin"), and enamels are fixed by firing at very high temperatures, which must increase gradually and regularly. Craftsmen can also resort to several firings for a single piece of glass, a procedure very commonly used during the nineteenth century. Modern kilns are generally electric, which allows for more regular firing. The pieces of glass are placed on metal trays which are covered with a layer of dried plaster. Each kiln contains a varying number of trays. Once the firing process is complete, at least twenty-four hours elapse before the glass is removed, though there are some flash firing techniques in which the glass can be removed sooner (firing time fifteen to twenty minutes, cooling time two hours).

□ GLAZING

Glazing or leading up consists of inserting each piece of glass into cames made of lead, which, being a very malleable metal, adapts perfectly to the contours of the piece. A lead came is composed of two leaves and a heart, all of which vary in thickness and width. Modern ones are normally mass-produced, but where delicate restoration work is involved the master glazier makes them himself and copies the shapes of medieval "cames," which have a broader heart and shorter leaves.

The glass is inserted into the grooves in the lead and held in place by pins or nails (see left), then the lead is cut flush with the glass pieces (A and B). This process is repeated until the panel is complete, with the cartoon pinned to the wall acting as a guide. The leaves are then flattened out using a boxwood spatula (C). Tin solder is applied at the junction of each came, acting as a means of assembling and reinforcing the lattice (D). The glass pieces are thus inserted into the lead and can be removed by raising the leaves of the cames, which allows for minor restoration work to be carried out on the spot without having to take the whole panel down.

□ WATERPROOFING

Since one of the functions of a stained-glass window is that of enclosure, it must also be watertight and prevent wind and water from penetrating the building. This is achieved through the use of a cement or

FIXING

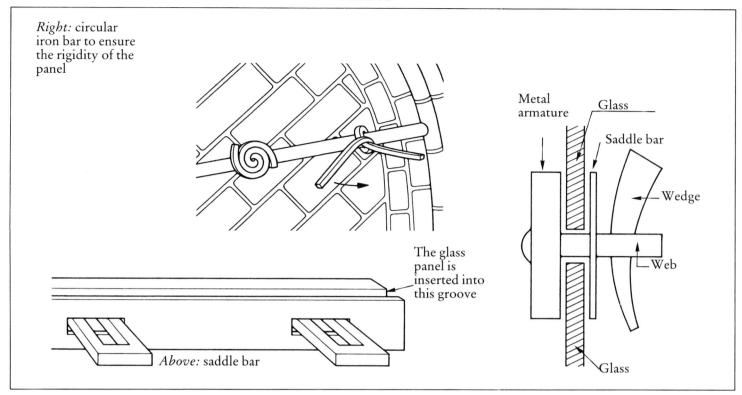

Right: circular iron bar to ensure the rigidity of the panel

The glass panel is inserted into this groove

Above: saddle bar

Metal armature

Glass

Saddle bar

Wedge

Web

Glass

glazing compound composed of whiting, linseed oil, and a drying agent, which is forced under the leaves of the lead cames with a large brush. The surplus is then removed with sawdust or powdered whiting (calcium carbonate), which soaks up the remaining cement. The window is thus rendered waterproof, with the cement also imparting a certain rigidity to the panels. The glass should not be handled for some days in order to allow the cement to dry.

□ FIXING

A stained-glass panel will not normally exceed one square meter (1.196 square yards) in area; it would otherwise be too heavy and also hard to handle. Each panel is set into a metal frame and fitted into grooves in the surrounding masonry, which must be in excellent condition. When the panel is in place, the gap between it and the masonry should be filled with sealant (mortar or mastic gum).

To ensure the rigidity of the panels, saddle bars are placed across the panels. They are held in place by copper ties soldered to the lead cames.

DALLE DE VERRE OR FACETED GLASS

The *dalle*, which was for a long time little appreciated, is now being increasingly widely used by glaziers, even in old buildings. The technique of making a window in this way initially involves the same processes needed to create a leaded window: a design on a scale of 1 to 10, a full-size cartoon, a tracing, and paper templates. Apart from the cutting, there are special procedures involved in making a glass *dalle*.

□ CUTTING

The templates are placed on slabs of glass several centimeters thick. The shape of the piece is then created by a lapidary saw or even a glass cutter. This rough shape is then worked on with a knapping or chipping hammer, with two edges often fitted with small plates of tungsten carbide, until the correct shape is obtained. The knapping hammer gives a "chipped" cut which will create special effects of light refraction.

□ CASTING

The pieces are arranged to correspond with the cartoon in a wood frame that exactly matches the complete panel in width, length, and thickness. Before casting, a metal armature—a reinforcement framework—is prepared for each panel; iron rods are bound between them. Once the casing is completed, the glazier pours an initial layer of concrete into the gaps up to the halfway mark. The metal armature is then placed on top of this concrete, with the iron rods in the middle of the interstices. Next, a second layer of concrete is poured into the casing, filling it up to the brim. After several hours the panel is covered in sawdust, which is then brushed away to remove the surplus concrete. The *dalle* technique is constantly evolving, particularly in the way that the binding agents have been greatly improved. This technique allows for the insertion of pieces of glass placed on their edge and other elements, resulting in a new dimension to the art of stained glass.

10
A Few Words from the Middle Ages on Stained Glass

A few extracts from the most important medieval texts dealing with stained glass will allow the reader to appreciate the essential role played by this medium during the Middle Ages. These texts fall into two categories. Some are concerned with aesthetics, glorifying stained glass as a manifestation of divine power, while others deal with technical information.

□ TECHNIQUE

The first technical work published in the West at the beginning of the twelfth century devotes one of its three sections to the manufacture of glass and stained glass. A vital contribution to the history of technique, the *Treatise on Divers Arts* (*De diversis artibus*) was written by a Benedictine monk called Theophilus who worked in precious metals in a Rhenish monastery between 1100 and 1140. The text is contained in several manuscripts, two of which date back to the twelfth century. Since the end of the eighteenth century it has been the subject of numerous editions and analyses. In his treatise Theophilus was following in an ancient tradition, that of making a compilation of recipes relating to artistic technique. There were already two such works in existence: the *Mappae clavicula*, written probably in the ninth century, and Eraclius's *De coloribus et artibus Romanorum*, from the twelfth century, but completed at a later date. These two writings are of less interest than Theophilus's work, but they serve to complement it, since several chapters of the latter—those dealing with the colouring agents used in making glass—have been lost.

Theophilus, who in his introduction to the first book defines himself as "a humble priest, servant of the servants of God, unworthy of the profession of monk . . ." shows himself to be a very attentive observer. The work is divided into three books, each preceded by an aesthetic and moral introduction glorifying God. The first book is devoted to the art of the painter, the second to the art of the worker in glass, and the third to the art of the metalworker. This division of Theophilus's work into three books in indicative of the spirit of its author, which itself reflects the concerns of the century in which he lived and the environment in which he had trained. The different techniques were complementary to each other and some craftsmen were able to master several of them. The sources of inspiration and the "pattern books" were often the same, despite the different backing materials.

The first three chapters describe the construction of the kilns necessary for making glass. Theophilus has proved to be so exact in his descriptions that it has been possible to build examples and make them work on the basis of his instructions. In Chapter 4 he gives the recipes for preparing the basic glass paste:

CHAPTER 4. *The Mixture of Ashes and Sand*

When you have arranged all this, take beechwood logs completely dried out in smoke, and light large fires in both sides of the bigger furnace. Then take two parts of the ashes of which we have spoken before, and a third part of sand, collected out of water, and carefully cleaned of earth and stones. Mix them in a clean place, and when they have been long and well mixed together lift them up with the long-handled iron ladle and put them on the upper hearth in the smaller section of the furnace so that they may be fritted. When they begin to get hot, stir at once with the same ladle to prevent their melting from the heat of the fire and agglomerating. Continue doing this for a night and a day.

He then explains the method of blowing glass using a blowpipe (Chapter 6). He goes on to describe the production of yellow glass and purple glass before outlining the methods used for making glass vessels. In Chapter 17 he details the laying out of windows and, in the following one, the way in which to cut glass:

CHAPTER 18. *Glass Cutting*

Next heat on the fireplace an iron cutting tool, which should be thin everywhere except at the end, where it should be thicker. When the thicker part is red-hot, apply it to the glass that you want to cut, and soon there will appear the beginning of a crack. If the glass is hard [and does not crack at once], wet it with saliva on your finger in the place where you had applied the tool. It will immediately split and, as soon as it has, draw the tool along the line you want to cut and the split will follow.

When all the pieces have been cut like this, take a grozing iron, a span long and bent back at each end, and trim and fit together all the pieces with it, each in its proper place. When everything has been laid out in this way, take the pigment with which you are to paint the glass and which you will prepare in the following way.

There then follows the recipe for grisaille in Chapter 19:

CHAPTER 19. *The Pigment with which Glass Is Painted*

Take copper that has been beaten thin and burn it in a small iron pan, until it has all fallen to a powder. Then take pieces of green glass and Byzantine blue glass and grind them separately between two prophyry stones. Mix these three together in such a way that there is one third of [copper] powder, one third of green, and one third of blue. Then grind them on the same stone very carefully with wine or urine, put them in an iron or lead pot and with the greatest care paint the glass following the lines on the board. If you want to make letters on the glass, completely cover the appropriate parts with this pigment and write the letters with the point of the handle of the brush.

He also deals with how to apply the pigments in three "values" of varying intensity:

CHAPTER 20. *Three Shades of Colour for Highlights on Glass*

If you have applied yourself diligently to this work, you will be able to make the shadows and highlights for robes just as you did in coloured paintings, as follows. When you have made the painted areas in robes out of the above-mentioned pigment, smear it about with the brush in such a way that while the glass is made transparent in the part where you normally make highlights in the painting, the same area is opaque in one part, light in another, and still lighter [in a third], and distinguished with such care that there seem to be, as it were, three pigments placed side by side. You ought also to do the same under the eyebrows and around the eyes, nostrils, and chin, around the faces of young men, and around bare feet and hands and the other limbs of the nude body, and it should look like a painting composed of a variety of pigments.

In Chapter 21 he describes the enrichment of painting on glass, in Chapters 22 and 23 the firing of glass, and in Chapters 24 to 27 the preparation and installation of the lead mounts; these latter chapters are very specific. In Chapter 28 he describes the process of "the setting of gems in painted glass," without resorting to cutting, but by fixing pieces of glass by means of thick vitreous paints onto the glass and then firing them together in the kiln. The smaller pieces will then adhere firmly. For a long time this recipe was thought to be impossible to achieve, but the art historian Louis Grodecki discovered that this process had indeed been used in a Romanesque window in Ratisbon Cathedral in Germany.

CHAPTER 28. *The Setting of Gems in Painted Glass*

If in these window figures you want to set on the painted glass precious stones of another colour—hyacinths or emeralds, for example, on crosses, books, or the enrichment of robes—you can do it in this way without using lead [cames]. Wherever in their proper places you made crosses on the head of [Christ in] Majesty, or a book, or an enrichment of the hem of robes, things which in a painting are made of gold or orpiment, these things in windows should be made of clear saffron yellow. When painting the goldsmith's work on them, leave bare the places where you want to set the stones, and take pieces of clear blue glass and shape from them as many hyacinths as there are places to fill. Shape emeralds out of green glass. Do this so that an emerald always stands between two hyacinths. When they have been carefully fitted and set in position, paint an opaque pigment around them with a brush, in such a way that none of the pigment flows between the two pieces of glass. Fire them in the kiln with the other pieces and they will stick on so well that they never fall off.

Finally, Theophilus describes "how a broken vessel should be repaired."

☐ AESTHETICS

"The Father is light, the Son is light, the Holy Ghost is light," wrote St. Ambrose. Since the time of St. Augustine, the Fathers of the Church always interpreted light as being a manifestation of divine power. Within this perspective, stained glass was destined to play an essential aesthetic role. Thanks to glass and to its changing effects, light could penetrate a building, turning it into a heavenly city, the "celestial Jerusalem of the Apocalypse" made of "walls of light." (On the mystique of light in the Middle Ages, see E. de Bruyne, *Études d'esthétique médiévale*, Bruges, 1946, III, pp. 16–29; L. Grodecki, with the collaboration of C. Brisac and C. Lautier, *Le Vitrail roman*, Fribourg, 1984, 2nd edition, pp. 12–15).

A large number of exegetes and liturgists glorified stained glass, especially because its translucence created different, almost conflicting effects depending on the time of day. Guillaume Durand (1230–96) wrote at the end of the thirteenth century: ". . . Stained-glass windows are divine writings that spread clarity of the true sun, who is God, through the Church, that is to say, through the heart of the faithful, bringing them true enlightenment" (*Rationale divinorum officiorum*). But it is in the writings of Abbé Suger that this aesthetic speculation on stained glass was expressed in particular detail. Suger, a friend of Louis VI, was elected Abbot of Saint-Denis, the burial place of the kings of France since the late Middle Ages, in 1122. During the 1130s he started rebuilding the abbey of which he was in charge, restoring the Carolingian nave and building a narthex. In 1140 he began to rebuild the choir in accordance with the principles of the nascent Gothic style of architecture. He succeeded in erecting a masterpiece in which the new system of building attained perfect coherence, contrary to what had happened with earlier and even contemporary structures. The bays were enlarged and Suger had them fitted with stained-glass windows, which were already installed by the time that this part of the building was consecrated on July 10, 1144. Suger described the ceremony in a tract that he wrote, devoting a few lines to the windows: ". . . whereby the whole church would glow with the wonderful, continuous light of the very holy windows, illuminating the beauty of the interior." But it is mainly in another text, which has frequently been commented upon, most notably by Erwin Panofsky and Louis Grodecki, that Suger deals at greater length with the windows which he had commissioned. He mentions their expense and gives directions as to their conservation, establishing a post, retained right up until the Revolution, which related to their upkeep and was entrusted to a master glazier.

It is the most generous God who, among other things, has also provided us with craftsmen for these admirable stained-glass windows, and a sufficient quantity of the sapphire material, and ready funds of around seven hundred livres or even more, and has not allowed for any lack of the means for us to achieve the work.

We have also from the hand of numerous masters of divers nations a splendid variety of new stained-glass windows, from this first one which begins [the series] with the Jesse Tree in the chevet of the church right up to the one which surmounts the main door at the entrance to the church, and that above as well as below . . .

This is why, as [these windows] are of marvellous work and with a great wealth of painted glass and of blue glass material, we have created an official post for a master craftsman who will take care of their upkeep and repair, in the same way as we have a post for an experienced goldsmith in charge of the ornaments of gold and silver, who will receive their prebends and what is given to them in addition, namely monies from offerings at the altar and contributions from the common fund of the brothers, so that they will never absent themselves.
(*De Administratione*, Lecoy de la Marche, ed., Paris, 1867)

But Suger's attitude in describing the windows that he had just had created is exceptional. People during the Middle Ages did not generally pass aesthetic judgements on their gifts. Suger's high regard for these works is made even more touching by the fact that several of his windows have been destroyed, while others have been obscured by restoration work, as has been demonstrated by Louis Grodecki in his work *Les Vitraux de Saint-Denis, I* (Paris, 1976, *Centre national de la Recherche scientifique et Arts et Métiers graphiques*).

Collections of Stained Glass in Museums

Chantal Bouchon

Curator at the Bibliothèque
des Arts décoratifs, Paris

The trade in old stained glass, first begun in the mid eighteenth century, gave rise to private collections which subsequently formed the nucleus of the public ones now in existence.

This inventory lists only public collections, meaning those that are open to the general public. It does not contain those religious buildings, of which there are a certain number in Great Britain and the United States, which possess stained-glass windows taken from elsewhere; Rivenhall Church in Essex, therefore, which contains windows incorporating a series of French panels bought during the nineteenth century, does not appear. Similarly, no reference has been made to panels of stained-glass windows preserved in ecclesiastical treasuries, such as the Romanesque panels from Châlons-sur-Marne Cathedral on display in that cathedral's treasury.

AUSTRIA

— GRAZ, Alte Galerie am Landesmuseum Johanneum
● Very important collection of panels from the thirteenth to the fifteenth century.
Bibl.: Bacher, Ernst. *Die mittelalterlichen Glasgemälde in der Steiermark, I-Graz und Strassengel*, Vienna, Böhlaus, 1979. Corpus Vitrearum Medii Aevi, Austria, vol. 3, pp. 57–110 and 190–95.
— KLAGENFURT, Bischöfliches Diözesanmuseum
● Collection of panels from the thirteen to the fifteenth century.
Bibl.: Frodl, Walter. *Glasmalereien in Kärnten*, Klagenfurt and Vienna, 1950.
— VIENNA, Museum des 20. Jahrhunderts
● Stained-glass window after a cartoon by Matisse.
Bibl.: Bony, Paul. "Vitrail de Matisse pour le musée du xxᵉ siècle de Vienne," *Cahiers de la Céramique et des Arts du feu*, 1962, 26, pp. 145–49.

BELGIUM

— BRUSSELS, Musées royaux d'Art et d'Histoire
● Panels from Mechelen.
Bibl.: Helbig, Jean. "Les Plus Anciens Vitraux conservés en Belgique," *Bulletin des Musées royaux d'Art et d'Histoire*, 1937, 3 d, ser. 1, pp. 2–11.

CANADA

— MONTREAL, Museum of Fine Arts
● Thirteenth-century panel from the Abbey of Saint-Germain-des-Prés.
Bibl.: Verdier, Philippe. "The Medieval Collection of the Montreal Museum of Fine Arts, Stained Glass from the Lady Chapel, Abbey of Saint-Germain-des-Prés," *Apollo*, 1976, 171, pp. 363–64.
— TORONTO, Royal Ontario Museum
● Small collection of non-Canadian panels, including a few Austrian examples dating from the fourteenth century.
Bibl.: Hickl-Szabo, H. "Seven Stained-Glass Panels," *Rotunda, Bulletin of the Royal Ontario Museum*, 1968, 1, pp. 24–31.

CZECHOSLOVAKIA

— PLZEŇ, West Bohemian Museum
● Cistercian panels from the fourteenth century.
Bibl.: Makous, Frantisek. "Sklomalby ze Zëbuice: Několik poznamek k jejich slohu," *Sbornik narodniho Musea v Praze. Historia*. Prague, 1967, 21, pp. 233–38.

FRANCE

— ANGERS, Château, Chapel of Saint-Geneviève
● Fifteenth-century window.
Bibl.: *Les Vitraux du Centre et des Pays de la Loire*, Paris, C.N.R.S. edition, 1981 [Corpus Vitrearum Medii Aevi. France. Recensement II], pp. 297–98.
— ANGERS, Musée de l'ancien hôpital Saint-Jean
● Panels and fragments derived mainly from buildings in Angers.
Bibl.: *Les Vitraux du Centre et des Pays de la Loire*, Paris, C.N.R.S. edition, 1981, pp. 299–301 and 308–10.
— BOURGES, Musée du Berry
● Fragments from the cathedral and other buildings in Bourges from the thirteenth and fifteenth centuries and also some heraldic panels.
Bibl.: Gatouillat, Françoise. "Les Vitraux conservés au musée du Berry," *Archéologia*, 1979, 134, pp. 26–30.
— CHANTILLY, Musée Condé
● Acquired by the Prince de Condé in 1817, the forty-four panels illustrating the loves of Cupid and Psyche as related by Apuleius date from the mid sixteenth century and come originally from the château of Écouen.
Bibl.: Perrot, Françoise. "Les Vitraux du château d'Écouen. Contribution à l'étude du vitrail civil à la Renaissance," *Actes du colloque international de Fontainebleau* (Fontainebleau, Paris, 1972), Paris, 1975, pp. 175–84.
— ÉCOUEN, Musée national de la Renaissance
● Heraldic panels of the mid sixteenth century removed from the château of Écouen.
Bibl.: Perrot, Françoise. "Vitraux héraldiques venant du château d'Écouen au musée de la Renaissance," *Revue du Louvre*, 1973, no. 2, pp. 77–82.

— NANCY, Musée de l'École de Nancy Émile-Gallé
● Important collection of stained glass by Jacques Gruber.
Bibl.: Musée de l'École de Nancy, *Le Vitrail*, Nancy, Imprimerie du Centre, 1981.
— PARIS, Musée des Arts décoratifs
● A few thirteenth-century panels; important collection of nineteenth- and twentieth-century stained glass: Grasset's *Spring*; Hector Guimard; Jacques Gruber.
Bibl.: Exhibition catalogue *Les Métiers de l'Art*, Musée des Arts décoratifs, Paris, 1980.
— PARIS, Musée du Louvre
● The Louvre collection comprises a number of collections assembled during the mid nineteenth century; numerous Swiss windows.
Bibl.: Grodecki, Louis. "Les Vitraux soissonnais du Louvre, du Musée Marmottan et des collections américaines," *Revue des Arts*, 1960, nos. 4–5, pp. 163–68. Wartmann, W. *Les Vitraux suisses au musée du Louvre, catalogue critique et raisonné précédé d'une introduction historique*, Paris, Librarie centrale d'art et d'architecture (1908).
— PARIS, Musée d'Orsay
● Collection of French and non-French panels from the end of the nineteenth century and beginning of the twentieth.
Bibl.: *Catalogue sommaire illustré des nouvelles acquisitions du musée d'Orsay*, 1980–83. Paris, R.M.N., 1983.
— PARIS, Musée des Thermes et de l'Hôtel de Cluny
● Important collection of old French and non-French panels (twelfth to sixteenth century) formed from the collection assembled by Alexandre du Sommerard.
Bibl.: Perrot, Françoise. *Catalogue des vitraux religieux du musée de Cluny à Paris* (typewritten thesis), Dijon, 1973.
— ROUEN, Musée départemental des Antiquités de la Seine-Maritime
● Collection of old panels, including four thirteenth-century examples from the Sainte-Chapelle in Paris.
— SAINT-GERMAIN-EN-LAYE, Musée du Prieuré
● Collection of windows from the end of the nineteenth century and beginning of the twentieth based on cartoons by Maurice Denis.
Bibl.: *Musée du Prieuré. Symbolistes et Nabis. Maurice Denis et son temps*, 1980.
— SENS, Musée municipal
● Thirteenth-century window (*Passion of Christ*) returned to France by an American collector.
— STRASBOURG, Musée d'Art moderne
● Collection of nineteenth-century windows by Sophie Taeuber-Arp, Théo van Doesburg, Serge Poliakoff, Roger Bissière.
Bibl.: Beyer, Victor. *Les Vitraux des musées de Strasbourg*, 3rd ed., completed by M.-J. Forté. Paris, 1978.
— STRASBOURG, Musée de l'Oeuvre Notre-Dame
● Important collection of early panels dating from the eleventh to the eighteenth century.
Bibl.: See above.

GERMANY

— BERLIN, Kaiser-Friedrich Museum
● Museum destroyed in 1945.
● Late twelfth-century panels from the Abbey Church of Maria-Laach (Mid-Rhine region).

— BERLIN, Kunstgewerbemuseum
● This museum possessed a magnificent collection of early stained glass (Soissons Cathedral, thirteenth century; Dijon Cathedral, fifteenth century), which was almost totally destroyed in 1945.
Bibl.: Schmitz, Hermann. *Die Glasgemälde des königlichen Kunstgewerbemuseums in Berlin mit einer Einführung in die Geschichte der Deutschen Glasmalerei*, 2 vols. Berlin, Julius Bard, 1913.
— COLOGNE, Schnütgen-Museum
● Museum containing a department devoted exclusively to stained glass. Panels dating from the thirteenth to the nineteenth century, including an important number of works by Cologne craftsmen.
Bibl.: Lymant, Brigitte, *Die Glasmalereien des Schnütgen-Museums*, Cologne, 1982.
— DARMSTADT, Hessisches Landesmuseum
● Possibly the most important collection of panels from the ninth to the twentieth century (head from Lorsch Abbey, ninth century; panel from the Church of Saint Victor at Xanten, twelfth century; panels by Peter Hemmel, fifteenth century; window by Melchior Lechter, nineteenth century).
Bibl.: Beeh-Lustenberger, Suzanne, *Glasmalerei um 800–1900 im Hessischen Landesmuseum in Darmstadt*, 2 vols., vol. 1, Frankfurt, Sozietäts Verlag, 1967, vol. 2, Peter Verlag, 1973.
— ERFURT, Angermuseum
● Panels of early stained glass (thirteenth to sixteenth century).
Bibl.: Drachenberg, Erhard and Maercker, Karl-Joachim. *Mittelalterliche Glasmalerei in der Deutschen Demokratischen Republik*. Berlin, Union Verlag, 1979.
— FRANKFURT, Historisches Museum and Museum für Kunstbrandwerk
● The collection of panels preserved in these two museums comes basically from churches in Frankfurt.
Bibl.: Beeh-Lustenberger, Suzanne. *Glasgemälde aus Frankfurter Sammlungen*, Frankfurt-am-Main, Waldemar Kramer, 1965
— FREIBURG IM BREISGAU, Augustinermuseum
● Panels from the fourteenth to the sixteenth century from the Konstanz region.
Bibl.: Becksmann, Rüdiger. "Die ehemalige Farbverglasung der Mauritiusrotunde des Konstanzer Münsters. Erkenntnisse aus einer historisierenden Restaurierung," *Jahrbuch der Staatlichen Kunstsammlungen in Baden-Württemberg*, 1968, 5, pp. 57–82.
— MARBURG, Universitätsmuseum
● Collection of thirteenth-century panels.
— MUNICH, Bayerisches Nationalmuseum
● Collection of panels from the thirteenth to the sixteenth century.
Bibl.: Schinnerer, Johannes. *Katalog der Glasgemälde des Bayerischen Nationalmuseums in München*, vol. 9. Munich, Verlag des Bayerischen Nationalmuseums, 1908; Witzleben, Elisabeth Schürer von. "Mittelalterliche Glasmalereien im Bayerischen Nationalmuseum," *Zeitschrift für Kunst*, 1948, 2, pp. 141–44.
— MÜNSTER, Landesmuseum
● Several panels, including the Romanesque ones from the ancient Abbey Church of Arnstein (property of Count G. von Konitz on loan to the museum).
Bibl.: Becksmann, Rüdiger, *Meisterwerke mittelalterlicher Glasmalerei aus der Sammlung des Reichsfreihern von Stein-Museum für Kunst und Gewerbe*, Hamburg, 1966.

COLLECTIONS OF STAINED GLASS

— NÜRNBERG, Germanisches Nationalmuseum
  ● Important collection of German, Austrian, French, and Swiss panels from the thirteenth to the eighteenth century.
  Bibl.: Essenwein, August von. *Katalog der im germanischen Museum befindlichen Glasgemälde aus älterer Zeit*, Nürnberg, 2nd ed. 1898; Bremen, Walter. *Die alten Glasgemälde und Holgläser der Sammlung Bremen in Krefeld, Katalog*, Cologne and Graz, 1964.
— STUTTGART, Württembergisches Landesmuseum
  ● Collection of panels dating from the twelfth to the sixteenth century (Alpirsbach Abbey, twelfth century).
  Bibl.: Balet, Léo. *Schwäbische Glasmalerei*, Stuttgart, 1912.
— WEIMAR, Goethe Nationalmuseum
  ● Collection assembled by Johann Wolfgang von Goethe, including several panels from the twelfth to the fourteenth century.
  Bibl.: Giese, Leopold. "Die mittelalterlichen Glasgemälde in Goethes Nachlass," *Goethe. Vierteljahresschrift der Goethe Gesellschaft*, 1936, 1, pp. 99–104.
— WIESBADEN, Museum
  ● Panels dating from the twelfth to the fifteenth century.
  Bibl.: Wentzel, Hans. "Fragmente aus den Tübinger Farbfenstern im Museum zu Wiesbaden," *Nachschriftenblatt der Denkmalpflege in Baden-Württemberg*, 1960–61, 3, pp. 10–15.

ITALY

— MILAN, Museo del Duomo
  ● Important collection of windows dating from the fifteenth and sixteenth centuries.
  Bibl.: *Tesoro e Museo del Duomo*, vol. 1, Milan, Electa, 1973.
— MILAN, Museo Poldi-Pezzoli
  ● Nineteenth-century panels by Giuseppe and Pompeo Bertini.
  Bibl.: Zanni, Annalisa. *Ceramiche-Vetri-Mobili e arredi* (Catalogue), Milan, Electa, 1983.
— PERUGIA, Galleria Nazionale
  ● Collection of Italian panels from the thirteenth to the fifteenth century.
  Bibl.: Marchini, Giuseppe. *Le Vetrate dell'Umbria*. Rome, De Luca, 1973 [Corpus Vitrearum Medii Aevi, Italy, vol. 1].
— RAVENNA, Museo Nazionale
  ● Colourless crown dating from the sixth century (?).
  Bibl.: Grodecki, Louis. *Le Vitrail roman*, Fribourg, Paris, Office du livre, pub. Vilo, 1977, p. 298.
— ROME, Vatican Museum
  ● Collection of windows based on cartoons by French, German, and Dutch artists: Georges Rouault, Fernand Léger, Jacques Villon, Georg Meistermann, Anton Wendling, Heinrich Campendonk.
  ● Important collection of modern religious art
  Bibl.: Ferrazza, M., Pignatti, T. *L'Appartamento Borgia e l'arte contemporanea in Vaticano*, p. 43, Vatican Museum, 1974; Mariani, V., Mascherpa, G. *Collezione Vaticana d'Arte Religiosa Moderna* (Catalogue), edited by M. Ferrazza and T. Pignatti, plate 59, pp. 112–13, Silvana, 1974.

NETHERLANDS

— AMSTERDAM, Rijksmuseum
  ● Sixteenth-century panels attributed to Arnold of Nijmegen.

Bibl.: Wayment, Hilary G. "An Early Work by Arnold of Nijmegen in the Rijksmuseum," *Miscellanea I.Q. van Retgeren Altena*, Amsterdam, Scheltema, and Holkema, 1969, pp. 33–35 and 257–59.

POLAND

— KRAKÓW, National Museum
  ● Panels from the fourteenth and fifteenth centuries.
  Bibl.: Pienkowska, Hanna, "Konserwacja witrazy Dominikanskisch w Krakovie," *Ochrona Zabytkow*, 1949, pp. 182–89 and 216.

RUSSIA

— KIEV, Historical Museum
  ● Panels from France.

SWITZERLAND

— BERNE, Bernisches Historisches Museum
  ● Heraldic panels.
  Bibl.: Lehmann. Hanns. "Die Glasmalerei in Bern am Ende des 15. und Anfang des 16. Jahrhunderts," *Anzeiger für schweizerische Altertumskunde*, 1913, 1914, 1915.
— GENEVA, Musée d'Art et d'Histoire
  ● Former collection of the Ariana Museum in Geneva, containing thirteenth-century panels from Burgundy.
  Bibl.: Lapaire, Claude. *Vitraux du Moyen Âge*, Geneva, 1980.
— ROMONT, Musée du Vitrail
  ● Collection of panels dating from the thirteenth to the eighteenth century taken from buildings throughout Switzerland, but also including a number of modern ones by Alexandre Cingria, Joseph de Mehoffer, and Sergio de Castro.
  Bibl.: *Musée du Vitrail, Romont*, Fribourg, Imprimerie St-Paul, 1981.
— ZÜRICH, Nationalmuseum
  ● *Virgin* from the end of the twelfth century from Flums, the only surviving example of Swiss Romanesque stained glass.
— ZÜRICH, Schweizerisches Landesmuseum
  ● Collection of heraldic panels from the sixteenth and seventeenth centuries.
  Bibl.: Schneider, Jenny. *Glasgemälde. Katalog der Sammlung des schweizerischen Landesmuseums*, 2 vols. Zürich, 1907.

TURKEY

— ISTANBUL, Archaeological Museum
  ● Fragments found during excavations, probably dating from after the capture of Constantinople by the Crusaders (1204); the glass is not blown, but "moulded" in the ancient tradition.
  Bibl.: Lafond, Jean. "Découverte de vitraux historiés du Moyen Âge à Constantinople," *Cahiers archéologiques*, 1968, 18, pp. 230–38.

UNITED KINGDOM

— ELY, Stained Glass Museum
- Collection of panels from the fourteenth century to the modern day: panels from Hadzor (Worcestershire) (fourteenth century); windows by Burne-Jones (nineteenth century).
— GLASGOW, Art Gallery
- Important collection of German, English, Flemish, and French (ancient Abbey Church of Saint-Denis and Clermont-Ferrand Cathedral) panels from the twelfth to the seventeenth century. Also collection of Victorian stained glass.
Bibl.: Donnelly, Michael. *Glasgow Stained Glass.* Glasgow, Glasgow Museums and Art Galleries, 1981.
— LONDON, Victoria and Albert Museum
- Very important collection of panels dating from the twelfth to the nineteenth century, assembled since the nineteenth century. Numerous panels of the twelfth century (Abbey Church of Saint-Denis; St. John's Cathedral, Lyon; St. Peter's Cathedral, Troyes), the thirteenth century (Abbey of Saint-Germain-des-Prés and Sainte-Chapelle, Paris), the sixteenth century (Flemish panels), and the nineteenth century (windows by William Morris and Burne-Jones).
Bibl.: Rackam, Bernard. *A Guide to the Collection of Stained Glass in the Victoria and Albert Museum*, London, Board of Education, 1936.

UNITED STATES

— BALTIMORE, Walters Art Gallery
- Collection of panels, basically French, from the thirteenth to the sixteenth century.
Bibl.: Verdier, Philippe. "An Exhibition of Stained Painted Glass from the Thirteenth to the Seventeenth Century," *Bulletin of the Walters Art Gallery*, 1960, 12, no. 5.
— BOSTON, Isabella Stewart Gardner Museum
- Thirteenth-century panels from Soissons, probably from the cathedral, and sixteenth-century examples from Milan Cathedral.
— BRYN-ATHYN (Pennsylvania), Glencairn Museum
- Probably the most important group of French panels from the twelfth to the sixteenth century assembled by an American collector. Part of it was presented to the Cloisters in New York in 1982.
Bibl.: Hayward, Jane. *Radiance and Reflection. Medieval Art from the Raymond Pitcairn Collection.* New York, Metropolitan Museum of Art, 1982.
— CHICAGO, The Art Institute of Chicago
- Thirteenth-century French panels.
Bibl.: Goetz, Oswald. "Hie henckt Judas," *Form und Inhalt, Festschrift O. Schmitt*, 1950, pp. 105–35.
— CORNING (New York), Corning Museum of Glass
- This is the most important museum devoted to glass and its technology. It contains some panels from old stained-glass windows (Bourges Cathedral, Church of Saint-Urbain, Troyes) and a series of modern windows by Louis Comfort Tiffany, John La Farge, and Hans Arp.
— DETROIT, Institute of Arts
- Collection of fifteenth-century German panels and a panel by G. Marcillat, one of the masters of Vasari.
Bibl.: Hayward, Jane. "Stained-Glass Windows from the Carmelite Church at Boppart am Rhein," *Metropolitan Museum Journal*, 1969, 2, pp. 75–114; Atherly, Susan. "Marcillat's Cortona Nativity," *Bulletin of the Detroit Institute of Arts*, 1980, 58, no. 2, pp. 73–82.
— KANSAS CITY (Missouri), William Rockhill Nelson Museum
- Different panels, including one from the fifteenth century by the Alsatian Peter Hemmel of Andlau.
Bibl.: Wentzel, Hans. "A Late Gothic Window from Strasbourg in Kansas City," *Art Quarterly*, 1953, 16, pp. 328–30.
— LOS ANGELES, County Museum of Art
- Panels dating from the thirteenth to the sixteenth century.
Bibl.: Normile, James. "The William Randolph Hearst Collection of Mediaeval and Renaissance Stained and Painted Glass," *Stained Glass*, 1946, 41, no. 2, pp. 39–44.
— NEW YORK, Metropolitan Museum of Art and the Cloisters
- Important collection of French and other European panels (twelfth to eighteenth century). Nineteenth- and twentieth-century American stained glass by Louis Comfort Tiffany.
Bibl.: Hayward, Jane. "Stained Glass Windows," *The Metropolitan Museum of Art Bulletin*, 1971–72, no. 30.
— PHILADELPHIA, Museum of Art
- Collection of panels from the thirteenth to the sixteenth century; panels from the Sainte-Chapelle (thirteenth century), heraldic windows.
Bibl.: *Catalogue of the Collection of Stained Glass and Painted Glass in the Pennsylvania Museum.* Preface by Arthur Edwyn Pye. Philadelphia, 1925.
— ST LOUIS (Missouri), City Art Museum
- Romanesque window from the church at Montreuil-sur-le-Loir.
— TOLEDO (Ohio), Museum of Art
- Outstanding collection of early glass (thirteenth to nineteenth century) and a few panels from early windows.
Bibl.: S[Kinner], O[rin]e. "Stained Glass in the Toledo Museum of Art," *Stained Glass*, 1936, 31, no. 2, pp. 37–47; *Art in Glass. A Guide to the Glass Collection.* Toledo, Toledo Museum of Art, 1969.
— WASHINGTON (D.C.), Corcoran Gallery of Art
- Thirteenth-century panels from Soissons Cathedral.
Bibl.: Grodecki, Louis. "Les Vitraux soissonnais du Louvre, du Musée Marmottan et des collections américaines," *La Revue des Arts*, 1960, 10, pp. 163–78.
— WINTER PARK (Florida), Morse Gallery of Art
- The most important collection of Tiffany lamps, windows, and vases.
— WORCESTER (Massachusetts), Museum of Art
- Important collection of medieval panels (French, Catalonian) and also of sixteenth-century Flemish examples.

Glossary

ABRASION (ETCHING)

Operation carried out to obtain gradations of colour or to reveal the underlying colour of flashed glass. The work is carried out by means of either a sharp metal implement or a mechanical device such as a grinding wheel, but the most common abrading or etching agent is hydrofluoric acid. Once the process has been completed, the bare patches can be highlighted with silver stain or painted with enamels.

ACIDING

The technique most commonly used for abrading flashed glass, whereby the surface layer is eaten into by the hydrofluoric acid to reveal the underlying colour.

AJOUR

Opening to let in daylight. In stained glass it refers to an individual element of the tympanum over a bay. Its shape varies according to its location in the tympanum and the period of the bay's construction.

ARMATURE

Set of metal bars (wrought iron, aluminum, copper, brass) fixed into the wall and designed to hold the panels of a stained-glass window.

BADGER (BADGER-HAIR BLENDER)

Round or rectangular brush, broad and not very thick, made out of badger's hair and used to spread the glass paint.

BAY

Opening made in a stone wall or wooden structure to create a window in which glass is to be placed. It can vary in size and shape, depending on the period of its construction. A bay may be divided by mullions or stone uprights into lancets and surmounted by a tympanum, itself forming an area of pierced stonework tracery. When the bay is circular, small in size, and not divided up by mullions, it is called an oculus; otherwise it is a rosette or rose window.

BLOWING

Action of blowing glass in order to obtain a plate of glass by either the muff or sheet method.

BRISTLE BRUSH

See FITCH

BULL'S-EYE

Excrescence or knot of glass at the center of the crown or sheet left by the pontil or gather. The sheet method of blowing glass.

CAGE À MOUCHE

Background painted in the form of a tight lattice. Used particularly during the thirteenth century for the painted background between the decorative motifs of pale or clear grisaille windows.

CAME

H-shaped lead rod used to assemble the pieces of glass in a panel. It is composed of a central part, called the *heart* or *core*, and *leaves* or *flanges*, which are of different thicknesses and widths and grip onto the glass. Old cames are different from those used since the nineteenth century. Their heart is thicker and their leaves shorter. Apart from lead, cames contain tin and antimony. Since the end of the nineteenth century other metals, such as copper and brass, have been used. Crucible lead, generally in very thin strips, was once used to repair a broken piece of glass, but nowadays, if at all possible, restorers prefer to use a reversible glue.

CARTOON

Full-size drawing of a stained-glass window on paper. The cartoon should contain all the information necessary for the creation of a window, from the metal armature right up to the colour of the smallest piece of glass.

CROWN

Disc of blown glass obtained by the sheet method. Pieces blown by this method are recognizable by the concentric striations that result from the movements to which the crown is subjected during its manufacture.

DALLE DE VERRE

Piece of cast glass, small in size and roughly 3 to 5 centimeters (c. $1\frac{1}{5}$ to 2 inches) thick. A *dalle* consists of these pieces of glass mounted in cement or resin.

DESIGN (SKETCH)

Scaled-down model of a stained-glass window, generally in a ratio of 1 to 10. The design is used as the basis for the full-size cartoon.

DIAMOND

Tool used for cutting glass, comprising a small particle of diamond set into a metal piece known in French as a *sabot* and equipped with a short handle.

DOUBLE-BLADED PATTERN SHEARS

These allow for the cutting-out of the templates because they consist of an upper part, of the same width as the heart of the lead came, and a lower section composed of two blades. With each cut of the scissors a small strip of paper is removed which matches the width of the cames.

ENAMEL

Powder of coloured frit that can be used for painting on glass. It is fixed by firing at temperatures between 1050° and 1250°C (1922° and 2282°F). The first enamels were introduced during the sixteenth century.

ETCHING

See ABRASION

FERMAILLET

Motif in the form of a clasp or fastening that serves to link scenes together. By extension, it can also be applied to the motifs that give a stained-glass window its rhythm.

FILLET

Narrow band of glass, either painted or unpainted, placed between two lead cames. It generally acts as a frame for a figurative medallion or border. It ensures that the different elements of a window lead smoothly into one another. The name fillet is also given to the broad border (c. 5 centimeters, 2 inches) surrounding a panel, which is placed in the groove of the bay at the point where the bay and the window meet. This fillet is generally stopped with lime mortar.

FITCH (BRISTLE BRUSH)

Brush of hard hairs of equal length. Its use allows for a granular surface to be imparted to the paint.

FIXING

Operation whereby the stained glass is positioned in the bay for which it has been designed.

FLUX

Mixture nowadays composed of lead oxide and borax, which has the effect of lowering the fixation temperature of the paint at the moment of firing.

FRIT

Blend of saline and earth-derived substances added at the moment of the glass paste's melting in order to accelerate the process.

GATHER

See PARISON

GATHERING

The action of taking the ball of molten glass, known as the *parison* or gather, in order to blow it.

GLASS

In the case of stained glass, the glass is blown. This glass is known nowadays as *antique*. Glass is a hard yet fragile substance, with a particular structure of elements containing potassium and vitrifiable elements (principally silica). During the Middle Ages, the potassic elements were provided by wood ash (beech, for example) and the silica by river sand. There are numerous grades of glass, only some of which are used for stained glass. *American glass* is a highly decorative glass in which the colours form streaks of differing intensity and differing shapes. *Cathedral glass* is a machine-made glass with undulating reliefs of varying sizes. *Dichroic glass* is an opalescent glass whose special qualities are produced by passing the melting glass through certain gasses. *Flashed* or *plated glass* is a coloured, blown glass generally composed of two layers, one of which is white, yellow, or blue. It is on this type of glass that the glazier employs the technique of abrasion or etching. Flashed glass is obtained by two or more successive gatherings at the moment of blowing. *Venetian glass* is composed of several colours forming regular bands.

GLASS PAINTING

Technique of painting on glass and, by extension, a synonym for stained glass as a pictorial technique. The latter meaning has come into common use mainly since the sixteenth century.

GRISAILLE

A clear or white window covered in painted or unpainted decorative motifs.

GROZING PLIERS (GROZER)

Generally flat-nosed pliers allowing the glazier to give a piece of glass its definitive shape and adjust it to that of the template.

HIGHLIGHT

Light touch paint, generally silver stain, used to enliven a particular section of a stained-glass window.

JEAN COUSIN (SANGUINE)

A red colour (trioxide of iron) the first use of which has been incorrectly attributed to a painter active at Sens during the first half of the sixteenth century, from whence its name. In fact, the use of Jean Cousin dates back to the mid fifteenth century. It allows for the colouring of faces with a pink tone similar to that of flesh.

KNAPPING HAMMER (CHIPPING HAMMER)

Small hammer with two panes used to tap a piece of glass that has already been cut with a diamond from a larger plate. There are several types of knapping hammer, including ones coated with tungsten carbide used to cut glass *dalles*.

LEAD ROD

See CAME

LINE

Line of paint of varying thickness. It can equally well be made using sanguine or silver stain. *Outline* is used to delineate the contours of a shape (e.g., a face or building) and provide the principal lines.

MAKING THE TEMPLATE

The cutting-out with a blade or double-bladed pattern shears of the traced outline of a stained-glass window in order to obtain the template for each piece of glass.

MASTIC (LEADED LIGHT CEMENT)

Used to make a panel completely watertight once the cames have been fitted. It is made up of a mixture of whiting, linseed oil, and fixative. The mastic is spread over both sides of the glass with a large brush. The glass is subsequently cleaned with sawdust, which soaks up any surplus mastic.

GLOSSARY

MELTING POT

Fireproof clay receptacle in which the glass paste is prepared and brought to melting point.

MODELLING

The technique of creating relief effects by means of vitreous paint. Such effects may be created with either paint or stain.

MOSAIC

Small-scale decorative background in thirteenth-century Gothic windows occupying the spaces between the narrative compartments.

MUFF

Cylinder of blown glass cut off at both ends and then flattened with a wooden spatula to form a glass plate.

PANEL

Element of a stained-glass window, generally no more than one meter (39 inches) square. Its shape varies according to its situation within the window, particularly where the latter includes tracery. A single window is as a rule made up of several panels. In the case of a narrative or figurative window, a panel may represent only part of the scene.

PARISON (GATHER)

Ball of molten glass that has just been gathered by the glass blower.

PICKING OUT

This is achieved by scratching away the paint, when it is wet or dry, by means of a needle, brush handle, etc. This allows for the creation of small patterns or for lightening the paint.

PONTIL

Iron rod used to gather the glass and create the parison. Using the pontil, the glazier can then impart a rotating motion to the parison while the sheet or crown is developing. Once the crown has been formed, the glazier removes the pontil, which leaves an excrescence called the bull's-eye.

ROSE WINDOW

Large circular bay divided by stone mullions, as a rule radiating from the center.

ROUNDEL

A small section of stained glass, generally circular, portraying a religious or profane subject, placed in front of a window. The fashion for these small panels never really caught on in France, contrary to what happened during the sixteenth century in England, the Netherlands, and the Germanic countries, where they were called *Kabinettscheiben*.

SADDLE BAR

Element of the T-bar metal armature designed to receive the panel. In France it is composed of several pieces. 1) a flat, rectangular iron rail is equipped with webs (*pannetons*) on which the panel is placed. 2) a strap iron or flat iron band, pierced with slots that correspond to the location of the webs, is threaded into the webs. 3) Wedges or small pins are placed in the webs, thereby enabling the panel to be held firmly against the rebate.

SANGUINE

See JEAN COUSIN

SCRATCHING OUT

Local removal performed on glass paint either when it is damp or when it is dry. It allows for less precise effects than those achieved by the picking-out process.

SILVER STAIN

Mixture of silver salts and neutral yellow ocher used from the 1300s onwards. It allows for white glass to be coloured yellow without resorting to a cut. It is applied to the exterior surface of the glass, while the painter paints the interior surface in the normal way. It is fired at low temperatures.

SOLDERING

Action of placing a spot of molten tin at the junction of two cames in order to bind them together. A fatty acid called stearin is used to allow the lead and tin to be soldered together.

SQUIRREL

Long, fine brush made from squirrel hair and used for painting lines.

STAINED GLASS

This is a manufacturing technique and an art involving the combination of pieces of glass, generally painted, and lead cames.

STAINED-GLASS WINDOW

Decorative enclosure of a bay, normally with a window, comprising pieces of coloured or uncoloured glass set in cames. There are different typological categories of stained-glass window. The *figurative window* contains one or several figures. The *narrative window* contains religious or profane scenes. The *legendary window*, which is composed of small compartments or scenes, as a rule is intended to be viewed from close quarters (e.g., the lower windows in cathedrals). The *mixed window* associates full-colour panels, generally depicting figures and rarely scenes, and decorative panels in pale or clear grisaille.

STRAP IRON

See SADDLE BAR

TIE

Pliable lead or copper rod soldered onto a panel and acting as a means of fixing the hoops or bars.

TIN

Tin rod used to solder two lead cames together at their point of intersection.

TRACERY

Stone openwork in the tympanum of a window that determines the *ajours*.

VITRE

Maîtresse-vitre, a term used, mainly in Brittany, to designate the stained-glass window which occupies the axial bay of the nave or chevet.

WASH

Procedure that involves covering the glass with a thin layer of glass paint, sometimes barely discernible. It has the effect of modifying the translucence of glass.

Bibliography

This bibliography follows a chronological system, with each section listing books or articles in order of publication. The titles in the Corpus Vitrearum Medii Aevi collection have been listed in a separate section; this work as a whole bears witness to the importance of studies carried out in the field of stained glass since the inception of this series of volumes in 1954.

Not all the works and articles consulted have been included here; only those which are of general interest, such as overall studies of the subject, have been included. Works on general history, therefore, and also on iconography, which are indispensable to the study of stained glass both ancient and modern, have been omitted.

Reference works and articles on public collections mentioned in the chapter Collections of Stained Glass in Museums have not been listed again in this bibliography.

Bibliography

Gessert, M. A. *Geschichte der Glasmalerei in Deutschland und den Niederlanden, Frankreich, England, der Schweiz, Italien und Spanien, von ihrem Ursprung bis auf die neueste Zeit*, Stuttgart and Tübingen, 1839.
Geró, J. *Bibliographie du vitrail français* (MS), Paris, 1983.
Caviness, M. H. (with E. R. Staudinger), *Stained Glass before 1540. An Annotated Bibliography*, Boston, 1983 (MS).
Evans D. *Bibliography of Stained Glass*, Woodbridge, 1984.

General Works

Warrington, W. *History of Stained Glass from the Earliest Period of the Art to the Present Time: Illustrated by Coloured Examples of Entire Windows in the Various Styles*, London, 1848.
Viollet-le-Duc, E. "Vitrail" in *Dictionnaire raisonné de l'architecture française du XIe au XVIe siècle*, vol. 9, Paris, 1868, pps 373–462.
Westlake, N. H. J. *A History of Design in Painted Glass*, London and Oxford, 1881–94, 4 vols.
Ottin, L. *Le Vitrail, son histoire, ses manifestations à travers les âges et les peuples*, Paris, 1896.
Day, Lewis F. *Windows: A Book about Stained and Painted Glass*, London, 1897.
Connick, C. *Adventures in Light and Color: An Introduction to the Stained Glass Craft*, New York, 1937.
Sowers, R. *The Lost Art: A Survey of One Thousand Years of Stained Glass*, New York, 1954.
Boom, A. van der *De Kunst der Glazeniers in Europa 1100–1600*, Amsterdam and Antwerp, 1960.
Beyer, V. *Offenbarung der Farbe, Kunst und Technik der Glasmalerei*, Berlin, 1963; *Stained Glass Windows*, Philadelphia, 1965.
Lafond, J. *Le Vitrail*, Paris, 1966 (*Je sais-Je crois* series), second edition, Paris, 1978.
Frodl-Kraft, E. *Die Glasmalerei: Entwicklung, Tecknik, Eigenart*, Vienna and Munich, 1970.
Lee, L., Seddon, G. and Stephens, F. *Stained Glass*, New York-London, 1976; *La Merveilleuse Histoire d'un art*, Paris, 1977.
Rollet, J. *Les Maîtres de la lumière*, Paris, 1980.
Cowen, P. *Rose Windows*, London 1979; *Die Rosenfenster der gotischen Kathedralen*, Freiburg im Breisgau, Basle and Vienna, 1979; *Roses Médiévales*, Paris, 1978.

Specific Works

Didron, E. "Le vitrail depuis cent ans à l'exposition de 1889" in *Revue des Arts Décoratifs*, 1889–90.
Grodecki, L. "Glasmalerei" [15th century] in *Propyläen Kunstgeschichte*, vol. 7, Berlin, 1972, pps 239–46.
Grodecki, L. (with Brisac, C. and Lautier, C.), *Le Vitrail roman*, Fribourg, 1977, second edition, 1984; *Die Romanische Glasmalerei*, Munich 1977.
Grodecki, L. and Brisac, C. *Le Vitrail gothique au XIIIe siècle*, Fribourg, 1984; *1200–1300 Gothic Stained Glass*, Cornell, 1985.

Technique

Neri, A. *Dell'Arte vetraria*, Florence, 1612.
Haudicquer, B. de *L'Art de la verrerie*, Paris 1718.
L'Escalopier, C. *Théophile prêtre et moine; essai sur divers arts*, Paris 1843; reprinted Nogent-le-Roi, 1977.
Ballantine J. *Treatise on Painted Glass, Shewing its Applicability to Every Style of Architecture*, London, 1845.
Merrifield, M. P. *Original Treatises on the Arts of Painting*, London, 1849; reprinted New York, 1967.
Bontemps, G. *Guide du verrier*, Paris, 1868.
Appert, L. *Notes sur les verres anciens*, Paris, 1896.
Magne, L. *L'Art appliqué aux métiers. Décor du verre: gobeleterie, mosaïque, vitrail*, Paris, 1913.
Ottin, L. *L'Art de faire un vitrail*, Paris, 1926.
Théobald, W. *Technik des Kunsthandwerks im zehnten Jahrhundert. Des Theophilus Presbyter. Diversarum artium schedula*, Berlin, 1933.
Lafond, J. *Pratique de la peinture sur verre à l'usage des curieux: suivie d'un essai historique sur le jaune d'argent et d'une note sur les plus anciens verres gravés*, Rouen, 1943.
Dodwell, C. R. Theophilus, *De diversis artibus: Theophilus The Various Arts*, London, 1961.
Hawthorne, J. G. and Smith, C. S. *On Divers Arts: The Treatise of Theophilus*, Chicago, 1963; reprint, New York, 1979.
Reyntiens, P. *The Stained Glass Technique*, London-New York, 1967.
Metcalf, R. *Making Stained Glass: A Handbook for the Amateur and the Professional*, New York-Toronto-Mexico, 1972.
Juteau, J. and M. *Le Vitrail*, Paris, 1978.
Brisac, C. "Les Maîtres verriers au Moyen Âge" in *L'Histoire*, no. 15, 1979, pps 49–57.

Preservation

Unwin, M. "A Treatment for the Preservation of Glass" in *Museums Journal*, 51, 1951.
Knowles, J. A. "Early Nineteenth-Century Ideals and Methods of Restoring Ancient Stained Glass" in *Journal of the British Society of Master Glass-Painters*, 11, no. 2, 1953, pps 73–79.
Frodl-Kraft, E. "Mittelalterliche Glasmalerei: Restaurierung und Erforschung" in *Österreichische Zeitschrift für Kunst und Denkmalpflege*, 9, 1955, pps 30–36.
Verrier, J. "De la conservation et de la mise en valeur des vitraux anciens" in *Les Monuments historiques de la France*, 1955, pps 20–26.
Lowe, W. "The Conservation of Stained Glass" in *Studies in Conservation*, 5, 1960, pps 139–49.

BIBLIOGRAPHY

Sowers, R. "On the Blues in Chartres" in *Art Bulletin*, 48, 1966, pps 218–22.

Brill, R. "Scientific Studies of Stained Glass: A Progress Report" in *Journal of Glass Studies*, 12, 1970, pps 185–212.

Caviness, M. H. "De convenientia et cohaerentia antiqui et novi operis: Medieval Conservation, Restoration, Pastiche and Forgery" in *Intuition und Kunstwissenschaft: Festschrift für Hanns Swarzenski*, Berlin, 1973, pps 205–21.

Newton, R. G. "Bibliography of Studies of the Deterioration and Conservation of Stained Glass" in *Art and Archaeology: Technical Abstracts (Supplement)*, 10, 1973, pps 132–78.

Frodl-Kraft, E. "Mittelalterliche Glasmalerei: Erforschung, Restaurierung-Bemerkungen zu Verwittungsformen, und Konservierungsmassnahmen and mittelalterliche Glasmalereien" in *Österreichische Zeitschrift für Kunst und Denkmalpflege*, 28, 1974, pps 200–209.

Newton, R. The Deterioration and Conservation of Painted Glass: A Critical Bibliography and Three Research Papers, *Corpus Vitrearum Medii Aevi, Great Britain–Occasional Papers*, London, 1, 1974.

Bettembourg, J-M. "La Dégradation des vitraux" in *Revue du palais de la Découverte*, 6, no. 53, 1977, pps 41–50.

Bettembourg, J-M. "La Conservation des vitraux anciens" in *Revue du palais de la Découverte*, 6, no. 57, 1978, pps 27–38.

AUSTRIA

General Works

Kieslinger, F. *Die Glasmalerei in Österreich: Ein Abriss ihrer Geschichte*, Vienna, 1920.

Kieslinger, F. *Gotische Glasmalerei in Österreich bis 1450*, Vienna, 1929.

Specific Works

Frodl, W. *Glasmalerei in Kärnten, 1150–1500*, Klagenfurt-Vienna, 1950.

Frodl-Kraft, E. "Die Kreuzgangverglasung und der Ambo des Nikolaus von Verdun" in *Österreichische Zeitschrift für Kunst und Denkmalpflege*, 19, 1965, pps 28–30.

Frodl-Kraft, E. "Die Figur in Langpass in der österreichischen Glasmalerei und die naumburger Westchor-Verglasung" in *Kunst des Mittelalters in Sachsen; Festschrift Wolf Schubert*, Weimar, 1967.

Niemetz, P. *Die Babenburger-Scheiben im Heiligerkreuzer Brunnenhaus*, Heiligenkreuz, 1976.

BELGIUM AND THE NETHERLANDS

General Works

Boom, A. van der, *Monumentale Glasschilderkunst in Nederland*, vol. 1, Antwerp, 1940.

Levy, E. *Histoire de la peinture sur verre en Europe et particulièrement en Belgique*, Brussels, 1960.

Specific Works

Cauwenberghs, C. Van, *Notice historique sur les peintres verriers d'Anvers du XVe au XVIIIe siècle*, Antwerp, 1891.

Helbig, J. "La peinture sur verre dans les Pays-Bas méridionaux" in *Annales de la Société royale d'archéologie*, 42, 1938, pps 147–8.

FRANCE

General Works

Le Vieil, P. *L'Art de la peinture sur verre et de la vitrerie*, Paris, 1774.

Langlois, E. H. *Mémoire sur la peinture sur verre et sur quelques vitraux remarquables des églises de Rouen*, Rouen, 1832.

Lasteyrie, F. de *Histoire de la peinture sur verre d'après ses monuments en France*, Paris 1853–7, 2 vols.

Merson, O. *Les Vitraux*, Paris, 1895.

Gruber, J-J. "Quelques aspects de l'art et de la technique du vitrail en France, dernier tiers du XIIIe siècle, premier tiers du XIVe" in *Travaux des étudiants du groupe d'histoire de l'art de la faculté des lettres de Paris*, Paris, 1928, pps 71–94.

Grodecki, L. "Les Vitraux de France du XIe au XVIe siècle" (exhibition catalogue), Paris, musée des Arts décoratifs, 1953.

Aubert, M., Chastel, A., Grodecki, L., Gruber, J-J., Lafond, J., Mathay, F., Taralon, J., Verrier, J. *Le Vitrail français*, Paris, 1958.

Specific Works

Martin, A. and Cahier, C. *Monographie de la cathédrale de Bourges: vitraux du XIIIe siècle*, Paris, 1841–4, 2 vols.

Hucher, E. *Calques des vitraux peints de la cathédrale du Mans*, 1864, 2 vols.

Bruck, R. *Die elsässische Glasmalerei vom Beginn des XII. bis zum Ende des XVIII. Jahrhunderts*, Strasbourg, 1902, 2 vols.

Bégule, L. *Les Vitraux du Moyen Âge et de la Renaissance dans la région lyonnaise*, Lyons, 1911.

Roussel, J. *Vitraux du XIIe au XVe siècle d'après les clichés des archives de la commission des monuments historiques*, Paris, 1913, 3 vols.

Delaporte, Y. and Houvet, E. *Les Vitraux de la cathédrale de Chartres*, Chartres, 1926, 4 vols.

Ritter, G. *Les Vitraux de la cathédrale de Rouen: XIIIe, XIVe, XVe et XVIe siècles*, Cognac, 1926.

Boissonnot, H. *Les Verrières de la cathédrale de Tours*, Paris, 1932.

Ranquet, H. *Les Vitraux de la cathédrale de Clermont-Ferrand (XIIe–XVe siècles)*, Clermont-Ferrand, 1932.

Zschokke, F. *Die romanischen Glasgemälde des strassburger Münsters*, Basle, 1942.

Lafond, J. "Le vitrail en Normandie de 1250 à 1300", in *Bulletin Monumental*, III, 1954, pps 317–8.

Lafond, J. "Le Vitrail du XIVe siècle en France" in L. Lefrançois-Pillion, *L'Art du XIVe siècle en France*, Paris, 1954, pps 187–238.

Grodecki, L. "Le Maître de saint Eustache de la cathédrale de Chartres", in *Gedenkschrift Ernst Gall*, Berlin, 1965, pps 171–4.

"Hommage à Jean Lafond", special issue, *Revue de l'Art*, no. 10, 1970.

Popesco, P. *Chefs-d'oeuvre du vitrail européen: la cathédrale de Chartres*, Paris, 1970; *Berühmte Glasmalerei in Europa: Glasmalerei einer bedeutenden Kathedrale*, Augsburg, 1970.

Beyer, V., Choux, J. and Ledeur, L. *Vitraux du Moyen Âge à la Renaissance*, vol. 1, Alsace, Lorraine, Franche-Comté, Colmar, 1970.

Perrot, F. *Le Vitrail à Rouen*, Rouen, 1972.

"Découvrir et sauver les vitraux", special issue of *Dossiers de l'archéologie*, January-February, 1978, no. 26.

Lillich, M. *The stained glass of Saint-Père de Chartres*, Middletown, (Connecticut), 1978.

Grodecki, L. "Les Problèmes de l'origine de la peinture gothique et le Maître de saint Chéron" in *Revue de l'Art*, nos 40–1, 1978, pps 43–64.

Bouchon, C., Brisac, C., Lautier, C., Zaluska, Y. "La Belle Verrière" de Chartres, in *Revue de l'Art*, 46, 1979, pps 16–24.

Ancien, J. *Les Vitraux de la cathédrale de Soissons*, Reims, 1980.

Raguin, V. *Stained Glass – Burgundy during the Thirteenth Century*, Princeton, 1982.

Zakin, H. *French Cistercian Grisaille Glass*, New York-London, 1979 (MS).

Barrié, R. and Brisac, C. "Les Vitraux de la cathédrale du Mans", in *La Cathédrale du Mans*, Paris, pps 60–69, 102–26, 139–46.

Brisac, C. "Viollet-le-Duc, cartonnier de vitraux", *Actes du Colloque international Viollet-le-Duc, Paris, 1980*, Paris, 1982.

Inventaire général des monuments et richesses artistiques de la France (Commission de Bretagne), *Le Vitrail en Bretagne* (exhibition catalogue), Rennes, 1980.

Brisac, C., Pérez, M-F., Ternois, D. "Les Vitraux du XIXᵉ siècle des églises de Lyon", *Bulletin de l'art français*, 1982, pps 159–79.

Inventaire général des monuments et richesses artistiques de la France (Commission Rhône-Alpes), *Objectif Vitrail Rhône-Alpes* (exhibition catalogue), Lyons, 1982.

Inventaire général des monuments et richesses artistiques de la France (Commission Lorraine), *Le Vitrail en Lorraine* (exhibition catalogue), Nancy, 1983.

Perrot, F. *Le Vitrail français contemporain*, Lyons, 1984.

GERMANY

General Works

Oidtmann, H. *Die rheinischen Glasmalereien vom 12. bis zum 16. Jahrhundert*, Düsseldorf, 1912–29, 2 vols.

Fischer, J. L., *Handbuch der Glasmalerei*, Leipzig, 1914, second edition, 1937.

Wentzel, H. *Meisterwerke der Glasmalerei*, Berlin, 1951; second edition, 1954.

Specific Works

Haseloff, A. *Die Glasgemälde der Elizabethkirche in Marburg*, Berlin, 1907.

Boeckler, A. "Die romanischen Fenster des augsburger Domes und die Stilwende zum 12. Jahrhundert" in *Zeitschrift des deutschen Vereins für Kunstwissenschaft*, 10, 1943, pps 153–82.

Frankl, P. *Peter Hemmel, Glasmaler von Andlau*, Berlin, 1956.

Korn, U-D. *Die romanische Farbverglasung von St. Patrokli in Soest*, Münster, 1967.

Krummer-Schroth, I. *Glasmalereien aus dem freiburger Münster*, Freiburg im Breisgau, 1977.

Becksmann, R. *Die architektonische Rahmung der hochgotischen Bildfenster: Untersuchungen zur oberrheinischen Glasmalerei von 1250–1350*, Berlin, 1967.

Becksmann, R. "Das schwarzacher Köpfchen, ein ottonischer Glasmalerei Fund", in *Kunstchronik*, 23, 1970, pps 3–9.

Becksmann, R. and Waetzoldt, S. *Vitrea dedicata: Das Stifterbild in der deutschen Glasmalerei des Mittelalters*, Berlin, 1975.

Drachenberg, E., Maercker, K-J., and Richter, C. *Mittelalterliche Glasmalerei in der Deutschen Demokratischen Republik*, Berlin, 1979.

Remmert, E. *Jugendstilsfenster in Deutschland*, Weingarten, 1984.

ITALY

General Works

Marchini, G. *Le Vetrate italiane*, Milan, 1955; *Italian Stained Glass Windows*, London-New York, 1957.

Castelnuovo, E. "Vetrate italiane" in *Paragone*, 8, no. 103, 1958, pps 3–24.

Specific Works

Monneret de Villard, U. *Le vetrate del Duomo di Milano: Ricerche storiche*, Milan, 1918–20, 3 vols.

Carli, E. *Vetrate duccesca*, Florence, 1946.

Cecchelli, C. "Vetri da finestra del S. Vitale di Ravenna" in *Felix Ravenna* vol. 35, 1930, pps 1–20.

Wentzel, H. "Die ältesten Farbenfenster in der Oberkirche von S. Francesco zu Assisi und die deutsche Glasmalerei des XIII. Jahrhunderts" in *Wallraff-Richartz-Jahrbuch*, 14, 1952, pps 45–72.

Lafond, J. "Guillaume de Marcillat e la France" in *Scritti di storia dell'arte in onore di Mario Salmi*, Rome, 1963, 3, pps 147–61.

Soldano, B. T. *Miniature e vetrate senesi del secolo XIII*, Genoa, 1978.

Haussherr, R. "Der typologische Zyklus der Chorfenster der Oberkirche von S. Francesco zu Assisi" in *Kunst als Bedeutunsträger: Gedenkschrift für Günter Bandmann*, Berlin, 1978, pps 95–128.

SPAIN

General Works

Ainaud de Lasarte, J. "Vidrieras", in *Ars Hispaniae*, 10, Madrid, 1952, pps 374–97.

Specific Works

Nieto, A. V. M. "El maestro Enrique Alemán, vidriero de las catedrales de Sevilla y Toledo" in *Archivo español de arte*, 40, 1967, pps 55–82.

Nieto, A. V. M. *La vidriera del Renacimiento en España*, Madrid, 1970.

Arenas, J. F., Espino, J. C. F. *Las Vidrieras de la catedral de León*, León 1983.

SWITZERLAND

General Works

Zschokke, F., *Mittelalterliche Bildfenster der Schweiz*, Basle, 1946, *Mediaeval Stained Glass in Switzerland*, London, 1947; *Vitraux du Moyen Âge en Suisse*, Basle, 1947.

Yoki, *Vitraux modernes en Suisse*, Fribourg, 1971.

Specific Works

Maurer, E. *Das Kloster Königsfelden* (Die Kunstdenkmäler des Kantons Aargau, III), Basle, 1954.

Thuillier, J. *Les Prophètes, vitraux de Sergio de Castro*, El Viso, 1984.

BIBLIOGRAPHY

UNITED KINGDOM

General Works

Nelson, P. *Ancient Painted Glass in England, 1170–1500*, London, 1913.
Le Couteur, J. D. *English Mediaeval Painted Glass*, London, 1926.
Read, H. *English Stained Glass*, London-New York, 1926.
Baker, J. *English Stained Glass*, London, 1960; *English Stained Glass of the Medieval Period*, London, 1976.

Specific Works

Bouchier, E. S. *Notes on the Stained Glass of the Oxford District*, Oxford, 1918.
Garrod, H. W., *Ancient Painted Glass in Merton College, Oxford*, London, 1931.
Knowles, J. A. *Essays in the History of the York School of Glass-Painting*, London-New York, 1936.
Woodforde, C. *Stained Glass in Somerset, 1250–1830*, London, 1946.
Rackham, B. *The Ancient Glass of Canterbury Cathedral*, London, 1946.
Woodforde, C. *The Norwich School of Glass in the Fifteenth Century*, London, 1950.
King, D. *Stained Glass Tours around Norfolk Churches*, Norwich, 1974.
Sewter, C. *The Stained Glass of William Morris and his Circle*, New Haven-London, 1974.
Caviness, M. *The Early Stained Glass of Canterbury Cathedral circa 1175–1200*, Princeton, 1976.
Harrison, M. *Victorian Stained Glass*, London, 1980.

UNITED STATES

Rigan, O. B. *New Glass*, New York, 1976.
Duncan, A. *Tiffany Windows*, London, 1980.

CORPUS VITREARUM

AUSTRIA

Eva Frodl-Kraft, *Die mittelalterlichen Glasmalereien in Wien*, Graz-Vienna-Cologne, 1962.
Eva Frodl-Kraft, *Die mittelalterlichen Glasgemälde in Niederösterreich*, Graz-Vienna-Cologne, 1972.
Ernst Bacher, *Die mittelalterlichen Glasgemälde in der Steiermark, l. Graz und Strassengel*, Graz-Vienna-Cologne, 1979.

BELGIUM

Jean Helbig, *Les Vitraux médiévaux conservés en Belgique, 1200–1500*, Brussels, 1961.
Jean Helbig, *Les Vitraux de la première moitié du XVIe siècle conservés en Belgique. Provinces d'Anvers et de Flandres*, Brussels, 1968.
Jean Helbig and Yvette Vanden Bemden, *Les Vitraux de la première moitié du VIe siècle conservés en Belgique, Brabant et Limbourg*, Brussels, 1974.
Yvette Vanden Bemden, *Les Vitraux de la première moitié du XVIe siècle conservés en Belgique. Provinces de Liège, Luxembourg, Namur*, Ghent-Ledeberg, 1981.

CZECHOSLOVAKIA

Francisek Matous, *Mittelalterliche Glasmalerei in der Tschechoslowakei*, Graz-Vienna-Cologne, 1975.

FRANCE

Marcel Aubert, Louis Grodecki, Jean Lafons, Jean Verrier, *Les Vitraux de Notre-Dame et de la Sainte-Chapelle de Paris*, Paris, 1959.
Jean Lafond, with François Perrot and Paul Popesco, *Les Vitraux du choeur de l'église Saint-Ouen de Rouen*, Paris, 1970.
Études 1. Louis Grodecki, *Les Vitraux de Saint-Denis. Étude sur le vitrail au XIIe siècle*, vol. 1, *Histoire et restitution*, Paris, 1976.
Louis Grodecki, François Perrot, Jean Taralon, *Les vitraux de Paris, de la région parisienne, de la Picardie et du Nord-Pas-de-Calais, Recensement des vitraux anciens de la France*, vol. I, Paris, 1978.
Recensement des vitraux anciens de la France, vol. II, Paris, 1981.

GERMAN DEMOCRATIC REPUBLIC

Erhard Drachenberg, Karl-Joachim Maercker, Christa Schmidt, *Die mittelalterliche Glasmalerei in den Ordenkirchen und im Angermuseum zu Erfurt*, Berlin, 1976.
Erhard Drachenberg, *Die mittelalterliche Glasmalerei im Erfurter Dom*, Textband, Berlin, 1980; vol. II, illustrations, 1982.

GERMAN FEDERAL REPUBLIC

Hans Wentzel, *Die Glasmalereien in Schwaben von 1200–1350*, Berlin, 1958.
Herbert Rode, *Die mittelalterlichen Glasmalereien des Kölner Domes*, Berlin, 1974.
Rüdiger Becksmann, *Die mittelalterlichen Glasmalereien in Baden und Pfalz (ohne Freiburg i. Br.)*, Berlin, 1979.

GREAT BRITAIN

Vol. suppl. I. Hilary Wayment, *The Windows of King's College Chapel Cambridge*, London, 1972.
Peter A. Newton, *The County of Oxford. A Catalogue of Medieval Stained Glass*, London, 1979.
Madeline Harrison Caviness, *The Windows of Christ Church Cathedral Canterbury*, London, 1981.

ITALY

Giuseppe Marchini, *Le vetrate dell'Umbria*, Rome, 1973.

SCANDINAVIA

Aron Andersson, Sigrid Christie, Carl-Axel Nordman, Aage Roussell, *Die Glasmalereien des Mittelalters in Skandinavien*, Stockholm, 1964.

SPAIN

Victor Nieto Alcaide, *Las vidrieras de la catedral de Sevilla*, Madrid, 1969.
Victor Nieto Alcaide, *Las vidrieras de la catedral de Granada*, Granada, Universidad de Granada, 1974.

SWITZERLAND

Ellen J. Beer, *Die Glasmalereien der Schweiz vom 12. bis zum 14. Jh.*, Basle, 1956.
Ellen J. Beer, *Die Glasmalereien der Schweiz aus dem 14. und 15. Jh., ohne Königsfelden und Berner Münsterchor*, Basle, 1965.

INDEX

INDEX

Acknowledgments

Catherine Brisac and the publisher wish to thank Chantal Bouchon for her collaboration.

The publisher wishes to thank all the institutions and persons consulted for their valuable assitance in the creation of this book. Particular thanks are due to Filippo Alison, Daniele Baroni, Ernesto Brivio, Dott. Mario Ferrazza, Padre Gherardo Ruff, master glaziers Lindo and Alessandro Grassi, Milan, Polloni e C., Florence.

Picture Sources